FRACTURED *dance*

The C. Henry Smith series is edited by J. Denny Weaver. As is expected to be true of many future books in the CHS series, Volumes 1 and 2 are being published by Pandora Press U.S. and copublished by Herald Press in cooperation with Bluffton College and also Mennonite Historical Society. Bluffton College, in consultation with the publishers, is primarily responsible for the content of the studies.

Some time ago and far up north, the conversation at a table of Mennonites turned to homosexuality. A farmer bluntly insisted the church must affirm its traditional stance or forever lose its way.

One woman said to me, "Isn't homosexuality an issue down your way?"

Someone else said, "Yes, at Germantown, isn't it?"

Suddenly it hit them. Years ago I was pastor at Germantown Mennonite Church, which was at the time of this anecdote in trouble with the larger church for its gay/lesbian-welcoming stance and has since been excommunicated.

"Uh, end of discussion," the woman said, "no offense."

"No," I said. "Let's work at this."

So we did. I described my thinking and stressed to the farmer that though we differed, I thought the issue was so complicated the body of Christ needed all our stances, and his could help mine grow.

I cannot explain exactly what happened. I can only say I genuinely believed the farmer had things to teach me. He reciprocated. Eventually, tears in his eyes, he said, "Maybe it really is true that we need each other. It scares me, but that means I need you." He drew my own tears.

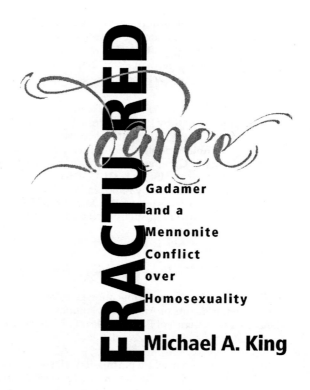

FRACTURED dance

Gadamer
and a
Mennonite
Conflict
over
Homosexuality

Michael A. King

Foreword by
Herbert W. Simons

Series Editor Introduction by
J. Denny Weaver

C. Henry Smith Series, Volume 3

Pandora Press U.S.
Telford, Pennsylvania

copublished with
Herald Press
Scottdale, Pennsylvania

Pandora Press U.S. orders, information, reprint permissions:
pandoraus@netreach.net
1-215-723-9125
126 Klingerman Road, Telford PA 18969
www.PandoraPressUS.com

The paper used in this publication is recycled and meets the
minimum requirements of American National Standard for Information
Sciences—Permanence of Paper for Printed Library Materials, ANSI
Z39.48-1984.

All Bible quotations are used by permission, all rights reserved and unless
otherwise noted are from *The New Revised Standard Version of the Bible*,
copyright 1989, by the Division of Christian Education of the National
Council of the Churches of Christ in the USA

Library of Congress Cataloging-in-Publication Data
King, Michael A., 1954-
    Fractured Dance : Gadamer and a Mennonite conflict over homo-
sexuality / Michael A. King ; foreword by Herbert W. Simons.
        p. cm. -- (C. Henry Smith series ; v. 3)
    Includes bibliographic references and index.
    ISBN 1-931038-03-1 (pbk. : alk. paper)
    1. Homosexuality--Religious aspects--Mennonites. 2. Church contro-
versies--Mennonites. 3. Franconia Mennonite Conference. 4. Gadamer,
Hans Georg, 1900- I. Title. II. Series.

BX8128.H67 K56 2001
289.7'3--dc21

                                                                    2001036236

        10 09 08 07 06 05 04 03 02   10 9 8 7 6 5 4 3 2

To Joan, from whom I have most deeply learned
what it means to be "We" without losing you and me;

to Warren, who knows better than I
how he helped me survive and find joy;

and to that moment of epiphany
some time ago and somewhere up north.

CONTENTS

FOREWORD

Fractured Dance, says J. Denny Weaver, is about two conversations; I want to write about a third. In his Preface, King describes a journey from study in Christian settings to study at Temple as a shift between "being in the church looking out at the world" to "sitting in the world looking back at the church." True enough. Yet on another reading, King had been educated "in the world" long before he came to Temple and remained "in the church" while he studied at Temple.

Indeed this duality, which seems so much at the center of the continuing debate among Mennonites over homosexuality, was also the recurring tension of a book King presented to me when we first met. On the surface, his *Trackless Wastes and Stars to Steer By* can be seen as a guide to internal conflict resolution for Anabaptist discussion groups, but King let on that its conflicts had been—continued to be?—his own.

The third conversation, then, is the one that has been going on in Michael King's head. What makes that conversation special is less its subject matter or duration and more King's uncommon ability to move the conversation forward without losing his anchors in world and church. The method is dialectics, and King practiced it long before he read my favorite dialectician, Kenneth Burke. (See Burke's "Four Master Tropes," an appendix to his *Grammar of Motives*.) In the face of seemingly opposed ideas or ideologies, it is tempting to opt for one over the other, then to dig in one's heels, find social support, and aim to support as well the conclusion that all who disagree are mad, bad, or sad.

Whether out of religious conviction or secular training (or both), King inclines in a different direction. A clue to his philosophy (theology?) is to be found in a recent exchange on the listserv of the Kenneth Burke Society. I had initiated the exchange, putting forward a model of ideal conversation not unlike Gadamer's, which I call persuasion dialogue.

"Such conversations are not possible between people with power differentials," said a correspondent.

"Never?" asked another. "Do you mean absolutely never?"

"Absolutely not." said the first commentator. "My experience," he said, "has been contrary to the hopeful wish for a civil, transformative conversation."

King could not categorically disagree. It is true, he said, that "power runs through and often risks subverting any attempts at 'PD'; thus it must in some way be accounted for." King added, however, that the analysis of power should not in itself be allowed to become disempowering:

> It is interesting to note how often PD is never even tried because potential participants immediately raise the specter of power and say that it can only work in an ideal world such as we never encounter in the power-saturated "real" world.
>
> I think the challenge, then, is how to theorize power effects without letting power analysis call all the shots. As a personal practitioner of something akin to PD, I regularly encounter power differentials, either the greater power the other has or the greater power I have, and I have found that even amid them a central question is whether I myself, regardless of what the other chooses to do, regardless of the power equations which are always surely present, am willing to listen respectfully and with some humility and openness to the other. If I am, this not always but frequently changes the character of the dialogue. The other more often than not begins at least partly to meet me. In such conversations I don't sell out my own position but expect the other to grant it the same respect I intend to offer.
>
> The key move, I believe, is my readiness to offer the respectful openness first, since it's a human tendency to meet generous listening with generosity but suspicious listening with suspicion. The outcome is so often more fruitful than power-foregrounding "hermeneutics of suspicion" that I suggest, "Try it, you just might like it"—but hey, I'm willing to listen to why you might not!

These, I believe, are core assumptions of *Fractured Dance.* Let none of us assume for a moment that applying them is easy, especially in the heat of a controversy like that which divides Mennonites and so many other Christians and religious groups over homosexuality. The usual practice between disputants is that each talks past the other, exhibiting what Barbara Herrnstein Smith has felicitously called the "microdynamics of incommensurability." But, having worked first with Mennonite leader Ervin Stutzman on a dissertation and then with Michael King, I've learned that the resources for peacemaking are woven into the very fabric of the Mennonite tradition out of which King launches the quest for understanding described in this book.

—*Herbert W. Simons, Professor of Communication,*
  Temple University; and Coordinator, Temple Issues Forum

SERIES PREFACE

C. Henry Smith began teaching at Goshen College, 1903-1913, then taught history at Bluffton College, 1913-1948, except for 1922-1923 at Bethel College. The first Mennonite in North America to earn a Ph.D. and remain in the Mennonite church, Smith was the premier North American Mennonite historian of his era. He wrote many articles for Mennonite periodicals and was a central figure in planning the *Mennonite Encyclopedia*. He had published five major works over thirty-five years, more full-length works than any other Mennonite historian of his time. Also a church leader, Smith was on the publication board of the General Conference Mennonite Church and the Peace Committee of Middle District.

Producing the C. Henry Smith Series (CHS) with cosponsorship of the Mennonite Historical Society is one dimension of the service Bluffton College seeks to provide the Mennonite church as well as Anabaptists at large. Smith's historical expertise, commitment to pacifism and nonresistance, commitment to the church, and wide-ranging interests beyond the discipline of history all represent the values and interests that characterize the series bearing his name. Naming the series for an individual of multiple interests and talents signals a vision to publish works that use a variety of disciplines and modes of inquiry to serve Anabaptist and Mennonite churches.

Works in the CHS Series reflect the assumption that a peace church worldview holds potential to shape discussion of any issue. These books present no consensus view, however, since none exists. Instead, they address aspects of Anabaptist and Mennonite studies pertinent to the future of these churches. Precisely that future dimension compels CHS publication.

SERIES EDITOR'S FOREWORD

Fractured Dance, the third volume of the C. Henry Smith Series, carries on two distinct conversations. One conversation concerns the philosophy of rhetoric. In this venue, author Michael A. King analyzes the philosophical hermeneutics of German philosopher of communication Hans-Georg Gadamer. King's methodology charts a new chapter in rhetorical analysis. *Fractured Dance* is among the few works not only to apply Gadamer's hermeneutical philosophy to actual conversations but also to assess at the level of theory the possibilies and problems with such an application. It thus promises to be a milestone in hermeneutic and rhetorical studies in general and a touchstone for future Gadamer studies in particular.

The second conversation concerns Mennonite conversations about homosexuality, a discussion that has occupied much of the energy and creativity of the Mennonite Church and General Conference Mennonite Church for the final decades of the twentieth century and into the present. While the second focus of the book comes from that ongoing discussion, it is important to realize that *Fractured Dance* is not about homosexuality per se. Rather, it is about talking about homosexuality. Conversations on any other agenda—such as denominational mission strategy, divorce and remarriage, military members in the peace church—might at another time serve equally well to test Gadamer's theory of conversation.

To obtain the source material for this project, in April 1997 King and an assistant sat in on three cluster groups of Franconia Conference and transcribed the dialogue as these groups struggled with how to respond to the Germantown congregation that did not accept the Conference's official stance, which excludes gays and lesbians who actively engage in sexual practice from church membership. It is these conversations which King uses as a case study to test

Gadamer's theory of genuine conversation and to assess how Mennonites do—or do not—know how to process conflict.

For King, these two conversations intersect at the juncture of conflict resolution. With Jesus' injunction to "love your enemies" in mind, King is drawn to study Gadamer because of Gadamer's theory that deep commonality underlies even the most bitter conflict and enables those sharing in the conflict to understand each other. Genuine conversation, Gadamer theorizes, seeks to find that commonality present within differences when each participant is open to question his or her own truth and to consider the truth of the other. In *Fractured Dance*, King applies Gadamer's theory of genuine conversation to the dialogue on homosexuality within the two largest Mennonite denominations (just before their merger into Mennonite Church USA). And because *Fractured Dance* focuses on the conversation about homosexuality rather than on homosexuality itself, people on both sides of this issue will profit from reading this book.

With this positioning, *Fractured Dance* clearly reflects the agenda of the C. Henry Smith Series to show how an assumption of nonviolence can impact the discussion in virtually any academic discipline. It is a pleasure to include this book in the series as a fine example of scholarship in the service of the church.

Fractured Dance may also pose an unexpected challenge to Mennonites as a peace church. One component of Gadamer's hermeneutics involves understanding the "effective history"—the shared history of common experiences and assumptions—of the group or groups in question. In developing the effective history of Franconia Conference, King remarked that in the history that shaped their conversations on homosexuality and their efforts to resolve the conflict, there was virtually no reference to the Mennonite tradition of peace and nonviolence. In other words, being a peace church seems to have had little explicit impact on the conversations that aimed at finding a resolution to a quite impassioned conflict. I wonder what it bodes for the future of the peace church if the historic commitment to nonviolence was not visible in efforts to resolve this conflict.

It is my prayer that King's observation will spur a new commitment to be more explicit about maintaining the peace church as a peace church. I fear that "use it or lose it" applies to the church's understanding of and commitment to continuation as a peace church. King's observation also invites research in other settings, as he asks whether conversations about homosexuality in other denominations would differ from the Mennonite conversation that occurred in the Anabaptist tradition of the historic peace churches.

I am deeply grateful to Michael King for his cooperation and colleagueship in all phases of the preparation of this manuscript for publication. In particular I am thankful for his superb responses to suggestions from reviewers and the editor. Readers will share that gratitude.

—*J. Denny Weaver, CHS Editor*
Bluffton College

IOR'S PREFACE

acknowledgments below make clear, *Fractured Dance* began
rtation completing the requirements for a Ph.D. in rhetoric
nunication from Temple University, Philadelphia. Two fac-
it statement are worth highlighting. First, J. Denny Weaver
: unknown (to me) consultants who reviewed the manuscript on behalf of the C. Henry Smith Series deserve special credit
for helping this material move from a dissertation to a publishable
book.

Second, even as it has hopefully moved a significant distance
from its dissertation origins, this book emerged from studies at Temple University in Philadelphia. Significant here is that after considerable exploration of educational options, I deliberately opted to pursue doctoral studies at a secular rather than religious or Christian
school. Up to that point all my post-high schooling had unfolded in
such Christian settings as Eastern Mennonite University and Eastern Baptist Theological Seminary. These were wonderfully productive milieus in which to study—yet they always placed me in the position of being in the church looking out at the world. I chose Temple to see what could be learned by aiming to sit in the world looking back in at the church.

The tone of *Fractured Dance* is very much connected to that out-
looking-in perspective. I aimed throughout my Temple years to remain rooted in the church. During much of that period I was always
at least either a part-time pastor, part-time book editor for Herald
Press (Mennonite Church denominational publisher), and sometimes both. And often I raised Christian perspectives in Temple class-
room settings.[1] But I also always held myself accountable to learn
how to speak about the church within those academic languages and
concepts that tend to be the native "dialect" of academia.

My assumption was not that this language was better than church language—sometimes it is not[2]—rather, my conviction was that if I at least provisionally worked at seeing the world through the spectacles provided by this academic discourse, I would glean insights not available if I insisted only on forever treating it as a foreign dialect. Much of *Fractured Dance* is thus a record of insights gained through the quest to take seriously the learnings available at Temple University, that alternate "temple" of secular worship (rooted, ironically enough, in the Christian vision of Temple founder Russell Conwell).

Among Temple-focused learnings I aim to record are those gleaned from applying the work of Hans-George Gadamer to a case study. In this regard I hope the book proves of interest to scholars regardless of how they may view its church-oriented material. This points to the fact that the book tells two intertwining stories. One is the story of what happens in an attempt such as this one to apply Gadamer to an actual set of conversations. Since this is a path not often taken, the story of how Gadamer fares in that process deserves attention in its own right, which is why it threads its way throughout the book. Here the question is what is learned about Gadamer.

The other story is the church-related tale of what unfolds in a set of denominational discussions. Here the question is what is learned about the conversations themselves. I hope those less fascinated with the nuances of the scholarship will either bear with me or skip to this story even as they grant me space to tell the story of Gadamer for those who will find it of interest.

This church story is also gaining fresh emphasis as the book is released within a series of volumes that explore Anabaptist-Mennonite concerns. With such publication, I hope to continue to talk with the conversation partners who were so important at Temple and are so often addressed in these pages. At the same time, I hope those who share my Christian passions will now also join the conversation. They and I may then find yet another layer of insights as together we stand in the church but gaze through this book at the church as if from outside. I hope that in some way this inside-outside juggling can be helpful to us all, no matter how far in or out we are.

Having explained why much of the book reads as if from a perspective of standing outside the church looking in, let me add one more explanation regarding the introduction and the epilogue. There I have sought to bracket the book in material that turns its perspective briefly the other way: inside looking out. There I have aimed to show how the rest of the book, though in some ways standing at such great distance from the church, does finally integrally connect with church agenda.

In the introduction I write as clearly and simply as I know how why the topic and approach of *Fractured Dance* matters to me, above and beyond my concerns as a scholar. I hope this will in at least a small way bridge any potential gap between church and academia. I hope also that, given the complexities of Gadamerian thought, this material will offer enough of a "Cliff Notes" summary of the book that anyone who gets lost in its mazes can always turn back to it for an overview of where I meant to go, even if I too sometimes risked getting lost in the labyrinth. Then in the epilogue I mean simply to bridge the church-academia gap one last time. My goal there is to offer one modest example of how the principles explored in *Fractured Dance* might actually be applied to ongoing church discussions.

Let me add yet that this is a living project, this quest for ways we become, indeed, a "We" amid all that sometimes appropriately and sometimes tragically divides us. I hope my investment in the project is evident. I hope it shines with some of the lifelong yet still growing passion I have felt to seek better ways to live with each other than the worship of one or another ideology, one or another partial truth worshipped as the whole truth, we humans so often fall into.

I hope evident at least implicitly are the roots of that passion in my journey through the tangled thicket of homosexuality and other controversial issues. I well remember the early 1980s days when I preached the sermons at Germantown that among many other influences probably contributed to setting the congregation on its fateful road toward head-on collision with Franconia Conference, its parent denominational body. I remember thinking I and we were so right and others so wrong.

Then I remember as well the gradual awakening to the realization that self-righteusness was probably not more to be celebrated when I was the one convinced I was right than when it showed its ugly face in those with whom I disagreed. I came increasingly to suspect that no way forward that allowed one side the smug conviction that it had cornered the truth was likely actually to be the whole truth. Year by year grew my conviction that whenever we face the thorny thickets of our most basic conflicts, there where we feel that everything dearest to us is at stake, the way forward is not likely to come by wielding the machete of one-sided righteousness. Rather, each of us will have to find our way through thorn by thorn, delicately pushing aside for each other the brambles, pondering carefully each step of the way where our truth is contributing to a way through and where it actually is one more branch obstructing our passage toward redemption.

But if I risk (as I am sometimes told I do) becoming one more dogmatist in my passion for dialogue, then I hope also that not only that passion but also my awareness of my own finitude (to preview Gadamer) is evident. I too need to risk my prejudice for dialogue and grow in response to the criticisms this book will surely generate.

I think often of a good friend of mine, who tells me mine is a romantic quest for forms of community likely to be rare indeed in a world where, he says, people actually do not want to trust and seek to learn from each other so much as to "turn each other into road-kill." There is plenty of evidence on his side, and I aim to address some of it in later chapters. But I hope he will not mind if I add that the evidence on my (and Gadamer's) side may include the mutual learning he and I find in the very act of debating whether his view or mine is truer to the actual condition of the world. The answer, I would guess, is that both of us are right and both of us are wrong, and that is why we have so much to offer each other on the way.

—*Michael A. King*
  Telford, Pennsylvania

ACKNOWLEDGMENTS

First in line to receive thanks for my having reached this point can be none other than Joan K. King, love of my life and partner in our shared juggling of parenting, homemaking, schooling, careers. She had faith I was smart those countless days I was sure I was stupid—and reminded me I was dumber than I thought those rarer days I believed I was smarter than I was.

I remember reading, long before I was a father, author acknowledgments of torments their children had suffered. Now I too understand. Thereby the parent says, "Oh, now I remember who you are; do you remember me? Will you have me back?" Kristy, Katie, and Rachael surely did live through too many weeks of "I'm sorry I've been so distracted by my writing," and "After I get through this stage I'll make you real suppers again." Candidly and repeatedly they described my scholarly personality as "Very grumpy."

Happily, after I finished the dissertation that undergirds this book they did let me return. I'll never forget the day. Katie and Rachael brought me a cake they had spent four hours making which said, "Congrats this far, Dad." Later that day, Kristy made supper as a gesture of support. With interest I wait to learn whether someday they in turn will all write books or flee screaming from the terrors they have observed. In the meantime I cherish the many times, as their minds grow ever keener, that we sit around the supper table or in the family room wrestling with issues such as this book addresses, and learn from each other perhaps even more than we ever can from books what it means truly to talk and listen and grow.

Members of my Temple dissertation committee deserve mention. I owe a tremendous debt to these veterans of the dissertation process who understood so much better than I, the apprentice, why early dissertation proposals were unworkable.

More specifically, I owe much to Herbert W. Simons, my adviser from beginning to end. Without Herb's rich and exotic blend of support alternating with pointed and perceptive criticism, I would never have made it through my course work, much less the dissertation from which this book has emerged. Arabella Lyon introduced me to Gadamer, warts and beauty both. Though she deserves no blame if I came to appreciate Gadamer perhaps even more than she might wish, without her, my passion for philosophical hermeneutics would not have flourished. Anita Pomerantz patiently and painstakingly helped me to see how many devils were in the details and to exorcise as many as I had the wit, with her help, to discern. Each will recognize in this book, imperfect though it remains, the many points where I am indebted to their feedback. My thanks also to David Watt, fourth reader, who responded with warm wit and provocative questions to a semi-final draft.

I am grateful to Germantown Mennonite Church and to Franconia Conference for suffering (perhaps uneasily, in which case I do not blame them) my observation of the conversations that became my case study. I hope they find scattered through these pages evidence their difficult journey has contributed to my own quest for ways those who disagree may still experience with each other at least a fractured dance.

As mentioned in the preface, I owe special thanks to J. Denny Weaver, C. Henry Smith Series Editor. I am grateful for the exceptionally careful, detailed, insightful reading he gave the manuscript. In addition, Denny oversaw the blind peer review which generated another round of revision suggestions but whose author(s) remain unknown to me. When I submitted the manuscript to the series, I hoped if it were accepted I would receive at least modest help shoring up weak points, but I received considerably more direction than I anticipated. At a few points perhaps it was even more than I bargained for, not because inappropriate but because demanding, yet from this vantage point I am thankful for all aspects of the feedback, including the demanding ones, since I at least am convinced that they have much improved the book.

Finally I honor my parents, Aaron and Betty King. If at times, following Gadamer, I have had to understand my tradition differently to understand it at all, without them there would have been nothing passed down to understand.

INTRODUCTION:
DREAMING ACROSS THE DIVIDE

This book is not, from one angle, about homosexuality. It is about what is involved in the process of coming to an understanding of texts or of stands taken by other persons. When one person has understood another, what has happened? That is among the key questions. What it is that is being understood can actually be virtually anything at all. Thus there is a sense in which this book is about any and all matters that lend themselves to the quest to understand. This also helps explain why one concern threading its way throughout the book has to do with what is learned not only about what is being studied (conversations on homosexuality) but also about the tools (Gadamerian philosophical hermeneutics) used to conduct the study.

Of course *Fractured Dance* does address homosexuality, yet the emphasis is not primarily on homosexuality or same-sex relations in themselves. Rather, homosexuality serves as a case study within which to examine, under particularly trying circumstances, the process of understanding. Given that it is among the more controversial issues of our era, one in relation to which perhaps understanding of positions with which we differ is particularly likely *not* to be achieved, homosexuality provides an acid test of principles of understanding. If understanding succeeds here, it is also likely to succeed in other challenging circumstances. On the other hand, if it fails here, under trial by fire, that need not rule out the possibility that understanding may be feasible in more conducive contexts, even as the failure itself can be probed for learnings.

My hope is that lessons taught both by the ability to understand (rare) and the failure to understand (common) addressed in these pages may be applicable amid any number of issues that divide, that polarize, that lend themselves more to conflict than the quest to grasp why others hold whatever position it is they cherish. I will also be pleased if such learnings can benefit denominations, congregations, or any communities wrestling with the persistent breakdowns of understanding that seem so inevitably to accompany all discussions of homosexuality and sometimes other contested matters.

Certainly breakdown has at points appeared to afflict my own denomination. A few years before this book was completed, for example, discussions of homosexuality pervaded the Mennonite binational assembly held at St. Louis in 1999. Polarized voices called the church to be faithful either by rejecting or affirming homosexual practice. However, perhaps a quest for understanding is beginning to unfold, since at the assembly held in 2001 at Nashville the rhetoric was less heated. In fact, guidelines for membership in the new Mennonite Church USA voted into existence in Nashville provide some space for continuing conversation on homosexuality. Athough the Purdue/Saskatoon agreements (see chapter 2) calling homosexual practice sinful continue to be seen as representing the core understandings of the new denomination, also receiving affirmation is the need for continuing dialogue on the issue.

A THIRD WAY

Amid this mix of polarization and hints of readiness to move past it, one possibility I hope *Fractured Dance* helps underscore is that the time may have come for a third set of prophetic voices to speak. Even as I grant the integrity of the calls many experience to speak for or against specific positions on homosexuality or other hotly argued issues, I believe some are called to a different stand, which is not primarily to choose a side and be its advocate. Rather, we are called to ask what we might learn if our focus were less on defending a given stand and more on what it means to understand each other, even—or maybe especially—across polarization.

What learnings might then emerge if, for instance, those who in relation to homosexuality have come to see each other as enemies were reconciled? What fresh understandings might be gained if together they contributed to a view of homosexuality or of the LGBT (gay, lesbian, bisexual, transgendered) agenda—the very choice of labels having itself now become a potential indicator of taking sides—larger than either alone is finding?

We whose prejudice is toward the quest to understand are also advocates, as fallible as any others, as prone as anyone to so worship our own bias toward dialogue that we lose our ability to see where our view of truth must grow. But amid our own brokenness, our call is to be advocates for the dialogue itself, to speak up for a way of looking at how we understand each other across differences that treats the one on the other side not only as enemy, not only as one whose dubious motives are to be unmasked, not only as one who wants to keep the church forever in the dark ages or as one happily ready to jettison all church values and boundaries. Our call is to ask what in the other's position, above and beneath the wrongness of it that seems so painfully obvious to so many, may nevertheless have its own valid contribution to make to our quest for truth.

My personal involvement with the Franconia research that contributed to such conclusions began early in 1997. At that point I wrote hundreds of Mennonite pastors in search of data for dissertation research into how Mennonites communicate successfully amid conflict. When I received few responses, my Temple University adviser asked me where else among Mennonites conflictual conversation might be available for study. I mentioned Franconia Conference, then processing whether to excommunicate Germantown Mennonite Church, but stressed I had no interest in being drawn into the tensions of that situation. My adviser's eyes brightened.

He won. So I observed, transcribed, and analyzed conversations of clusters of delegates who met before an April 1997 assembly. The conversations focused on the preliminary Franconia recommendation of a "third way" between the poles of full exclusion or full affirmation of congregations which accepted gays and lesbians into membership. The desire was for an imperfect, complicated, but redemptive outcome that called persons on all sides of the issue to remain in conversation and relationship.

Those who followed the story know what happened. Others will find it detailed in the latter chapters of this book: Franconia eventually voted to disfellowship Germantown. But if the outcome is not in suspense, perhaps my analysis of the process that preceded that vote can be useful to a still-battling church as well as to any groups at war with each other over their most basic beliefs and values.

TRUE UNDERSTANDING

There are many ways a researcher could specify what makes communication across differences successful. My definition is indebted to Hans-Georg Gadamer, a German philosopher whose lifelong project has been to investigate what it means truly to understand another. Among many reasons I was drawn to Gadamer was sensing connections between his views and the Apostle Paul's vision in 1 Corinthians 12-13 of a body of Christ which must learn to love its many different parts as all contributing to one body. Leaving aside the complexities which gain their full hearing in the rest of this book, let me focus here on just one key precept that seems to me to emerge from Gadamer's thought: *Each speaker's ability to grasp why the other speaker finds her or his own position persuasive is what enables the true understanding that defines conversational success.*

Gadamer believes that as we seek to understand another we must always begin through the lenses of our own biases and prejudices. We have no way to get outside ourselves to see in some neutral or objective way what is "really there." We can only start from how we see as a result of who we uniquely are, and Gadamer wants us to treasure our initial perspectives as our only way of beginning to perceive each other.

But Gadamer then asks us to risk having these initial stances enlarged, transformed, or at least in some way affected, by placing them in contact with other views. He asks me to converse with another's prejudices, and that person with mine, so profoundly and genuinely that little by little we see why the other's position seems right to her or him. Success (an evaluative term slated to receive much more attention later) does not require fully agreeing with each other but does demand our entering the other's position deeply enough to sense why the other person holds it and why it deserves our respect and readiness to learn from it.

If we do such learning, our own initial core position may remain in place, yet it will at a minimum have been enlarged by our awareness that another's position can stand beside it as having its own merit. In more dramatic if perhaps least usual cases, our readiness to learn from the other's position may impel us to allow more radical changes in our initial stand as we take into account the validity of what we may initially have opposed.

THE FRANCONIA CONVERSATIONS

My main job, then, was to look in the Franconia conversations for instances of persons ready to risk their own prejudices and to value and be enlarged by other prejudices. Sadly, I reached two key conclusions among many. First, the original third-way proposal, which emerged from conversations between Conference and Germantown representatives and was signed by both, could be viewed as moving a considerable distance toward Gadamerian conversation. It respected the initial prejudices all parties brought to the conversation and invited all to grow in valuing the perspectives of others. Second, in Gadamerian terms the conversations regarding whether to implement the third way tended to fail. Let me briefly summarize why I say this, then explore responses.

SOURCES OF FAILURE

To oversimplify, I observed three interrelated sources of failure: closure, certainty, and power dynamics. In contrast to Gadamer's belief that genuine conversation can only proceed in a spirit of mutual openness, participants tended to seem closed. We seemed to have come together less to grow than to figure out how the positions with which we disagreed would be dealt with. Second, we tended to see such closure as justified because we were already certain our own positions were right, complete, needing little adjustment.

Now closure and certainty seemed shared by persons on all sides. Many did call for openness and growth, but what seemed sometimes wanted was the openness and growth of those being spoken *to*, not those speaking. I need to be careful here; as will be seen, one research task was to investigate how my tools were insufficient for analyzing my data, and it is likely more growth unfolded than I could identify. But whether due to poor tools or actual lack of progress, I had trouble detecting significant growth.

Inadequate tools also affected my assessment of power dynamics, because Gadamer provides insufficient help with analyzing power. But if I cannot reliably say more than some modest words about power (see chapter 6), I do want to note that its effects likely helped produce the conversations as well as contributed to conversational failure. Among its many and often complex dimensions, power has to do with who decides, who defines the issues and how, who is in or out. When those aspects of power that entail setting explicit boundaries are implicated, power issues may tend to make a group see its tasks as finding closure and clarity in a defined period of time and in awareness that some may be able to impose their preferences on others. This means participants may find it hard to see their tasks as openness to others and growth in their own views.

RESPONSES

Although my bias toward pursuing understanding is clear throughout, in my study itself I aim to retain at least a modicum of scholarly distance from what I formally analyze. My formal conclusions (see chapter 7) thus largely address scholarly agenda. But here, while drawing on research results, let me also move briefly beyond them to comment not only as scholar but also as participant in the dynamics under scrutiny. When I view the Franconia conversations from within, as church member pondering implications for my denomination or others facing similar agenda, I discern a number of potential responses to the observed failures to understand. I offer them for continued testing.

First, and probably obviously, I suggest our accepting that even for Mennonites, other peace church adherents, or any people of faith—or not—committed to love of enemies, communication amid conflict is messy. There is no simple formula for success nor for assessing blame for failure. It is hard to know who could have led or participated in conversation more effectively than did Franconia delegates, I among them. The Franconia polarization grieves me, but there we see the reality that in some conflicts flawed humans may find no obvious happy way forward.

Second, we need to continue studying how power affects our deliberations. Though power dynamics are inevitable, there may be ways to structure denominational handling of them to make conversational success more likely.

Third, if we want conversation in which we value all stances as potentially contributing to Christ's one body, those of us with closed minds may need to open them. There can be little true conversation among those certain of the truth *before* we work at discerning it.

Fourth, those of us who value open minds—maybe especially Gadamerian researchers!—may also need to learn how to close them. Rigidly open minds are closed in their own way. In great conflicts, much is at stake. Here the church intends responsibly if imperfectly to exercise what members often understand (based on Matthew 18 in the New Testament) to be a God-given mandate both to loose and to bind. There *are* times to bind, to reaffirm as well as open boundaries. For those whose prejudice is that God *always* sides with loosing, growth may involve sensing when the time to bind has come.

Fifth, no matter which side we choose, evidence that *we* remain open to growth is likely what lets the *other* side trust that it is safe to grow.

Sixth, despite failures the Franconia conversations did in one crucial way succeed. Amid polarization, we delegates were present to each other. As elaborated later, Gadamer says that "The mere presence of the other before whom we stand helps us to break up our own bias and narrowness, even before he [or she] opens his [or her] mouth to . . . reply" (1989a, 26). Even when presence does not produce instantly visible mutual growth, it may set in motion reflection which over time leads me to see merit in your stance as well as mine.

Seventh, our conversations are an ongoing process unfolding amid mysterious nudgings from somewhere beyond our own understandings. Who knows, in that topsy-turvy realm, precisely when success is failure and when from failure will arise success?

A MOMENT OF GRACE

Finally I point to an anecdote (one so key to my thinking that I risk reporting it on the fourth page of this book and then again in chapter 5 in addition to alluding to it here). Such evidence counts little in hard research, but maybe it is like the tiny mustard seed from which can grow a great tree, an image Jesus uses to speak of what great things can can from what seems small and insignificant. When that farmer up north and I first disagreed then came to cherish each other's truth across our differences, this book was born. It took more months before I accepted that in fact studying conflictual conversation regarding homosexuality was to be my privilege and fate, but as that destiny became clearer, and during the many phases when I nearly lost my way in academic abstractions, I turned repeatedly for inspiration to the cherished memory of that day.

Even after our sense of truly hearing each other across our differences brought tears to each of us, we still did not fully agree. If we ever meet again, I at least will be nervous, unsure whether our journeys since then have moved us closer together or farther apart. It could be that we were offered just that brief moment of grace to hear each other, one moment of epiphany in which to transcend our ordinary earthbound tensions and see the lovely human with which we were faced.

Yet still the memory persists. If only for those few minutes, we during that time not only abstractly but truly experienced being knitted together, even amid, and in some ways because of, our contrasting stances, as members of a common body headed by Christ and surging with the power of what Christians often call the Holy Spirit and Gadamer might call—who knows? Play? Not play in the frivolous sense but the deeper import of being carried along by something larger than ourselves with which Gadamer infuses the word. Surely there is room even in Gadamer for some such spirit, given Gadamer's love for the "beautiful that captivates us. . . . before we can come to ourselves. . ." (1994, 490). My research leaves me barely glimpsing how more of us might reach that destination, but it shines for me as the dream I wish we someday all would wake to find come true. That is why I share this book.

FRACTURED dance

ONE CHAPTER

SEARCHING THROUGH GADAMER FOR A "WE" THAT DANCES WITH DIFFERENCE

INTRODUCTION

The dancers glide onto the floor of the ballroom. The waltz begins. Each dancer contributes steps not quite like any other. Each, bringing to the listening a unique way of being in the world, hears and responds to the music in different ways. Yet the music and its beat weave these varied responses into a community of movements.

Put it that way. Or this way: seeking a "we" that respects and incorporates difference; theorizing, refining, or modifying it through the philosophical hermeneutics of Hans-Georg Gadamer; exploring its presence or absence in a set of local religious conversations; assessing to what extent Gadamer is suited to such an application—these are the key ingredients of this study.

Dance. We. Simultaneously seeking the whole of the parts, the parts of the whole. Looking for togetherness amid apartness. Pursuing difference amid commonality and the commonalities that wed difference. Put it these ways and more, but each points in some way toward the quest.

Jean Bethke Elshstain helps set the study in motion through her contention that when contemporary politics of difference confront the challenge of maintaining a "we" that also respects difference, such politics refuse to work in the tension. They choose instead "smashing it to bits." She worries that focusing on "marks of difference" is generating a "public . . . world of many I's who form a we only with others exactly like themselves. No recognition of commonality is forthcoming." Elshtain concludes that "We are stuck with what the philosopher calls a world of 'incommensurability,' a world in which we literally cannot understand one another" (1995, 7).

Elshtain is pointing to a dynamic often bemoaned or celebrated in current culture: heightened awareness of difference. The popular media frequently echo Elshtain's concern. In *USA Today*, for example, Jill Lawrence (1996) comments on the "growing rudeness, even harshness, of American life" and reports on the quest for renewed civility. She quotes Pam Solo, head of the Institute for Civil Society in Boston, who contends that "What we need to do is have a civilized conversation and civilized disagreements, all with a commitment to solving problems and not winning points." And echoing Jameson's (1984) argument that postmodern emphases on difference are the "cultural logic of late capitalism," David Shenk (1997) mourns the "fragmentation and factionalism" which communication and computer technologies are fostering, as in addition to a cultural village they produce a "vast amount of cultural splintering."

My concern is not to assess whether such diagnoses are precisely on the mark. I am prepared, however, to stipulate at least that differences exist and that a We that respects difference and nurtures bridge-building, dance-fostering—or "civilized," to use Solo's term—conversation is worth pursuing. Or, to put it another way and begin to use one of the key Gadamerian terms I will shortly be elaborating, I am prepared at the outset to affirm a *prejudice*—a particular preconception—in favor of not merely celebrating differences but also bridging them. This leads to my project, which is amid the challenges posed by difference to probe the dance steps of a We that respects difference.

This also leads to my choice of *dance* as a metaphor for conversation significant enough to include in the title of this book. As partners in a dance do different things but cooperate to create a complete effect, so conversation depends on cooperation of two or more people doing different things to form a whole. In dance as in the type of conversation envisioned here, there is a complex joining of individuality and community, of freedom constrained yet not destroyed by contribution to a larger effect or outcome.

The dance imagery can also be interpreted to point to the potential problem with incommensurability, which is that at least as Elshtain arguably views matters, the potential partners are too often ceasing to dance with each other. Though the movements of a lone dancer can be beautiful, to imagine dancing only alone is to glimpse how much might be lost if the dance of partners mutually creating their ballet faded away. Similarly, though dancers engaged antagonistically or against the rhythms of the music might in their own way portray a potent dynamism, there would be much to grieve if such combativeness or at a minimum inability to share with the other complementary movements become the only interplay.

These are huge matters. Thus I propose to narrow them through a case study of Mennonites. "The calls to draw the lines are on the increase among us," contended Lorne Peachey (1996a, 16), who was editor of *Gospel Herald*, at the time circulating as one of the primary Mennonite denominational magazines, as I began this study.[1] "With those calls come temptations to assign labels and make assumptions about both belief and practices." Surveys of writings in *Gospel Herald* as well as other denominational periodicals and books (see further comment below under "Literature and Cultural/Mennonite contexts") support Peachey's perception. Peachey's rhetoric is not identical to Elshtain's, but their concerns are related. Increasingly Mennonites, Peachey can be understood to say, are fracturing the dance rather than waltzing toward a We able to respect difference.

What then are my narrowed questions? I want to ask in relation to Mennonites what instances of a Mennonite risking of prejudices and enlargement of horizons might look like, and what this might reveal concerning the requirements for sustaining a We that dances with differences. As a Mennonite myself, I am interested in the specifics of the question. And specifics are precisely what can narrow my initial broader question to a manageable scope. So Mennonite specifics will be much addressed in this study.

However, I remain interested as well in the larger implications for Western culture of how the question is answered. Thus my study proceeds at two levels. At the primary level, I focus on local Mennonite concerns. But at a secondary level I keep in mind the larger question of what may be required to encourage a cultural We that respects difference. The study is framed by that level, as in introductory and concluding comments I address possible broader implications of learnings gleaned from analysis of my local research site.

The primary resources I draw on in addressing my key questions are those provided by Hans-Georg Gadamer's philosophical hermeneutics (1976, 1994a). Gadamer, still active as a scholar even though a centenarian, deserves attention as a theorist of the process of understanding who has played a central role in shaping twentieth- and twenty-first-century thought. As Hugh J. Silverman notes,

"Gadamer's hermeneutics has permeated not only philosophy, literary study, and theology, but also legal studies, sociology, intellectual history, art history, and cultural studies" (1991, 2-3).

Gadamer (as will be seen) might interact with issues of difference and "We-ness" by speaking of prejudices and the "deep common accord" from which they spring (1976, 7). As Graeme Nicholson summarizes what will turn out to be crucial matters,

> By "prejudice" Gadamer means the finiteness of every understanding we achieve, the circumstance that every understanding and interpretation will be controlled to some degree by preconceptions that are not brought to consciousness and that reflect the viewpoint of the interpreter, and the times of the interpreter, rather than the interpreted text. (1997, 317)

Then, to link these issues more specifically to my project, Gadamer might contend that prejudices simultaneously produce and embody the differences in each interpreter's perspective yet point to a commonality that can be viewed as undergirding a We. This is because those who hold prejudices—namely, all of us—are not locked into but can experience them as "biases of our openness to the world" and to each other's perspectives (1976, 9).

Perhaps in mild but significant contrast to Nicholson's description, which speaks of prejudices which "control" the interpreter, Gadamer highlights their productive characteristics, their power not so much to control our vision as to enable us to see the world at all. To understand Gadamer it is crucial to understand this positive twist Gadamer gives to prejudices, which are more commonly and perhaps nearly universally viewed in negative terms. To be prejudiced is typically to be afflicted with an unfortunate condition. Not so for Gadamer, who claims "It is not so much our judgments as our prejudices that constitute our being" (9).

Aware that "This is a provocative formulation," Gadamer deliberately engages in the irony of turning the meaning of prejudice inside-out. Against the common view, which Gadamer blames on the Enlightenment, Gadamer insists that "Prejudices are not necessarily unjustified and erroneous, so that they inevitably distort the truth." Rather, wanting to restore to the term the "literal sense of the word," Gadamer claims that prejudices "constitute the initial directedness of our whole ability to experience" (9). Note again that Gadamer values prejudices particularly as avenues for gaining enlarged insight. As we allow our many different prejudices to intersect, interact, even combat, they lead us toward what Gadamer's thought might inspire us to view as the common music weaving our many different steps into one dance.

Although my research may have implications in many disciplines, the disciplines from in which I have approached Gadamer are primarily those of rhetoric and speech communication.[2] In addition, to the extent hermeneutics as well as Gadamerian scholarship are emerging as their own fields of discipline, I have clearly operated heavily in them. Thus my work joins rhetoric and speech concerns with those of Gadamerian hermeneutics.

As will later become evident (see particularly chapter 6), this is no uncontroversial union, and some would prefer to see the partners parted. One concern is that Gadamerian analysis may too easily conflate rhetoric and hermeneutics. Perhaps a more pressing concern, in light of my aims, is that by choosing to give Gadamer and his ontological hermeneutics as much weight as I have, I bias my entire project in the direction of equating successful management or bridging of differences with finding commonalities of understanding. The worry is this: the We-seeking prejudice of Gadamerian hermeneutics may shroud the ability of at least some rhetoric-weighted theories to envision management of differences that remains fruitful even if those who differ remain antagonists rather than seeking to understand each other.

Charles Altieri, for one, sees any weighting of "ontological" hermeneutics over rhetoric as potentially constructing a prison. As Altieri puts it, "Where ontology is trapped in terms like *same*, *relative*, or *other*, rhetorical analysis concentrates on how actions play among those various conditions." Ontological hermeneuts, Altieri claims, lock themselves in static and too often transcendent and apolitical categories that reward only ponderous musings far above the fray of the competing rhetorics which are the real stuff of real life. In contrast, rhetorical analysis, as Altieri conceives it, evades positing "static poles" and instead concerns itself "always with flexibility and malleability: claims to identity can be manipulated for the interests of difference, and fears about irreducible differences can be negotiated in ways that establish provisional shared concerns" (1997, 102).

Altieri's cogent reasoning deserves a response. What can I offer? Why proceed, as I have, precisely into what Altieri has identified as a trap? Although (again as discussed especially in chapter 6) I have come to see that views such as Altieri's have merit, the entirety of this study in one sense constitutes support for what Altieri criticizes. Repeatedly I have aimed to highlight the value of the hermeneutic emphases. I have hoped to demonstrate why Stanley Deetz contends authors like "Gadamer . . . have convincingly shown that the most basic conception of communication is the attempt to reach mutual understanding" (1990, 230-231). I have tried to make a case for the value of bridging differences through mutual understanding rather than only through the creation, say, of shifting alliances based on the similar goals of those who do not in the end understand each other.

This valuing of hermeneutic commonality has served as another prejudice, another bias of openness to the world, with which to begin a study—and also as yet another prejudice to be tested, enlarged, and potentially changed. No matter the outcome, a beginning must be made, and this is one of the crucial prejudices with which I set my project in motion.

The data for my explorations were provided primarily through transcripts of three conversations on homosexuality held by delegates of the Franconia Conference[3]—a geographic and administrative denominational subdivision of roughly seventy congregations.[4] The issue at stake was whether one congregation, Germantown Mennonite Church, should be expelled from membership in the Conference for accepting into membership gay and lesbian members engaged in active practice of their sexuality. As will be seen, these conversations unfolded in a highly polarized context. They thus provided a potentially fruitful setting in which to discern what prejudices are being expressed, to investigate what resources for managing prejudices they offer, and to assess to what extent a We can be perceived as existing even amid sharp differences.

The fact that these conversations provided the site for my study also helps explain my opting for an approach with a hermeneutic bias. As will be seen, I conclude there are normative ingredients to Gadamer's thought which would make application harder in settings where high value is placed on rhetoric's ability to enhance negotiation of Altieri's "provisional shared concerns." But Gadamer seems well-matched to a study of Mennonite data, because his norms have affinities with Mennonite norms. As chapter 2 details, Mennonites place high value on community even as they have historically struggled with how to manage differences of perspective in the community. Heterogeneity even amid Mennonites generates a variety of images of what it means to be Mennonite, but at least one common tendency is to see themselves as a people who gather to open themselves to the Bible's transforming wisdom and guidance.

A version of this emphasis is evident in Mennonite biblical scholar Willard Swartley's contention that the "believing community is an *interpreting community*" which "as a whole people of God"

(1983, 236) or "community of faith" (1990, 81) tests interpretations of individuals. As they come together in accountability to their biblical subject matter and each other's interpretations of it, Mennonites are inherently living by norms not distant from Gadamer's.

After laying introductory groundwork in this chapter (see also Appendixes A and B for more detailed comment on how and through what methods the study unfolded), I proceed in five steps described in six chapters:

- First, I introduce Mennonite "effective history" (ch. 2).
- Second, I explore in the Franconia conversations the characteristics of conversation successful in Gadamerian terms (ch. 3).
- Third, I investigate what characteristics might be judged as failures to engage in Gadamerian conversation (ch. 4).
- Fourth, I point to and wrestle with challenges in applying Gadamer that have become evident through this attempt to do so (ch. 5 and ch. 6). Key here is the fact that, as noted earlier, my goal is to tell not one but two stories: not only the story of what is learned about conversation, including the specifics of the Franconia discussions, when viewed through Gadamer, but also the story of how Gadamerian thought fares when applied as it is here. Thus an important question asked in these chapters is this: When failures to operate within a Gadamerian view of understanding occur, are they failures of the conversations or of Gadamerian theory?
- Finally I evaluate what has been learned, what has not, and what directions for further research into or application of Gadamerian thought might prove fruitful (ch. 7).

LITERATURE AND
CULTURAL/MENNONITE CONTEXTS

The paucity of significant literature on a practical Gadamerian appropriation such as I propose[5] suggests one of this project's contributions is, precisely, to explore how Gadamerian theory may be concretely applied. Applications of Gadamer *have* been made to communication studies (Deetz, 1978), ethnograpy (Huspek, 1994; McHoul, 1982), feminist studies (Buker, 1990), religious studies (Tracy, 1984) social theory (Palmer, 1987), sociology (Cotlar, 1986; McGowan, 1989; Hekman, 1984), homiletics (Bullock, 1996), and more. Often, however, applications either draw on mediating theories after relying on Gadamer for broad inspiration, or they tend toward the lack of specificity frequently characteristic of Gadamer's own treatment of his theory[6], which, as Czubaroff and Whelan note, is "extremely abstract." They add that "its denial of methods leaves one wondering how, indeed, to proceed if one practically wishes to achieve understanding of given texts or persons encountered in one's experience" (1995, 8). Their application of philosophical hermeneutics to pedagogy stands as one of the rare efforts to concretize Gadamer; I hope my project is another.

If the literature on philosophical hermeneutics does not provide significant guidance for my practical appropriation, my concerns nevertheless intersect with several bodies of literature. Throughout, I explore interrelated writings in hermeneutics, communication, rhetoric, and philosophy whose treatment of the issues makes them pertinent.

Most literature on homosexuality is ultimately tangential to my purposes, since homosexuality as an issue is not in focus except to the extent that it emerges in the Franconia conversations themselves. Nevertheless, some of the key or representative works in this literature, particularly those which intersect in some way with religion, Christianity, or Anabaptism provide a helpful survey of the range of thinking in this area, from the "welcoming but not affirming" stance of Grentz (1998) to the "queer theory" of Comstock and Henking (1996).

Among examples of pertinent literature are Abelove et al (1993), Armour (1999), Balch (2000), Boswell (1981), Brawley (1996), Brooten (1996), Clark (1997) , Collins (2000), Comstock (1996), Comstock and Henking (1996), Foucault (1990), Fulkerson (1994), Gaede (1998), Gies and Messer (1994), Glaser (1998), Goss (1993), Greenberg (1998), Halperin (1995) , Hanigan (1988), Hays (1986, 1991), Hefling (1996), Jones and Yarhouse (2000), Jordan (1997), Kotva (1989), Kreider (1998), McNeil (1995), Mollenkott (1992), Pronk (1993), Satinover (1996), Say and Kowalewski (1998), Schmidt (1995), Siker (1994a, b), Soards (1995), Stuart et al (1997), Sullivan and Landau (1997), Weed and Schor (1997).

Five sets of resources on homosexuality deserve more extended attention. First, Ralph R. Smith and Russel R. Windes are authors of two works whose goals differ from yet complement and even at one point explicitly overlap with my own. These are "The Progay and Antigay Issue Culture" (1997) and *Progay/Antigay: The Rhetorical War over Sexuality* (2000). Their analyses of North American cultural rhetoric related to homosexuality places priority on "highlighting instabilities of discourses on controversial public issues" rather than, in hermeneutic fashion, seeking the commonalities that unite more stable interpretive communities (1997, 30). Drawing on such theorists as Kenneth Burke and Joshua Gamson, they proceed consistent with Altieri's emphasis on the ability of rhetoric to trace shifting and unstable alliances and oppositions among those who do not necessarily aim to understand each other. They highlight ways

> oppositional discourse in public controversy over variant sexuality shapes presentation of collective identity, influences definition of controversy, contributes to understanding of the relationship between antagonists, and heightens dissent among sponsors of any one interpretive package. (1997, 30)

However, even as Smith and Windes place "emphasis on oppositional engagement" (2000, 183) in analyzing progay/antigay rhetoric, they seek "prescriptions for preventing the development of tragic conflict out of moral disagreement" (197). Among their prescriptions is to recognize that "polarized public debate can be supplemented by dialogic communication" (198). Interestingly, they cite in this regard the earlier dissertation from which this book emerged:

> Employing the Gadamerian insight that every misunderstanding presupposes common accord, rhetorician Michael King (1998) suggests that "what we hold in common is what allows us to recognize difference in the first place" (p. 18). Consequently, there is a need to encourage dialogic search for commonality in which difference is translated through symbols of consubstantiality into a more civil and productive discourse. (198)

Second, for those interested in a synopsis of the history of debates on homosexuality among religious groups, the Internet provides invaluable resources. Key is the work of Ontario Consultants on Religious Tolerance. Although their very name likely flags a prejudice, sometimes evident in their interpretive comments, their site provides a largely factual, carefully annotated overview of the current positions of the major Christian denominational bodies, from Anglican through American Baptist to Presbyterian to Roman Catholic and many more, including Mennonite (2000).

As can be seen in the Ontario Consultants resources, the Mennonite debate studied in this book is just one of countless similar conversations unfolding across Christendom, and the range of positions are also roughly comparable, ranging (as will be elaborated later in relation to Franconia) from exclusion of homosexuals from membership through conditional inclusion and full inclusion. The bulk of denominations tend toward some form of exclusion, typically at least denying membership to any involved in same-sex erotic activity. Some, such as the Southern Baptists, are even ready to countenance some forms of discrimination against gays and lesbians to protect, as they see it, heterosexual family life. Only a few denominations, such as United Church of Christ, appear largely to have resolved the tensions by moving wholeheartedly toward full inclusion of practicing gays and lesbians. UCC commitment to full inclusion is symbolized by unusual readiness to ordain practicing gays and lesbians on the same terms as heterosexual ordinands (2000).

A third resource on homosexuality deserving notice is among the few careful academic treatments to date to assess not only Mennonite discourse but also the same Germantown-Franconia conversations I am exploring. In "Mennonite Public Discourse and the Conflicts over Homosexuality," Gerald Biesecker-Mast reaches conclusions similar to mine though by a different path. Using analytic tools indebted to Ernesto Laclau and Chantal Mouffe, Biesecker-Mast suggests combatants in church wars can learn to treat each other as enemies to be loved in recognition that whether in war or peace, they together make each other who they are (1998).

Biesecker-Mast is asking how Mennonites might bring to bear on conflict "our radical, self-endangering love for the necessary enemy and thus our openness to the possibility of miracles that transcend ongoing communal antagonisms" (299). By reaching this Gadamer-like place on a different path, Biesecker-Mast shows there is more than one way to get here. However, he reaches this destination by drawing on theorists who are in turn influenced by Foucault. As particularly my chapter 6 discussion indicates, I see Foucaultian thought as potentially less suited than Gadamerian emphases to the healing of antagonisms Biesecker-Mast joins me in seeking. Nevertheless, Biesecker-Mast makes his own strong case for his path, suggesting that a fruitful way to approach our respective emphases is to place them in mutually transforming conversation.

A fourth resource on homosexuality is a modest (in length) yet significant article by Richard A. Kauffman on "A Third Way Beyond Fight or Flight" (2000), which was published in the denominational weekly magazine *The Mennonite*. As he calls for a ratcheting down of denominational battle cries over homosexuality, readiness to live with ambiguity, and the need for more humble respect for positions other than our own, Kauffman eloquently explores a variety of themes which overlap with the concerns explored in this book. In a memorable conclusion that dovetails with some of the central Gadamerian themes, he states that

One thing I know for certain is that we can't be absolutely certain about these matters. The people who make me most skeptical and guarded are those—on either side—who are so sure of themselves. And I've sensed that there's more than enough self-righteousness to go around. If we can't find a third way and a church split results, I don't know which group I'd want to join. I'm willing to be part of a church committed to wrestling with the issues, but I'm not willing to be part of a church defined by homosexuality, either for it or against it. A measure of humility would help us all. (8)

A final resource on homosexuality is *To Continue the Dialogue: Biblical Interpretation and Homosexuality*, edited by C. Norman Kraus (2001). Among reasons to mention this book are these: first, this collection of chapters by many Mennonite authors is among the first Mennonite book-length treatments of homosexuality to be published. Second, that book was shaped by this one. On behalf of Pandora Press U.S., I oversaw development of the Kraus book and its dialogic framework. Although I make no claim to have contributed to a perfectly dialogic outcome (whatever perfection might look like in this case), principles of understanding reported on in *Fractured Dance* explicitly and regularly guided my efforts to shape *To Continue the Dialogue* (whose foreword is by Richard Kauffman) into a resource guided by a quest for mutual understanding rather than one primarily made up of position papers.

Also deserving comment is literature emerging from and contributing to an intellectual and cultural milieu in which dissensus and difference are emphasized. Pertinent here are literatures intersecting, for instance, with postmodernism, poststructuralism, and Foucauldian understandings of power. Echoing to some extent the perspectives attributed above to Altieri, Calvin O. Schrag (1997) helps place such literature in context. He suggests that the hermeneutic bias is "broad and deep in its orientation toward a solidarity of consensus against the backcloth of a valorization of unity and totality. . . ." Meanwhile the rhetorical bias is "to problematize the ideals of solidarity and consensus in recognition of the need to live with multiplicity and difference" (136).

But even as Schrag values the problematizing of hermeneutic desires by rhetoric, he wants to show the need for hermeneutics to problematize rhetoric. Schrag contends there is a "tendency to valorize and celebrate difference over sameness" to such an extent that "the proper disposition of discourse is . . . seen as being dissensus rather than consensus, disagreement rather than agreement" (136).

As I proceed, I make no claim to resolving the extent to which difference or commonality predominates in the West. Nor do I claim to maintain delicate scholarly distinctions between the meanings of such interrelated terms as difference, pluralism, fragmentation, multiplicity, heterogeneity, dissensus, on the one hand; or such terms as sameness, unity, oneness, totality, homogeneity, consensus on the other hand. The differences among them do matter; much of my application of Gadamer has to do with showing, for example, that though Gadamer is often viewed as supporting only the set of terms that might be viewed as clustering around sameness, his thought actually leads to seeing the sameness- and difference-related terms as interpenetrating. However, the finer nuances of such terms are addressed primarily as they relate to Gadamerian thought, since my concern is not so much to interact with the many literatures related to such matters as to remain close to Gadamer's handling of the nature and implications of prejudices in favor of connecting differences or celebrating their separateness.

Nevertheless, and as one who concurs with at least the broad strokes of Schrag's assessment, let me briefly point to evidence that the presence and valorization of difference is indeed significant and has implications for how I situate my own study. For instance, Michel Foucault calls for a genealogical thought which searches not for foundations but rather "disturbs what was previously considered immobile; it fragments what was thought unified; it shows the heterogeneity of what was imagined consistent with itself" (1977, 147). And Richard Rorty claims any "solidarity which is not parochial" could only be "the expression of an ahistorical human nature" (1991, 23). Yet even Rorty's parochial consensus is distrusted by some as a mirage or even a form of terrorism (Lyotard, 1984; Lyotard and Thébaud, 1985; Kent, 1992) which must yield in turn to the differences of each lingual community, of each individual, and of each fragmentary identity in the illusory unified self. Patricia Ticineto Clough approves an ever-fragmenting feminism and its production of a "subjectivity which never becomes unified and which speaks in many tongues" (1994. 129).

It is with such valorizing of dissensus as backdrop and potential critic of my own quest for some sort of We that I proceed. As I do, I show how Gadamer is challenged by such emphases as well as how he addresses difference even as he provides an alternative which highlights commonalities.

Finally deserving mention is literature on the Mennonite context and its own contrasting and sometimes conflicting tendencies toward on the one hand community maintenance and on the other hand fragmentation (tensions explored in chapter 2). Sociological surveys of Mennonite attitudes, such as Leland Harder and J. Howard Kauffman (1975); and Kauffman and Leo Driedger (1991), provide noteworthy data. Pertinent as well are results of Kauffman and Driedger's exploration of Mennonites and modernization. Their study, they conclude, confirmed their expectation that "modernization would lead to. . . . more heterogeneity and pluralism" (46).

Also significant are studies by Rodney J. Sawatsky (1992), who comments that "For those who know Mennonite reality, pluralism is, if not *the*, at least *a* central reality" (141); and Harder (1993), who draws on Sawatsky as well as the Kauffman and Driedger study to compare and contrast separatist, conservative, liberal, and transformative Mennonites. Sociologist Fred Kniss (1997) deserves mention for his studies placing in cultural context intra-Mennonite tensions over preserving tradition versus maintaining community.

Anabaptist rhetorician Susan Biesecker-Mast wrestles in significant ways with how Derrida's thought might inform Anabaptist responses to postmodernity and difference. In calling for an Anabaptism courageous enough to pursue "the traces of those truths which would undo our truths," Biesecker-Mast pursues a goal that overlaps with my own call for risking of prejudices even as she might contend that her Derridean approach is more truly risky than a Gadamerian understanding which always sees difference as undergirded by commonality (1999).

One indicator of Mennonite heterogeneity is a history of splits at all levels of denominational life, from congregational to national fellowships. Repeatedly Mennonites facing differences have opted to separate from rather than coexist with opponents. Among many splits that could be noted, two in particular deserve mention.[7] One is the 1690s split in which Mennonites became a more culturally (though still separatist) mainstream group and the Amish a different group characterized by dramatically greater withdrawal from the larger culture.

The other is the 1847 Pennsylvania split in which the conservative and progressive wings of one group became alienated from each other and elected to separate. In 1861 the progressive Pennsylvania wing joined several Iowa congregations to form the General Conference Mennonite Church (GC). Meanwhile the conservative wing formed the roots of what remained into the 1990s the Mennonite Church (MC). The GC and MC became the two largest North American Mennonite denominations.

In eastern Pennsylvania, the initial site of the 1847 division, the split can be visually observed: various congregations exist across fields or roads in plain sight of each other, here MC, there GC, each split pair mute testimony to the original preference of members to ratify their own stances rather than seek a way for their different prejudices to remain in dynamic and potentially enlarging contact. As will be seen, this history of splits has affected the Franconia conversations in various ways, including a renewed quest for a commonality able to "avoid the schism and brokenness of past decisions" (Miller, 1997).

GADAMER'S HERMENEUTICS

This section summarizes central emphases of Gadamer's philosophical hermeneutics. This brief treatment is intended to set the stage for following more detailed accounts of Gadamer's thought. Here key terms in addition to prejudice, already introduced, and their relevance to my study are explored. In addition, two key issues are highlighted. The first issue is the potential of Gadamerian thought to acknowledge and affirm the difference highlighted by poststructuralism and postmodernism yet still weave connections and commonalities. The second is the crucial question of how, amid difference, risking of initial prejudices or understandings to dance to a common music might unfold.

DIFFERENCE AND COMMONALITY: A CREATIVE TENSION

The potential of philosophical hermeneutics to hold difference and commonality in creative tension is eloquently highlighted by Gerald L. Bruns, who sees Gadamer as providing a

> figure of commonality or mutual belonging, where what is common, what is shared, is not an identity but a difference—and moreover not a dialectical or systematic difference in a totality but a radical difference that is not to be overcome or subsumed in a higher order, one that calls for acknowledgment and acceptance, much the way a limit or one's own mortality calls not so much for knowledge as acknowledgment. What is it to share a difference or to hold a difference in common? It is perhaps like sharing a history or a mode of being historical. But is a sharing in which neither side gives up its singularity, its freedom, its otherness or self-refusal. . . . (1992, 206)

Gadamer himself can of course be intepreted in innumerable ways as different interpreters bring different prejudices to bear on his thought, but for my purposes, Bruns' interpretation of Gadamer is critical and shapes mine. As Bruns and I both understand Gadamer, from the beginning he assumes commonality *and* difference.

Although there is much more to be said on this later, here is one key response to those who see Gadamer as so privileging commonality that no room is left for the dance with difference. Their concerns are important, because if Gadamer does not respect difference, then his valuing of commonality indeed risks becoming the imperialistic devaluing of difference he is sometimes viewed as fomenting. While deferring full discussion of these matters, the key point to be made in these introductory comments is that it is possible to interpret Gadamer as weaving difference into the core of his thought. Without difference, there would be no need for philosophical hermeneutics, which emerge from asking how, when striving to understand the text, object, person which is other than us, "we can break the spell of our own fore-meanings" (1994a, 268). How to relate to what is other, to what confronts us across the rifts of difference: this is Gadamer's quest. How we can be affected by, even transformed by the other and the other's differentness (and vice-versa) is a central Gadamerian question.

But note—and of course here is where he is sometimes viewed as vulnerable to criticism—that for Gadamer *other* is always joined to *relate*. For Gadamer the very ability to recognize difference points to deeper commonality. "Is it not, in fact, the case," he famously asks, "that every misunderstanding presupposes a 'deep common accord'?" (1976, 7). The very recognition of difference or misunderstanding points to commonality that enables such recognition. Thus for Gadamer there is always a byplay between difference and commonality. The quest to understand is made necessary by difference. But what we hold in common is what allows us to recognize difference in the first place. Gadamer's project is to search for fruitful ways to manage this byplay.

Again it must be stressed that difference, according to this understanding of Gadamer, is always in view. Gadamer's "deep common accord" is sometimes interpreted by critics as affirming so primordial a commonality that difference becomes evanescent. This, it seems to me, is simultaneously a concern to be taken seriously and one that risks misreading Gadamer, who is not aiming to minimize difference with such a statement but rather claiming that a minimal commonality is necessary for difference even to register.

To give a pertinent example: if Altieri and I argue from our different perspectives over the relative merits of a hermeneutic or a rhetorical bias, we must both hold in common at least minimally overlapping understandings of what constitute hermeneutics and rhetoric, or there would be no point our even engaging each other over their relative merits. The commonality is what enables the discussion over our differences.

KEY GADAMERIAN TERMS

At the outset of his quest, Gadamer calls for an interpretive turn which places him at odds with the Enlightenment and modernist faith that humans can seek truth and knowledge undistorted by the knower. This entails moving from a search for solid foundations of knowledge and objectivity to an affirmation that human understanding is always, as both Martin Heidegger[8] and Gadamer might put it, a "thrown projection."

Understanding is thrown into an *effective history* (1994, 301-302) which predetermines the *prejudices* (1976, 8-9; 1994, 269-277)—the foreknowledges or prejudgments—I bring to a situation in any act of understanding. Effective history, then, points toward the crucial role the past plays in shaping my present. As I enter this effective history through my own acts of understanding, I project my understandings forward toward a future I cannot control or clearly foresee. I contribute my part toward the effective history which will be the medium in which my descendants understand.

Among crucial ensuing principles are that when one party in a conversation seeks to *understand another*—a crucial, hermeneutics-biased assumption weaving its way throughout this study—both must gather around the *subject matter* (*die Sache*) and *open* themselves (1994a, 361) to the *questions* (1994a, 299-301, 362-379) it asks of them. As they each extend the reach of the questions through wrestling with them within the *horizon* which produces and is made visible by their initial prejudices, their horizons are enlarged. As the wrestling proceeds, some overlap in horizons emerges; Gadamer calls this overlap the *fusion of horizons* (1994a, 306-307). He refers to participants in hermeneutic conversation as linguistic circles who through putting their prejudices *at risk* in openness to the claim of the subject matter expand their circles to overlap with other circles (1976, 17).

LONGING FOR COMPLETION

What energizes the quest for common understanding? Why risk my prejudices in a quest to learn from yours? Why not rather affirm a ceaseless profusion of difference? Some clues for answering such questions are provided in Gadamer's essay on Plato's *Lysis* (1980). There Gadamer does not explicitly link hermeneutics to his comments. However, he provides a doorway through which to enter his vision of how prejudices which are initially my treasure or yours become mutual treasures.

Gadamer addresses the nature of friendship through commentary on Socrates' dialectic (as presented by Plato) with two boys regarding the issue. Gadamer concludes that crucial to friendship is recognizing that the other is both like and unlike me. The friend is sufficiently like me that I can connect with her (7-12). As Gadamer elsewhere says, I can only encounter the alien through the support of the common, the familiar, through an affinity with what in the other I already understand from in my own horizon (1976, 15).

At the same time, if the friend is merely like me, of what use or attraction is that? There is no spark there, no energy, nothing to draw us together. Needed as well is the pull of what is different than me. Yet if we push this insight too far, we conclude my best friend is my enemy—because he is most unlike me, therefore the energy released in the tension between us is greatest. Clearly anyone involved in friendship knows the friend is not the same as the enemy (1980, 13).

A third option—the "neither/nor" Gadamer says Plato so often insightfully provides in his dialectics—is needed. That option is this: I am able to connect with the friend initially through what is like me, but there is also something unlike me in the friend which is "dear" to me, which sparks in me love for the friend, because though it is unlike me it is something which completes me, brings me home to myself. Through such exchange of what is "dear" to us Gadamer claims that friends—and by extension all who seek to understand— enter an *oikos* or household in which through our joint seeking of completion we launch ourselves into the buoyancy of play and abandonment to the subject matter (13-20).

Again and again it is evident that for Gadamer a crucial feature of life in the oikos as well as of the hermeneutic journey is a relationality of commonalities. There is an interpenetration of need and completion and love in the Gadamerian household which can only take place in relationships oriented toward rather than against the other. In an essay on art and the beautiful, Gadamer refers to a Greek fable in which the gods cut humans in half. They then become halves ever after seeking wholeness. Some such longing as this, which Gadamer compares to the love relationship or to marriage, brings people together in all hermeneutic processes or conversations (1986, 31-33).

This longing for completion in relationship is what drives our willingness to open ourselves to views of the world inherent in the prejudices of the other (1994a, 268). The longing impels us to listen to each other, and "anyone who listens is fundamentally open. Without such openness to one another there is no genuinely human bond" (1994a, 361). Here it becomes evident why *risk* is so crucial to Gadamerian thought. To make contact with the other we must be open to the other. Even though we long for those completions through the other which constitute our human bonds, it is risky to be open to the otherness of others. Such openness puts in question our prejudgments, our ways of foreknowing the world.

Indeed, Gadamer goes so far as to contend that true understanding has not taken place until the interpreter not only risks prejudices but assumes the superiority or at least completeness of what is being interpreted. This "foreconception" or "prejudice of completeness . . . implies not only . . . that a text should completely express its meaning—but also that what it says should be the complete truth" (1994a, 294). This is a key and radical statement. Through it Gadamer is insisting that until we have suspended judgment regarding the validity of what we seek to understand, or to put it even more radically, until we trust in the full truth of what we seek to understand, we cannot actually understand it. As we will see, much fruitful insight and many challenges flow from this claim.

TEXT OR PERSON?

Note here two things. First, Gadamer speaks in terms of "text" rather than person. This introduces an important problematic in applying Gadamer. Does he mean primarily to speak of understanding in relation to the reader of, say, an article or book? Or does he mean to address as well the "texts" exchanged by living persons seeking to understand each other? Gadamer himself claims that hermeneutics applies to "everything intelligible. Since it brings this whole breadth into play, it forces the interpreter to play with his own prejudices at stake" (1994a, 568). This conflation of text with "everything" else is a common Gadamerian move which seems to justify proceeding in the attempt to apply his hermeneutics not only to texts but also to conversational exchanges. Yet worries about Gadamer's textual bias remain and will receive their due in chapter 5.

NOT KNOWING BUT BEING GRASPED BY TRUTH

Second, Gadamer's radical claim is that until I assume the "completeness" of the other, I will not launch myself into the risk of openness that allows my being fully possessed by the truth of whatever I seek to understand. As Warnke explains, Gadamer intends in this way to ensure that the "thing itself" has opportunity to enlarge my prejudices rather than being merely subsumed in them. Gadamer wants to emphasize a view in which truth possesses, takes hold of, or "knows" me rather than in which I possess, control, fully know the truth. Truth, not I, takes charge. It is by accepting the possible superior validity of the thing that I risk my initial view of it (Warnke, 1987, 82-83). It is important to remember that the argument is not that in actuality the other is always true or complete. The claim here is not finally that whatever I come to understand is therefore by definition also true. Rather, the contention is that I cannot fully understand even what makes it false or incomplete if I have not first accepted the possibility of its truth or completion.

Shadow hermeneutics

Gadamer's arguments for risk imply the possibility of choosing against risk, as is evident in the envisioning above of what happens "without such openness." Thus underlying Gadamer's hermeneutics as a kind of shadow or counter-hermeneutics is an implicit vision of strategies for and consequences of denying the hermeneutic process. As is more fully explored in chapter 4, the counter-strategies might include ignoring, minimizing, distorting, or opposing other prejudices in the process of defending one's own against them. A major counter-strategy is the attempt to evade (as Gadamer believes objectivist, Enlightenment thought does) human finitude. This counter-strategy is evident whenever an effort is made to leap to de-historicized objective thought believed capable of transcending prejudice. The common feature uniting such counter-strategies is the tendency toward ahistorical certainty and closure, toward erecting walls against mutual understanding rather than building bridges across which such understanding might travel.

At least two grave consequences flow from such strategies. First, true (i.e. Gadamerian) understanding itself becomes impossible. Understanding simply cannot occur when the interpreter refuses to recognize that the subject matter "always speaks for itself," always aims to speak for the prejudices of the horizon from which it arises (1994a, 568). Thus it has never been fully understood until the potential persuasiveness of its perspective has been experienced. Second, counter-hermeneutic strategies make impossible any "genuinely human bond." For Gadamer the human bond exists only amid the exchange of risky hermeneutic openness.

Analyzing Gadamer's "shadow" hermeneutics highlights negative motivations for risk. But Gadamer's emphasis is finally on the positive payoffs. By risking opening ourselves to the other in the hermeneutic experience, we allow ourselves to be "possessed by something and precisely by means of it we are opened up for the new, the different, the true" (1976, 9).

Being possessed

Even as Gadamer calls us to risk ourselves, however, he always maintains the tensions of neither/nor, like/unlike. We open ourselves to the other "by putting *ourselves* in his position." Gadamer italicizes *ourselves* here to emphasize the implications. What we put in the other's shoes, when we seek to understand, is *ourselves* as the other. This means we do not somehow become the other but rather make radical contact with "the otherness, the indissoluble individuality of the other person" even as we maintain our own (305).

For Gadamer the risk of openness to the other is balanced by knowledge that each of our differences is irreducible. To open ourselves to the other is to relinquish neither our difference from nor similarity to the other. The indissolubility of my and your individuality is maintained even as the commonality and longing for completion that enables us to put ourselves in each other's position is affirmed.

Application

This balance is maintained as well in Gadamer's concept of *application*. Understanding depends on deep commonality yet also requires application to the particular. No subject matter has been properly understood until it has come alive in the immediate, the local, the concrete (1994a, 308-309). Thus the differences inherent in all interpreters are not dissolved in the hermeneutic process; rather, they reshape what they seek to understand even as they open themselves to be reshaped by it through a fusion of horizons in which differences are not dissolved but mutually contribute to a new understanding. This is the meaning of Gadamer's memorable comment that "we understand in a *different* way, *if we understand at all*" (1994a, 296-297).[9]

Power

Such insistence that true understanding does not permit dissolution of difference has a bearing on criticisms that Gadamer does not confront implications of power.[10] Indeed I grant power is undertheorized in Gadamer; it is striking to observe in the foregoing discussion of the household of love, for instance, that power issues do not intrude. This is a common silence in Gadamer (as detailed in chapter 6). However (as contended also in chapter 6), Gadamer's thought implicitly engages power agenda. It does so through its insistence that risking my prejudices includes affirming their integrity and inescapability, not exchanging them for yours, and through the related recognition that in application to the particular the interpreter's singularities always play a role in the hermeneutic process. To maintain my singularity, my difference, rather than to accede to its erasure, is to exercise a form of power (again see chapter 6). Thus Gadamer is finally in tension with any power configurations which promote coercive abolishing of differences.

But enough of introducing Gadamerian theory. Important as it is, key to this project is the effort to apply theory, to ask what tools it offers when brought to bear on specific instances of successful or failed human attempts to understand.[11] To that application, amid the halting efforts of those in Franconia Conference to understand each other, and their haunting, as we shall see, by the specter of failure, I now turn.

TWO
CHAPTER

EFFECTIVE HISTORY AND MENNONITES

As introduced in the previous chapter, a key Gadamerian concept is that of *effective history*, by which Gadamer refers to the complex intertwining of linguistic and historical factors that preconstruct the milieu we individually and communally enter even before conscious of it. An important aspect of Gadamaer's view here is that history and the cultures embedded in and embodying it are in motion, like a river, and carry us forward in their currents. Thus any of our understandings are part of this pre-shaping motion even before we begin to focus on them. The goal of this chapter, then, is to focus on the Mennonite "effective history" that might be argued to have produced or at least helped shape the prejudices in play in the Franconia conversations.

However, application of this concept of effective history in such a specific way—bringing it more fully "down to earth" than Gadamer himself usually does—involves a variety of challenges. Thus first some preliminary comments on problems and possibilities in such a meshing of Gadamer and Mennonites are in order.

JUSTIFYING A STARTING POINT

Perhaps the greatest challenge in beginning to apply Gadamer is finding a starting point. This is partly because Gadamer's hermeneutic thought is itself circular rather than linear. As Lawrence Schmidt argues, Gadamer's view of the process of understanding raises the "epistemological problem of the hermeneutic circle," which is that

To discover the truth of the projected unity of parts and whole
one must have discovered the truth of the prejudices underlying this interpretation, but to discover the truth of the prejudices one must have correctly projected the unity of the parts
and whole. (1996, 265)

What is the solution to this problem? If any thinker or researcher
must rightly know the whole in order properly to interpret the parts,
but the whole can only be known as a projection of the parts, how
can any movement take place? The answer, as Schmidt interprets
Gadamer, is two-fold. First, I must accept that there is no evading
the hermeneutic circle and its highlighting of the fact that all knowing happens in the stream of effective history and the foreknowledges or prejudices it has produced in me. There are thoughts thinking me before I begin to think. Second, however, through the act of
application I as interpreter allow the subject matter at hand to correct my initial prejudices. This happens when I "create an openness
into which the subject matter may emerge" as I allow my own prejudices to be called "into question and listen to and acknowledge the
possible correctness of the other" (266).

This is no neat, orderly process, neither in theory nor, certainly,
in practice. There can be no failsafe identification of precisely when
a prejudice is producing insight and when the subject matter is calling the prejudice into question. Achieving such success would be to
find a vantage point above history and its prejudices to evade precisely the historical situatedness which makes the hermeneutic circle inescapable.

This understanding of the hermeneutic circle suggests that one
fruitful way to begin applying Gadamer is to do so in two stages.
The first stage is to treat philosophical hermeneutics itself as providing the initial foreknowledges through which first to examine the
data. In this stage, Gadamerian thought provides the whole or framework in which to seek to place the parts. The second stage is to create an openness through which the data, the subject matter of the
parts themselves, have opportunity to call into question initial
Gadamerian prejudices—and as necessary to suggest a reconfigured
whole as travel through the hermeneutic circle continues.

Chapters 5 and 6 record my movement through the second
stage. There the tensions, the problems, the ambiguities of thinking
with and applying Gadamer are pondered at considerable length.
There the construction project achieved thus far through building on
Gadamer is probed, poked, deconstructed, as when a termite inspec-
tor prods joists for that tell-tale softness. At points Gadamer is reaf-

firmed, his contributions underscored. At other points, questions linger and, more personally, my own prejudicial alignment with Gadamer is risked.

Now, however, this chapter and the next document my journey through the first stage, detailing what I observe when, as introduced in the previous chapter, I use Gadamer to isolate key categories and "core themes" (Emerson et al, 1995, 157-160) in my data to generate a type of "focused coding" (160-162). Here the constructive project is undertaken. Here difficulties in the project are sometimes deliberately bracketed, the better to show just what it is that can be perceived when Gadamer is applied with some trust that this is worth doing.

The construction begins even before application of categories, however. As I began to analyze the three Franconia Conference delegate cluster conversations which form my primary database, it seemed to me that applying Gadamer's thought dictated taking two preliminary steps before placing my focus squarely on the data.

First, repeated references in the conversations to past documents or events made it necessary to trace the *effective history* which produced the current prejudices. Second, I needed to identify *which primary prejudices were in play* in the conversations as prelude to analyzing how these prejudices did or did not fit in particular analytic categories.

THE EFFECTIVE HISTORY
PRODUCING FRANCONIA CONVERSATIONS:
DEFINING ITS SCOPE

The quest for ingredients of effective history could have been impossibly broad. In theory, the entire history of Western views on homosexuality is implicated in producing the prejudices evident in the Mennonite Church. Certainly material for countless studies can be discerned in the complex crosscurrents of the societal, Christian, and multi-denominational views on homosexuality—or gay, lesbian, bisexual, transgendered agenda—observable just in the contemporary United States.

However, my Gadamerian research concerns focus not on homosexuality per se but on the process of negotiating differences observed in a particularly setting. These boundaries, implicitly set (as will be seen) by the Franconia conversations themselves, likewise set the limits of my study. Even if undoubtedly shaped by broader historical and cultural currents, the Franconia conversations emphasize instead local Franconia concerns in the context set by denominational statements on the issue. Nevertheless, I should forewarn that aspects of these limits are problematic, for at least two reasons. First, even an attempt to be limited by the data provides only modest guidance, given that to pull on any given thread of effective history is potentially to pull on countless more.

Second, the Franconia conversations and their effective history as portrayed below pay remarkably little explicit attention to the larger cultural context in which the discussions unfold. Yet it seems unlikely homosexuality would even have been in play as an issue if Mennonites had been as truly isolated from the cultural negotiations of the matter as their silence regarding their cultural context might imply.

That larger forces have influenced Mennonites in relation to this and countless other issues is a case Fred Kniss persuasively makes (1997, as elaborated in chapter 5). Thus of particular concern is the likelihood that my limitation of scope to what the data explicitly justifies excludes aspects of the larger cultural context likely to have played a role in shaping the conversations. I have opted nevertheless to proceed as indicated, amid recognition of the problems this entails. Then I return to the matter (chapter 5) as a challenge of applying Gadamer. As noted there, not only does Gadamer not provide tools for a systematic pursuit of effective history, he explicitly argues that the deepest, most fundamental effects of such history will by their very nature be inaccessible.

This suggests that actually attempting to discern the particular ingredients of effective history, as opposed to theorizing in the abstract that they are crucial forces, may already be a stretching of Gadamer. That is one reason it has seemed important to focus primarily on those aspects of effective history that seem required not only for participants in the conversations but also for readers of this study to "make (some) sense" of what is reported. Such a relatively informal application of Gadamer seems to exemplify in a small way what he means to address through the notion of effective history— while avoiding pressing the application too far beyond what the concept permits.

Having set such limits, I traced the history of the Franconia conversations particularly through sources of data that could be argued to present an explicit trail of historical effects resulting in the Franconia conversations. I sought such data particularly in news reports, editorials, and letters to the editor on homosexuality published in the weekly denominational magazine *Gospel Herald* from 1987— when the denomination adopted a statement repeatedly referred to in Franconia discussions—to 1997. In addition, from noting the grappling with the proper role of *community* so evident in the conversations, I inferred the need to trace briefly, through whatever sources proved pertinent, the effective history of this facet of the interchanges.

SEEKING THE COMMON
ACCORD EFFECTIVE HISTORY PRODUCES

"Even the total breakdown of communication," insists Gadamer,

> even misunderstanding and the famous admission that one does not know, presuppose that understanding is possible. The commonality that we call human rests on the linguistic constitution of our lifeworld. . . .
>
> For we live in what has been handed down to us. . . . never the world as it was on its first day but as it has come down to us. (1997a, 28-29)

Here Gadamer is repeating his nearly lifelong contention that the very legibility of even a misunderstanding, the very fact that the misunderstanding registers for us *as* a misunderstanding—rather than simply not registering—is contingent on the fact that anything which is legible to us, if only as a misunderstanding, is a product of the same effective history which generated ability to see the misunderstanding as what it is. Therefore, through noting our ability to misunderstand, we are being pointed toward the deeper ability to understand, the deep common accord, which makes what we misunderstand available to us. My quest here then is for what elements of deep common accord enabled through effective history may underlie the misunderstandings, conflictual stances, or opposing prejudices later to be identified as ingredients of the Franconia conversations.

Below I contend that the primary prejudices in play can be summarized as inclusion, exclusion, and third way—meaning that the primary biases are toward (1) finding a way to affirm in the conversation the stance of Germantown Mennonite Church, (2) to exclude it, or (3) to seek a mediating position which allows the polarities of inclusion and exclusion somehow to be reconciled. In naming these prejudices now I am foreshadowing a later turn in the plot. This exemplifies once more the workings of the hermeneutic circle. Because that later turn has been glimpsed, it is now possible to look back from its vantage point to that which may have brought it about. And at the same time probing the effective history which preceded it should deepen an understanding of that turn once it again becomes my focus.

What then might be one version (of the many that could be narrated, because no one version can ever, according to Gadamer, be definitively known) of the effective history which will be seen to have yielded such prejudices as in, out, and third way? To reverse the question, what aspects of effective history might particular observed dynamics be effects of? Or, to put the matter yet another way, what underlying commonalities produced by their shared history made these differences discernible and meaningful to the participants in the conversations?

Very different conversations taking place between very different participants than those in Franconia can be imagined. Take, for instance, any participants to whom the concept of sin is meaningless—for them there would have been no point to the Franconia discussions; the commonalities which allowed the Franconia participants to understand each other even when they differed would not have existed. Sin has to register for participants as an issue before they can hold different views regarding what is sinful.

In this chapter I want to introduce more generally four sources of effective history and their broader description. The first two, the body of Christ and the history of Germantown Mennonite Church, have a more implicit impact on the conversations yet can be inferred from them as factors without which it is highly unlikely the conversations would have unfolded as they did. The second two are the impact of the Bible and of the Purdue statement, the "official" (how official is itself part of the debate, as seen below) statement on homosexuality of the Mennonite Church, adopted at its 1987 national general assembly at Purdue University. The outlines of these two sources are particularly evident in the *Gospel Herald* and will be traced especially there. When later I turn to detailed analysis of the Franconia conversations, I comment more specifically on the role effective history plays as a Gadamerian category intersecting with other categories.

The first three sources of effective history can be viewed as centuries-old aspects of a larger category which might be labeled (see below) "Mennonite tradition" and which has had innumerable effects on Franconia. Together the various aspects of Mennonite tradition purvey Mennonite understandings of the Bible and of the God, Jesus, and Holy Spirit thought to be revealed through the Bible and accessible through prayer in the context of the discerning community. The final source, since it came into existence only in 1987, is much more local and recent one. Given its recent vintage, it is frequently referred to as "the Purdue 87 statement on homosexuality."

MENNONITE TRADITION

I turn first then to Mennonite tradition and discussion of the community, Germantown Mennonite Church history, and the Bible.

Emphasis on the community or body of Christ

In the Franconia conversations, the explicit textual evidence pointing to the importance of "maintaining the right fellowship"[1] is sparse. But James, who is from cluster 3 or C3[2] does stress that "the relationship between brothers and sisters is crucial." He adds, "Because *both*"—fellowship and rightness—"are so important, that's why the FC process has been so deliberate, why there has been meeting after meeting." Even if often implicit, this aspect of effective history can hardly have escaped shaping the Franconia discussions, and its tensions are discernible throughout the struggle to decide whether maintaining the *right* fellowship or the right *fellowship* are more important.

Grace: forgiveness or transforming power? The varying meanings of grace relate to which aspect of fellowship is given priority and will also be seen to intertwine with the prejudices affirmed by Franconia delegates. Amid the book-length comments that could be made, perhaps it is enough here to point to two contrasting visions of grace. According to Thomas Finger (1990, 352), the divergent emphases can be traced back to the varying denotations of the words for grace used in the New Testament, that part of the Christian Bible seen by so many Christians as the key source of right doctrine and theology. Finger contends that "forgiveness or favor bestowed on the undeserving" is sometimes the key meaning. "At other times," however, the terms for grace "indicate a living, transforming energy." As one or the other set of meanings is given priority, "differences in theological understandings of grace often arise. . . ."

Finger then argues that the Protestant Reformers developed a theology based on grace viewed as forgiveness. In this view God's grace made sinful humans acceptable to and forgiven by God *before* any human cooperation with the process through "works" or human actions.

In contrast, for the Anabaptists—those radical sixteenth-century reformers from whom Mennonites sprang—"grace was primarily a transforming power. Many of them spoke of being renewed by, or participating in, the divine nature." Noteworthy in the context

of the Franconia discussions is that if grace was not only "restora-
tive" (the Protestant view) but also "creative" (the Anabaptist view),
then God through grace could "recreate" and not only forgive sinful
people. "This understanding," believes Finger, "lay behind the Anabaptists' lofty behavioral standards."

Finger's view is influenced by Alvin Beachy's classic treatment
of *Grace in the Radical Reformation*, which Finger cites. There Beachy
takes pains to distinguish between the Anabaptist view of grace as
having the power to transform or "divinize" humans and the more
standard Reformed view, in which grace justifies humans before God
(as in 1977:28). In his analysis of nineteenth-century Anabaptist
views of the atonement, *Keeping Salvation Ethical*, J. Denny Weaver
makes the related case that an implicit and "lived" Anabaptist theology of that era can be discerned which understands Christ's atonement as calling for transformed living, in contrast to a "satisfaction-
ist" view in which Christ's death on the cross "pays off" the debt of
human sin (1997).

The connection with contrasting emphases on the meaning of
community now begins to come into view. As discussed and lived
out in actual communities, grace rarely comes neatly wrapped in
one or the other of two packages, and in fact Mennonites have made
efforts to analyze the strengths and weaknesses of various views of
grace. Arnold Snyder (1995, 384, 386), for one, has contended that
the Anabaptist view of grace has promoted legalistic and perfection-
ist tendencies "and the lack of an adequate means for dealing with
personal failure and sin. . . ." Yet if the matter is complex, provisional
observations regarding the intersection between views of grace and
of the meaning of community can nevertheless be made. If grace is
viewed as that forgiving gift of God by which God forgives human
sin, it is possible to develop an understanding of community in
which fellowship or relationship between God and humans and
among humans takes priority over eradicating sin. We may be sinners, but God loves us anyway.

Grace as forgiveness is not absent from the Franconia conversations, but this view of grace is not what lends the discussions their
urgency. The urgency arises when grace is viewed as transforming
power. Then affirming relationships *without* calling for the transformation of those who continue to sin is to cheapen grace, to rob it of
its potential to enable change.

In a pertinent overview of key Anabaptist emphases, Mennonite
historian C. J. Dyck (1995, 24) says that for Anabaptists "*Faith and
obedience* belonged together, as did the *individual and community*."

Given that faith here functions as at least partly a synonym for grace, what Dyck is saying is that in Anabaptism grace *is* a transforming power which enables obedience, or right living—and this process can properly unfold for individuals only in the context of community. If varying circumstances and emphases call forth different relative weightings of *right* versus *fellowship* as the right fellowship is sought, rarely is a Mennonite discussion of issues likely to unfold outside this tangle of tensions.

Traditionalism versus communalism. Fred Kniss (1997) introduces a different but comparable typology. He contends that in fact such controversy as the Franconia conversations exemplify are not unusual but to be expected. Thus if Mennonite effective history produces areas of recognizably Mennonite commonalities, in these very commonalities are tensions. This is because "There are several core elements of Mennonite culture that, rather than embodying a shared consensus about values, served to map the battleground of cultural conflict" (5). Kniss emphasizes particularly two of these core elements, which he terms *traditionalism* and *communalism*. He contends that "traditionalism has meant stressing traditional moral and spiritual values, the importance of the family, biblical and communal authority, and denial of individual interests in favor of the collectivity." The paradigm of communalism, on the other hand, includes the conviction "that the primary moral good is the community" and the role it plays in "creating a just social order" (6).

When the *rightness* of *traditionalism* is emphasized, splits result, as mentioned in the previous chapter, and the danger of this is evident in the Franconia meetings. During some periods in Mennonite history groups have not only split from each other but practiced "the ban" or shunning, in which the group in power cuts off fellowship with a member or members considered to have engaged in sinful practices beyond tolerating.[3] The shadow of this history is evident in Franconia, where Nelson (C2) explicitly refers to it: "To cut them off is like shunning. That's wrong. Even if what they're doing is sin. It's wise to keep fellowship."

When the *fellowship* of *communalism* is emphasized, means must be found for accommodating differences without a severing of relationships. The search for precisely such an outcome generates the third-way statement (introduced in chapter 1) which is so key to the Franconia process.

As is seen in the intertwining story of grace, such dynamics and tensions between the purity of traditionalism on the one hand and maintenance of the community on the other have been facets of Mennonite history from the beginning. Mennonites have always longed to maintain both an uncorrupted and an unruptured community. Dyck points out that the Anabaptists believed they were separated from sin and entered the presence of God

> Primarily within and in the brotherhood as supporting community—a rejection of individualism. The community becomes co-responsible for the salvation of its members and, by extension, for everyone through their mission calling. (1993, 144)

Commitment to community was no small matter; rather, "this practice of *community* was a total, lifelong yielding to each other, after first yielding to Christ. . . ." As introduced in chapter 1, Mennonites have inherited the understanding that "A key word in true community was *Gelassenheit*—meaning yieldedness, self-denial, trust" (144). *Humility*, a related Mennonite characteristic, is argued by Schlabach (1988) Liechty (1980) and others to to have played a key role in nineteenth-century Mennonite thought and practice. Schlabach argues that for "the first six or seven decades" of that century, "humility saturated ordinary Mennonite and Amish discourse" (96) and involved being lowkey, reticent, reserved in matters of dress, speech, cultural styles. Created was a "deferential and self-effacing kind of personality." A leader of that era is quoted by Schlabach as writing that "the humble man feels poor, bowed, cast down, and unworthy within himself, and esteems others more highly than himself" (102).

Interestingly, the very style of the church buildings in which most of the Franconia conversations were held was marked by humility theology, since the meetinghouses themselves were constructed according to its precepts. As one eastern Pennsylvania congregation explained in 1850, not intended was "a magnificent temple, with ornamentations, erected for pride" (quoted in Schlabach, 100).

Liechty contends that humility was a key trait of Mennonites in postcolonial America which perhaps reached its fullest expression in the latter half of the nineteenth century. He acknowledges that humility has faded somewhat as a trait of contemporary Mennonites "in a day when voices from all directions tell them they should feel good about themselves and be assertive," making it "difficult for modern Mennonites to understand and appreciate the humble personality" (17). Nevertheless, even the concept of effective history itself suggests that humility continues to have effects within the subcultural "gene pool" of Mennonites, which makes fascinating the affinities between Gadamerian thought and some of the traits of humility Liechty explores. For example, Liechty pays extended attention to Mennonite leader John M. Brenneman, author among other works of *Pride and Humility* (1886) and one who "incarnated the ideal" of the humble personality. Brenneman, reports Liechty, assured readers in a book on *Christianity and War* (1863) that "could the writer of this little work be convinced, from the doctrines of Christ and His apostles, that he is in error, he feels willing to lay aside the sentiments which he now holds, and to accept those that are better" (17).

It is hard to imagine a much more Gadamerian sentiment than that, a perception underscored by Liechty's assessment of Brenneman's stand:

> Those words expressed not an obligatory and merely academic openness, but his basic stance toward all his beliefs. These attributes—self-effacement, an awareness of personal weakness and a willingness to submit to correction—were the essential ingredients of the humble personality that Mennonites of the 1860s idealized. (17)

In remarks that seem particularly pertinent when placed in the context of the Franconia conversations, Liechty also argues that humility was key to nineteenth-century Mennonite handling of conflict, providing a way for Mennonites simultaneously to pursue a larger unity "yet keep strong beliefs about minute areas of life." Through humility Mennonites were able to experience more than simply the coexistence enabled by compromise. They sought also "a common mind" characterized by readiness of those in conflict to continue working through differences to a fundamental understanding within which traces of the original differences in emphases were preserved even as they were transmuted. The church splits that nevertheless still occurred during this era can then be at least partly explained, thinks Liechty, by the fact that "not all Mennonites were willing to practice humility" (17-18).

Community. Gelassenheit. Humility. Here it becomes evident why a Mennonite might be drawn to a hermeneutic bias; many values of Gadamer's hermeneutics are deeply congruent with this Mennonite valuing of community—and a normative one to boot.

Beulah Hostetler, focusing on Franconia Conference itself, helps bring the story up to date. She contends that by the late 1800s, those Mennonites who had settled in eastern Pennsylvania were finding threatened—by urbanization and other forces of modernization—their attempts to maintain this cohesive group life carried out in contrast to the surrounding culture. So they hardened the lines between church and world by "defensive structuring and codification of practice" (1987, 245ff.). Defining and maintaining "right" practices made even clearer who belonged in the fellowship. But then, notes Hostetler,

> In the quarter century following 1950, virtually all of the elements of defensive structuring disappeared from Mennonite practice. During the period of sloughing off of cultural identity symbols it appeared to some Mennonites that their only difference from Protestant neighbors was a certain inability to articulate beliefs. (329)

Hostetler appears to envision Mennonites as existing in a kind of limbo, uncertain how to navigate between the strong and perhaps extreme boundary lines drawn in the past and whatever boundaries may still be helpful. There is evidence this limbo persists. In a 1997 Sunday school lesson, James R. Engle asks Sunday school participants, "What are some practices you think all congregations should enforce, even to the point of excommunication?" In addition he wonders, "Are there periods of history when boundaries are necessary for survival?" (62).

As framework for addressing such questions, Engle cites at length a description of grounds for excommunication written (not necessarily approvingly) some forty years before by Harold S. Bender, one of the more prominent Mennonite leaders of his time and a figure who helped move the church in more progressive directions.

> At various times and places the following have been (and still are) grounds: immorality in any form, theft, lying, etc., drinking of alcoholic beverages or drunkenness, smoking tobacco, attendance at theaters (including motion pictures), gambling and card playing, military service and training, unethical economic practices including taking advantage of bankruptcy laws, wearing of jewelry and fashionable attire, violation of the requirements of uniform costume, etc. An earlier universal ground was intermarriage with "outsiders," often even with those of other Mennonite branches; it is still the rule in a number of the more conservative groups. (Bender, 1956, 277-278)

Engle places the Bender quote in conversation with the contemporary perspective of Ruth Detweiler Lesher, who notes that "As a Mennonite community, we may be in the stage of having loosened our boundaries considerably for good reasons." She is worried, however: "But some may say we have lost our criteria for membership altogether." Citing sociologist Robert Bellah, she makes the point that "when membership criteria for a community are lost, the identity of the community dissolves as well." She continues to seek balance. On the one hand, she notes, "Some families come to our congregations for some room to breathe and for God's healing love and grace." However, boundaries remain important: "Others come to our church because we are one of the few who still have the courage to take a stand on some Christian lifestyle matters" (Lesher, 1996).

With such words, Lesher helps articulate the tensions in which the Franconia conversations unfold. They have inherited and must somehow navigate a mixed legacy of focus on maintaining the right fellowship along with growing uncertainty regarding how to implement it.

The body of Christ. From another angle, Mennonite poet and literary theorist Julia Kasdorf evokes and puts flesh on the Mennonite community through the prisms of metaphor and memory. Kasdorf does so by remembering the days when Mennonites used the physical markings of plain clothing (much as the Amish continue to do to this day) visibly to symbolize their commitment to the community and also by showing how the metaphor of the body of Christ has helped the community organize itself.

> To belong to the Body of Christ was so important that you would gladly alter your own body. This was not physical torture or martyrdom exactly. It was simply how you chose to conform so that you could show others—and know yourself— that you belonged to a non-conformed group. (1997, 170)

Kasdorf also points out that

> Sitting on the bench among grandmas and aunts and great aunts and cousins both distant and close, you . . . knew that to belong to the Body had more than metaphoric meanings. You not only shared history, religious beliefs and practices with these people; you also shared genetic material: you were one body in flesh. You belonged with the people in your congregation because you were literally related to them; you experienced the Body of Christ as an extension of your own physiology. So while other Christians may have understood metaphorically 1 Corinthians 12:27 ("Now you are the Body of Christ, and each one of you part of it"), Mennonites in traditional ethnic communities could claim their community as a body in actuality. To be enmeshed like this can be pleasurable,

comfortable and secure, although it sometimes breeds freaks of body and soul. (171-172)

Two aspects of the body stand out in Kasdorf's depiction when joined to descriptions by Dyck, Kniss, Hostetler. First, to belong to the body of Christ has been crucial for Mennonites. Second, the body has been seen as made up of those who simultaneously share Mennonite values (not to mention, often, genes) and define themselves in contrast to the mistaken values of those outside the community to which Mennonites are "nonconformed." As Kniss notes, "the central idea that the Mennonite community is to embody a set of alternative religious and cultural values that do not conform to mainstream values has been a continuous unifying principle" (1997, 7).

These two meanings of the body of Christ, as that to which one intentionally belongs and as that through which one defines oneself in opposition to what is in error, play key roles as ingredients of the effective history in which the Franconia conversations unfold. Even as participants differ regarding whether to handle a dissenting congregation through exclusion, inclusion, or a third way, the cruciality of being in the community and defining properly who belongs are matters legible to all participants. This is the case because they are products of a shared effective history which has imprinted indelibly on them such features of the body of Christ.

The history of Germantown Mennonite Church

Because it plays little explicit role in the Franconia discussions, I will note only in passing a local aspect of effective history which nevertheless surely contributed to the dynamics. Germantown Mennonite, the congregation under threat of expulsion, was the first Mennonite church in North America, founded by Mennonite and Quaker emigrants from Europe.[4] It was from Germantown that Mennonites spread out to the Pennsylvania hinterlands to plant the congregations that were to become Franconia Conference. Germantown was thus also the founding church of Franconia Mennonite Conference. It can at least be speculated that the intensity of the concern regarding how to maintain the right fellowship was only heightened by the powerful symbolism entailed in the need to address the issue in relation to a congregation which not only founded the Conference but is the oldest in the hemisphere.

The Bible

Mennonites have for nearly 500 years seen themselves as a "people of the Book." They trace their beginnings largely to dissenting Roman Catholic men and women, some of them priests, such as the Menno Simons for whom Mennonites are named. The founders attempted (in their own intriguing effort to enlarge their prejudices even while being formed initially by Catholic effective history) to read the Bible anew and for themselves rather than only on the terms set by the established church of their day. Such Mennonite distinctives[5] as baptism of adult believers rather than infants, the refusal to bear arms, and the previously noted stress on the community as the body of Christ all emerged from their attempt to read the Bible as a guidebook for daily living.

A number of issues arise in considering the biblical contribution to effective history. One is that there is some tension between the great diversity of views seen as biblical and high Mennonite agreement on the importance of the Bible as guide to faith, thought, and life. Mennonites often do not agree on what it means in practice, in relation to particular issues, to be a people of this book. Basing his analysis on the 1989 Mennonite survey data reported in Kauffman and Driedger (1991), Leland Harder identifies separatist, conservative, liberal, and transformist Mennonites. Then he traces the associations between these four broad standpoints (or prejudices!) and a variety of specific views on such controversial issues as war and peace, capital punishment, abortion, homosexuality (1993).

Mennonite scholar Willard Swartley has also traced some of the wildly divergent understandings of slavery, the sabbath, war, and women judged to be biblical (1983). Swartley is primarily surveying the range of interpretations evident in Protestant Christianity rather than focusing explicitly on Mennonite varieties. However, Swartley credits a variety of largely Mennonite names and organizations with supporting this book, which was released by a Mennonite publisher, and includes in its appendix documents related to Mennonite church life, which has been frequently used as a text in Mennonite settings. Such factors point to the likelihood that Swartley is at least partly thinking out of and responding to diverse Mennonite approaches to interpretation of Scripture.

On the other hand, although Harder is able to isolate some modest variations in how those associated with the different standpoints view the Bible, he contends that the only significant variable is whether or not the word *inerrant* is seen as a satisfactory description. Otherwise he finds that "all have high views of biblical authority" (28). This squares with the Kauffman and Driedger finding that a full seventy-five percent of Mennonites are prepared to describe the Bible as the "inerrant Word of God" (70).

Another issue that arises in considering the Bible and effective history is the extent to which external forces have shaped the Mennonite interaction with the Bible. The very use of the word *inerrant* points to that larger cultural influence Kniss pursues. Kauffman and Driedger include this label for the Bible as one of the markers of religious fundamentalism, which they see as an external theological influence in contrast to the internal influence of Anabaptism (66-71). And as will be observed in chapter 4, one cluster participant does emphasize that "there are two bases for truth: either pluralism or objectivism. Pluralism keeps us all working together until we agree. Objectivism says there's right and wrong." These are strong hints that forms of thought potentially external to the intragroup effective history are making their mark.

But they are primarily hints, not definitive pointers toward external influences. One reason for this is likely that Mennonites have not traditionally emphasized systematic theological, philosophical, or analytic competence. They do not converse, so to speak, in this "lingo." As Harder asserts, "Mennonites . . . have always had fervent convictions which they believe to be based on the life and teachings of Christ." He contends that rather than placing emphasis on "intellectual assent" to "theological systems," they have emphasized "commitment of one's life to the Lordship of Christ." He quotes Menno Simons, who said that "The Scriptures do not need interpretation; they need to be obeyed" (98).

Thus despite clues that the story is indeed more complex than what the surface of the Franconia data reveals, there is no clearly blazed trail for the Gadamerian in pursuit of extra-Mennonite effective history. What can be asserted with some confidence is this: if, amid probable yet hard-to-pin-down external influences, Mennonites at times disagree over *how* to view and interact with the Bible, they rarely contest that they *are* a people of the Bible.

That Mennonites' view of the Bible and its importance is inextricably intertwined with their positions on homosexuality is amply evident in the *Gospel Herald*. Commenting on a report by a denominational Listening Committee on Homosexual Concerns (Reimer, 1993), one letter writer asks critically, "When did we as a church start listening more to psychology than to God and the Word? Check out 1 Cor. 6:9-11, for example" (Grove, 1993). Meanwhile other writers mourn the disbanding of the Listening Committee. In support of their plea for love of gays and lesbians, who are to be accepted— without changing—"for who they are now," they cite the biblical words of Jesus, "who condemned the self-righteous—even the religious establishment—and blessed the merciful" (Brethren/Mennonite Parents of Lesbian/Gay Children, 1993).

Thus whether in agreement or disagreement regarding how the Bible is to interpreted and applied, discussion of homosexuality is not conducted without repeated reference to the Bible. The Bible does appear to play a secondary role in some letters and documents, including the news report on the Listening Committee to which Grove is responding. Even then, however, precisely Grove's type of complaint—"But where is the Bible?"—is common.

Constant references to the Bible are made throughout the ten-year *Gospel Herald* archive of homosexuality materials. "Let us not forget that the Scriptures are quite clear on how to deal with *professed Christians* who are in sin. . ." (Green, 1987). "In response to Jack Derstine's letter. . . . All too often today we try to modify what the Bible says by applying new 'terminology' to old sins" (Helms, 1987). "Let's listen to the Word of God on homosexuality" (Godshall, 1987). "To me, the Bible makes it very clear that it is sin" (Hershey, 1992). "To those of us who still consider Scripture valid on this issue. . ." (Dudley, 1992). "I thoroughly agree with Bill Dudley's letter. . . . Is Scripture valid, or is it not?" (Gaboury, 1992). "The statistics as to how many are practicing any lifestyle cannot really alter what the Holy Scripture defines as sinful" (Yoder, 1993). "In his letters, Paul stresses that we are saved by faith in Jesus Christ, not by obedience to the law (Rom. 3:23-24)" (Mast, 1995). Reporting on a workshop on homosexuality, Rempel says, "In an opening Bible study, Tom Yoder Neufeld examined Acts 15, Matthew 18, and Romans 14 and 15—biblical texts about the church coming to agreement amid great conflict" (1995).

The Bible is interwoven into all facets of Mennonite effective history. No one can fully understand the prejudices at play in the Franconia conversations without understanding the key role the Bible has played in producing them.

THE PURDUE 87 STATEMENT

But if the Bible and the emphasis on the community are sources of two of the larger streams of effective history in which Mennonite thinking and speaking is carried along, the role played by the narrower channel into which the Bible's currents were funneled in 1987 must also be noted. Of course starting this part of the narrative here is arguable; what happened in 1987 was shaped by previous currents of church polity and conversation. But for my purposes starting with Purdue 1987 seems less than arbitrary, because the Franconia conversations were explicitly shaped not so much by what preceded 1987 as by the ripples sent out from and defined in Purdue.

At Purdue 87, held at Purdue University in Lafayette, Indiana, the Mennonite Church at its biennial North American assembly attempted to define its stance on homosexuality. The Human Sexuality in Christian Life Committee, a denominational body charged with helping Mennonites over six years to discuss and clarify their position, had produced a report which included concern to love "those with a different sexual orientation" but also clarified boundaries of acceptable sexual expression. Delegates voted to approve the report. These key words were to become those meant whenever the Purdue 87 statement was referred to and remained so significant they were reproduced in the 1997 Franconia delegates booklet:

> We confess our fear and repent our absence of love toward those with a different sexual orientation and our lack of understanding for their struggle to find a place in society and in the church.
>
> We covenant with each other to study the Bible together and expand our insight into the biblical teachings related to sexuality. We understand the Bible to teach that genital intercourse is reserved for a man and woman in a marriage covenant and that violation even in the relationship, i.e. wife battering, is a sin. It is our understanding that this teaching also precludes premarital, extramarital, and homosexual genital activity. We further understand the Bible to teach the sanctity of the marriage covenant and that any violation of this covenant is sin.
>
> We covenant with each other to mutually bear the burdens of remaining in loving dialogue with each other in the body of Christ, recognizing that we are all sinners in need of God's grace and that the Holy Spirit may lead us to further truth and repentance. We promise compassion and prayer for each other that distrustful, broken, and sinful relationships may experience God's healing. (*Praying for the Church Beyond Us*, 1997, 29)

That the delegates' adoption of this statement was a defining moment in an ongoing flow of effective history but not a damming of the current seems evident in this news report:

> Some delegates—especially those with a hardline position against homosexuality—seemed frustrated that six years of work had still not produced a clear denominational stand. A few others, like Sam Steiner of Ontario/Quebec, argued that the Bible itself "is not that clear" on homosexuality. Martin

[chair of the Human Sexuality committee] pleaded for compassion and tolerance, and Moderator-Elect Ralph Lebold asked the delegates to accept the fact that there are differences among them on the subject.

David Thomas of Lancaster suggested that the affirmation/confession/covenant section of the committee's report could be used as "a statement that we can take back to our congregations." The delegates agreed—by a large majority. (Gay and lesbian Mennonites in attendance at Purdue 87, through a statement they issued later, said they felt rejected by the action.) (Shenk, 1987, 533)

The plurality of delegate viewpoints, the call even by the Moderator-Elect (the denomination's top elected leader) for acceptance of different viewpoints, and the fact that a delegate helped turn what had been a "report" into a "statement"—such factors point to the inherent ambiguity of the delegates' action. What had they done? Had they approved rules binding on all Mennonites? Or a more informal report to their congregations? In addition, whatever the official or unofficial status of the statement, it called for Mennonites to "remain in loving dialogue . . . recognizing that . . . the Holy Spirit may lead us to further truth and repentance." What did this mean? Was the statement a provisional one, to be revised as further truth was glimpsed?

For eight years the status of the statement as well as the meaning of the "loving dialogue" phrasing remained unresolved. Precisely this ambiguity then became a resource for those who preferred that the church stance not be interpreted solely in exclusivist terms or as having churchwide authority. Tensions between rival interpretations led to a denominational need to lessen the ambiguity.

Efforts at clarification then involved such moves as a January 1995 consultation of Mennonite church leaders reported on by Peachey. There General Secretary (highest denominational staff position) James M. Lapp responded this way to questions about the role of the statement: "General Assembly statements have the authority conferences attribute to them. . . . If conferences accept them as authoritative, they are" (Peachey, 1995a).

In contrast, Mary Burkholder, executive secretary of the Mennonite Conference of Eastern Canada (one of the conferences, or regional clusters of congregations, to which Lapp was referring), noted, "I would have thought that when a statement is passed by General Assembly, it has authority for the life of the church" (Peachey, 1995a).

Other participants in the consultation noted the difficulty of determining at which level of denominational life accountability was finally lodged. No definitive conclusions were reached, but participants "agreed the answers need not come as 'either-or' in resolving the questions and tensions." They explored a range of options conferences had in "dealing with churches that adopt a practice different from the formal position of the Mennonite Church on homosexuality." These options included (1) terminating a congregation's conference membership or encouraging the congregation voluntarily to seek membership elsewhere, (2) accepting a congregation without question, or (3) continuing a relationship with the congregation while placing restrictions on it—such as by demoting it from full to "associate membership" in the conference. Additional possibilities included allowing "practicing homosexuals" to be congregational members but not leaders at any denominational level, or establishing a few "congregations of refuge" permitted to accept practicing homosexuals (Peachey, 1995a).

In this consultation report can be seen the continuing ambiguity regarding the denomination's position on homosexuality and what range of freedom congregations and conferences had to determine their own stand on the issue. Also evident in the report, however, are moves toward clarification, particularly in the outlines of the three options—exclusion, inclusion, or inclusion with restrictions—for conference handling of dissenting congregations that were to emerge as key in the Franconia discussions.

The report on these options marks a key shift in the denominational discussions. Here a significant move is being made from questions of whether or in what ways homosexuality is sinful to *how different stances should be dealt with*. This is evident in responses to the report by writers who hold contrasting positions but whose focus is on the managing of differences. On the one hand, Ryan Ahlgrim is disappointed that consultant participants did not address the possibility that a congregation could have homosexual members but not be at odds with the denominational positions. He contends that this could be the case, because the Purdue statement "identifies homosexual genital activity as a sin, but it says nothing about forbidding church membership to homosexuals" (1995). On the other hand, Ruth and Timothy Stoltzfus Jost "are dismayed and deeply concerned that our church would consider approving, or in any way accepting, any practice the Bible calls sin" (1995).

For some months, the *Gospel Herald* records show, ambiguity fostered continuing discussion along similar lines. Ambiguity persisted even as some conferences began to make decisions regarding congregations which accepted practicing homosexual members. In April 1995 Illinois Conference delegates "took steps toward the exclusion of two . . . congregations" even as a guest speaker "cautioned against rushing to judgment" (Hockman, 1995). In May, as Cummings reports, Franconia Conference delegates acted to place Germantown Mennonite Church on associate member status for two years, meaning that the congregation "may send nonvoting delegates to conference assemblies and members serving in conference capacities may complete their terms." During that period Germantown was asked

> not to advocate for a position on homosexuality different than the Conference, refrain from sanctioning same-sex covenantings, and support the Conference in upholding the ideals of heterosexual relationship and marriage. (1995)

Both Conference actions prompted numerous letters continuing the debate regarding the status of the Purdue statement and its meaning. Thirty-nine people signed a June 1995 open letter asking that "the efforts to expel churches that have gay and lesbian members be discontinued" because "Our church statements on homosexuality have not required exclusion from membership but, rather, openness to dialogue" (Ahlgrim et al, 1995). In early August, ten more persons added their names to the original 39, noting that the "Mennonite church statement on homosexuality calls us to openness to dialogue, not exclusion" (Borntrager et al, 1995).

In contrast, on August 29, fourteen members of a men's Bible class supported the Franconia action, contending that "Sin must be purged from among us if we expect God's blessing as a Mennonite Church" (Bachman et al, 1995). Twenty-seven members of another congregation expressed their strong concern "about the way that some people apparently desire to use Scripture to justify including practicing homosexuals into church membership" (Byrne et al, 1995).

The multiple-signatory letters were perhaps the last straw for *Gospel Herald* editor Lorne Peachey, who on August 29 (1995b), in the same issue in which he published the final such letters, declared a moratorium on letters to the editor on homosexuality except "if a letter addresses something we print." Peachey noted that up to then all letters had been published according to the "Mennonite Church official statement on homosexuality—which calls the practice sin but also urges continued discussion with those who disagree. . . ." But now perhaps a period of silence would be more beneficial, "to allow us to catch our breath" and "pray, study the Scriptures, and listen to what God may be saying to the church" (1995).

Still ambiguity persisted. Then, according to a December news report (*Gospel Herald*, 1995), a "news story in the church press about 12 Mennonite and Brethren congregations which have publicly stated that they welcome gay, lesbian, and bisexual people as members" led to a sharp clarification of lines. The Mennonite Church General Board asked the Council on Faith, Life, and Strategy (CFLS), which reports to it, to resolve the ambiguity. CFLS indicated that the Purdue statement "is the position of the Mennonite Church as well as of CFLS and the General Board" and stressed that

> The words "loving dialogue" found in this document should not be construed to mean that the homosexual issue is unresolved or that the position of the church is in question. . . . Rather, "loving dialogue" relates to the area of pastoral care in terms of biblical teaching on the denominational position, care of families and individuals who are touched by this issue, admonitions to those with a homosexual orientation, sponsorship of ministries that are directed toward calling persons out of homosexual practices and restoration in the body of believers, and dialogue that reflects the love of Jesus. (Council on Faith, Life, and Strategy, 1995)

Despite such efforts to reduce ambiguity, the fullest tests of the church's position continued to unfold in the conferences. The key debate continued to be how differences should be managed. *Gospel Herald* summarized 1996 developments this way:

> Three area conferences deal with homosexuality in annual meetings. Recommendation to oust two churches who [sic] don't make homosexual practice a test of membership fails by three delegate votes at Illinois Conference meeting. Indiana-Michigan Conference delegates pass statement on sexuality and membership, and Southeast Conference moves toward separation with congregation which accepted into membership a gay couple living in a covenanted relationship. (1996)

On April 15, 1997, precisely while the Franconia cluster conversations on which this study focuses were underway, a significant event took place. As *Gospel Herald* reported, by a roughly three-fourths vote Illinois Conference, whose earlier vote to expel two congregations had failed, agreed to place the congregations "under discipline" (Sommer, 1997). This was a new form of sanction delegates had created by amending their previous constitution. Such discipline stopped short of expulsion of congregations while removing from them conference voting privileges, possibly conference funds if they were receiving them, and the right to serve on conference commissions.

Such then was the effective history set in motion by the Purdue statement and helping to provide the currents in which were produced the prejudices placed in play in the Franconia conversations. To those prejudices I now turn.

CHAPTER THREE

DANCE: CHARACTERISTICS
OF GADAMERIAN CONVERSATION

THE PREJUDICES IN PLAY

In developing the Gadamerian categories to apply to the Franconia conversations, some seemingly useful avenues of inquiry turned out to less useful than first hoped.[1] One of them deserves mention here.

Before the conversations and my analysis of them as well as of the above effective history of the denomination unfolded, I expected the primary prejudices to represent a range of positions on the issue of homosexuality itself. Thus I anticipated that in addition to viewing the data through Gadamer, I would also first code prejudices discerned in the conversations according to such categories as provided by Philip Bakelaar (1997). After performing a wide-ranging study of North American Christian denominational attitudes toward homosexuality, Bakelaar identifies the range of initial stances as including the traditional, reform, compromise, progress, and radical positions. I expected after working with Bakelaar's categories to cross-compare the two sets of categories. This proved not the most fruitful approach. Let me explain, beginning with an elaboration of Bakelaar.

CATEGORIES OF HOMOSEXUAL PREJUDICES

According to the *traditional* prejudice, as Bakelaar taxonomizes, homosexuality is among the worst sins, so grievous it need not and should not be discussed. Pressure on homosexuals to remain in the closet should be maintained. In the *reform* stance, homosexuality is discussed, civil discrimination is opposed, the sin is considered one among many, and the homosexual who is celibate or seeks a changed orientation permitting sexual practice in heterosexual marriage is affirmed. The *compromise* position encompasses the reform tenets but adds to them support for homosexual "marriage" as a tolerated if less-than-ideal analog to heterosexual marriage. According to the *progress* position, stigmatization of homosexuals will cease as the church comes to see that such a view is as outmoded as old views regarding slavery and women. The *radical* stance incorporates progress affirmations. However, going beyond progress readiness to assimilate homosexuals into homosexualized versions of heterosexual institutions and practices, it celebrates joyous and non-institutionalized forms of sexual expression.

My informal knowledge of the Mennonite scene led me not to anticipate much if any evidence of the progress or radical prejudices. There were a few exceptions to my expectations. For instance, in a letter criticized by Green (1987) in the previous chapter, Jim Derstine protested the outcome of the Purdue 87 statement, arguing that *homosexual practice* should be deemed wrong because it applies to "typical"—i.e. heterosexual—men or women having same-sex relations. The phrase does not, however, accurately apply to relations by non-heterosexuals with each other, because these are persons of "mixed (or ambiguous) sexuality" who should be called "intersexuals" (1987, 594).

Through Derstine's effort to make space for full normalization of gay and lesbian sexual expression, he seems to position himself roughly in the progress position. He nevertheless appears to avoid the radical stance through his careful reference to gays as being in a "committed relationship" analogous to marriage. Since his comments are among the most radical to appear either in *Gospel Herald* or in the Franconia conversations, it appears that there are no instances of the radical stance.

Examples of all the remaining stances, particularly the traditional and reform positions around which most commentators cluster, can more easily be given. Andrew (C1) says in one conversational turn, "If we really believe we are sinners in common, then here we are being hypocritical. Why is this sin singled out and others not? This bothers me. I don't know why, but I can't keep quiet." Later he adds that "At the personal level I say, yes, homosexuality is a sin, however, I still can open my arms to those sinners; other sinners open their arms to me." Andrew does not place himself on record as supporting homosexual "marriage," so it is unclear whether he may be classed in the compromise position, but at a minimum his comments fit the reform willingness to evaluate homosexuality as one among many sins rather than a cardinal sin.

Meanwhile Lorraine (C2) argues that "It's not very charitable, for Germantown to want to have people living in sin. Why don't they leave instead of stirring up a hornet's nest? How loving is it, really, what they're doing?" She seems to articulate a traditional position. Homosexuals and their advocates belong in the closet, under wraps, not amid good Christians "stirring up a hornet's nest." Similarly Albrecht comments, "You say the debate must go on. Why? The Bible calls it sin" (1995, 5).

But if identifying prejudices in relation to stances on homosexuality seemed initially promising, and might indeed have been fruitful had a conversation revolving around such distinctions been the object of study, such categories proved on closer inspection not to be the ones best suited to analysis of the Franconia conversations. This was because homosexuality prejudices as typologized by Bakelaar turned out to be secondary to what might be termed *relationship* prejudices.

As is evident in my survey of the effective history rooted in the Purdue statement, the subject matter had become not primarily homosexuality itself, though of course the issue was repeatedly and inevitably implicated. Rather, most crucially at play was what the *relationship* between different stances should be. This emphasis is congruent as well with the broader Mennonite stress on the body of Christ—which as seen has involved maintaining an uneasy tension between the often conflicting priorities of maintaining the *fellowship* and doing so *rightly*.

Similar formulations of the key prejudices can be found in all clusters and are perhaps most succinctly summarized in Milton's (C3) statement that "It feels like the options are in, out, and third way," or in Robert's (C2) comment that the options "would be full inclusion, full discipline, this is in between." As will be seen, in the Franconia conversations as well as the larger denominational interchanges, prejudices regarding homosexuality itself did also remain in play. They were subsumed, however, within prejudices toward inclusion, exclusion, or finding a "third way" through which the tensions between opposing positions might be maintained in continuing relationship.

As chapter 2 details, participants were entering a discussion long underway and thus one in which the range of possible positions regarding homosexuality and arguments for them were well-known and even predictable. In addition, they had before them a specific question: what should be done about a congregation holding a stance at variance with the stated Franconia position? Such factors likely contributed to the fact that participants did not so much debate stances on homosexuality as what relational prejudices a given stance on homosexuality might justify.

CATEGORIES OF GADAMERIAN CONVERSATION

It is in this defining of the key prejudices that my analysis of the cluster conversations now proceeds. What I will be particularly assessing is within what sets of categories these in, out, or third-way prejudices can be placed as the conversations unfold. As introduced in chapter 1 and elaborated in Appendixes A and B, my refining process led to these categories of Gadamerian conversation: (1) effective history producing commonality, (2) goodwill highlighting of prejudices as yours and mine, (3) awareness of finitude, (4) openness, (5) risking prejudices in relationship.

ASSESSING GADAMER AND UTILITY, NORMATIVITY, AMBIGUITY

As I move now to detailing my analysis using these refined categories as headings, a word on what I hope to achieve is in order. A first goal, addressed in this chapter and the next, has been to report what utility such Gadamerian categories had as lenses through which to perceive and organize the data. In brief, I conclude that if conversation is conceived, in hermeneutics-biased terms, as a mutual quest for understanding, Gadamer provides a heuristically rich framework for assessing what is at stake and how a process of understanding and mutual enlargement unfolds or fails to take place.

Note that I speak of success and failure. This points to a second goal and also to an aspect of my assessment of Gadamer. First the assessment. After considerable pondering of Gadamerian thought and what is revealed about it by attempting to apply it to actual conversation, I conclude that it includes a strong normative component. Gadamer does not (nor should he, based on his view of the directedness of prejudices, including his own) begin with disinterested analysis of actual conversation, then inductively and descriptively work backward from what he observes to develop an account of what he there observes. Rather, he begins with a strong and perhaps paradoxically (as discussed in chapter 5) unwavering commitment to openness as the inviolable condition for understanding and conversation to unfold. Without openness, a conversation simply cannot be, in any full sense, genuine.

It may be that in fact Gadamer would argue that he arrives at this commitment to openess descriptively, based purely on observation that without it conversation ceases to be. However, it is difficult to escape the conclusion that Gadamer would treat any conversation lacking openness as failed rather than as reason to give up commitment to openness. Indeed, as noted in chapter 7, that is the conclusion I myself reach. Even as I observe countless failures in the Franconia conversations, I nevertheless conclude that commitment to openness remains a crucial marker of genuine conversation, and in this sense I join Gadamer in normative commitment.

Now to the goal: based on this assessment of Gadamer's normativity, I have aimed to explore insights produced by the prejudice that indeed some conversations can be seen in Gadamerian terms to succeed and some to fail. Thus this chapter and the next are structured by this normative bias—which treats as synonymous conversations which are on the one hand Gadamerian, genuine, or successful and on the other hand non-Gadamerian, non-genuine, or failed. However, I then (as so often!) turn to chapter 5 to examine liabilities of this prejudice, including its potential to create static categories unable to produce the insights made available by more nimble, less normative, rhetoric-and-ambiguity-friendly approaches.

This leads to a third goal (addressed particularly in chapters 5 and 6), which is to assess how the Gadamerian precepts in which the categories are rooted are clarified, enlarged, or contradicted through their application to the data. Again in brief I conclude that Gadamer is ill-suited to microanalytic studies. One turns to Gadamer to grapple, for instance, with how through "texts," written or spoken, persons may grope for an enlarging fusion of their horizons. One does not turn to Gadamer to analyze sentence structures.

As introduced above, running through these goals as an issue affecting them all is the question of how to handle ambiguity. As will become evident if it is not obvious already, any effort to apply the bulky and often normative Gadamerian apparatus to specific data will generate much ambiguity concerning whether there is a good "fit" between this or that aspect of the data and a given category, whether misfits are problems with the conception of the categories or the analysis of the data, whether seemingly "good" fits are evidence of sound research or inability to see how the square peg is being forced into a round hole.

Or to put it another way, what relationship do Gadamer and ambiguity have? Do they nurture or weaken each other? Does Gadamer provide a means for treating ambiguity as resource or for repressing ambiguity in the interests of his theory? In brief, particularly in chapter 5 I answer that Gadamer points to the resources of some ambiguities while repressing others. Gadamer has seen perhaps as clearly as anyone this century the rich ambiguities released, for instance, by the view that we understand differently if we understand at all. At the same time, through his relentless hermeneutic pursuit of the "deep common accord," combined with tendencies toward abstraction that allow him to downplay the ambiguities of living communicative processes unfolding in the "real" world, he risks overlaying ambiguity with an idealized and overly static portrayal of communicative exchanges.

Here, however, before that discussion, decisions must be made regarding how to manage ambiguities inherent in the effort fruitfully to match categories and data. I have tried to proceed by working with Gadamer's grain in this chapter and the next. Where his thought embraces ambiguity, I have aimed to show the benefits. Where his thought risks repressing ambiguity, I have likewise allowed my appreciation of ambiguity to be muted. Then in the evaluative chapters 5 and 6, I have assessed the rewards and price of the Gadamerian approach, as hopefully illustratively enacted in my own study. Now to the categories of analysis.

EFFECTIVE HISTORY PRODUCING COMMONALITY

As Richard Shusterman summarizes, Gadamer's understanding of effective history and the prejudices it "effects" leads him to believe "We can make no sense of something's being intelligibly different without being able to map that difference on some common background of coordinates" (1989, 220). This is not to say all conversation partners automatically share a common background; it is not, as Gadamer often stresses, to refuse the possibility of misunderstanding. Gadamer "would not want to say that the solidarities that bind human beings together and make them partners in dialogue always are sufficient to enable them to achieve understanding and total mutual agreement." He makes clear that "we speak past each other and are even at cross-purposes with ourselves" (1989b, 57).

Gadamer is not contending that the commonalities or solidarities produced by effective history necessarily encompass all humans at all times. But he *is* convinced that wherever humans speak to each other with any understanding whatsoever, they do so because of preceding commonalities. We could not be partners in dialogue at all "if we had not traveled a long way together, perhaps without even acknowledging this to ourselves" (57).

Gadamer's perspective here has affinities with that of philosopher Joseph Margolis. Framing the issues particularly in relation to Wittgensteinian language games, Margolis argues against those who see humans as trapped in incommensurate language games, with no hope of speaking a common language. Rather, he stresses, "the detection of conceptual incommensurability is a mark of cognitive and communicative competence, not evidence of its local defeat or failure" (1995b, 170).

Margolis does not intend to adopt a fully Gadamerian framework.[2] However, he agrees that Gadamer "affords a plausible sense in which the human world is historicized" (337) and joins Gadamer in making at least two related affirmations. First, if thought is historicized, then aspects of it are tied to the local and not the universal; this inevitably leads to varieties of misunderstanding and incommensurability (169). But second, because he sees incommensurability as a limited inability to detach given statements, concepts, ideas from their local contexts or "original entrenching practices" (170), he remains convinced that "incommensurabilities need not be indiscernible or unimaginable or unintelligible or even untranslatable" (169). It seems no great stretch to paraphrase Margolis here as affirming "deep common accord."

Barbara Herrnstein Smith, also attuned to the implications of historicized thought, makes her own related contribution.

> Incommensurability, it appears, is neither a logically scandalous relation between theories, nor an ontologically immutable relation between isolated systems of thought, nor a morally unhappy relation between sets of people, but a contingent, experiential relation between historically and institutionally situated conceptual/discursive practices. Some radically divergent ideas never meet at all, at least not in the experiences of mortal beings. In other cases, meetings are staged repeatedly but never come off, ending only in mutual invisibility and inaudibility. Sometimes, however, meetings do occur, perhaps intensely conflictual and abrasive but also, in the long run, mutually transformative. (1997, 152)

Here Smith does underscore what tends to be a secondary though, as noted above, discernible theme in Gadamer: misunderstandings, failures to meet, or failures of meetings which do take place, indeed occur. Smith seems considerably less ready than Gadamer to move quickly to affirmation of commonality. But Smith also stresses that incommensurabilities are mutable, bridgeable, potentially transformable. If she perhaps does not quite affirm a deep common accord, she does join Gadamer and Margolis in positing that differences evident in "situated conceptual/discursive practices" can meet (152).

The Franconia conversations help exemplify how commonality may be discerned beneath differences. Participants hold many different prejudices. They no doubt misunderstand each other, fail to meet, or suffer from varieties of incommensurability at levels no one researcher can fully discern. Yet they hold in common, as earlier introduced, the effects brought about in them by a history flowing from the Bible, Mennonite tradition, and that complex tissue of understandings, both theorizable and too "thick" for abstraction, of which the ingredients of effective history I have isolated are at least a form of shorthand.

To highlight what is meant here by a deeper commonality that underlies any smaller incommensurabilities, imagine that the Franconia delegates were variously adherents of, say, not only Mennonite Christianity but also Hinduism, Buddhism, neo-Nazism, or a fervent secular humanism. Clearly they would be less able to make at least the minimal sense of each other's understandings enabled, even amid differences, by a basic layer of shared Mennonite assumptions. If eventually they were able to fathom some of the other's positions even across chasms of Hindu or neo-Nazi prejudices, such understanding would in turn be feasible only to the extent they had begun to glimpse—by at least beginning to travel "a long way together," as Gadamer puts it—some underlying commonality, however minimal, as the medium through which to discuss their radical differences.

Or push the reasoning one step farther, to the level of science fiction: an intelligent alien life form reaches earth. Initially, however, human and alien intelligence is so different, so lacking, we might say, in effective history, that no meaningful commonality is present. In its absence, in fact, the life forms do not even discern each other's presence, much less communicate. What then might eventually, even if perhaps over many years, enable the beginning of rapport?

There may be multiple answers—but it seems likely that one viable one is that these life forms must spend enough time "traveling" together in a common enough space that eventually their shared history begins to give them glimpses first of each other's presence and then of each other's efforts at intelligible communication. If they are ever able to achieve this minimal commonality, they will simultaneously remain ineradicably different even as their emerging commonality is what enables them to initiate rudimentary relating across their differences.

Turning to a different issue, as chapter 6 explores, philosophical hermeneutics lacks an explicit theory of social institutions and structures. Thus it is unclear how through Gadamer to interpret the prejudices and functioning of those playing a formal institutional role in a conversation, such as the Franconia commentators and moderators (sometimes the same person) quoted below. Do they speak for themselves or the group? How has effective history produced them? Although definitive answers are impossible, perhaps Gadamer can at least be stretched to support the contention that even when the relation of their public and private positions is unclear, office holders help to represent—and present—what a group considers its core themes.

If so, commentator/moderator roles and cues provide important clues to the seeker of effective history. This makes significant as a possible product of effective history the practice, observed in all three clusters, of placing early in the conversation a reading of and commentary on a biblical text. Effective history, it can be argued, is what makes intelligible and meaningful the commentary on Romans 14:1-12, a New Testament text, by one such leader. After reading the text, cluster one commentator Harlan says that

> "There is a very direct application to our being together, to our purposes. We need to find a way faithfully in our day and in our circumstances to face and find insight to work as the body of Christ and hear what the Holy Spirit is saying to us and each other.
>
> "I've read this Scripture numerous times, but it has never meant more to me than this time. Paul calls us to welcome those 'weak in faith' but not to quarrel over opinions. Paul says we are to be more accepting."

Harlan concludes that in light of Paul's comments the issue is more how Christians welcome each other than homosexuality itself.

Here the emphasis is on the right *fellowship* long celebrated as one pole of the body of Christ. The fact that the commentator is the overseer of Germantown Mennonite Church, appointed to provide *the* formal institutional liaison between Germantown and Franconia and holding as much of the modest yet significant supervisory power the Conference apportions, seems likely to be meaningful, though here again the absence of Gadamerian institutional theory hampers assessment of that meaning. At a minimum perhaps it can be said that from whatever public or private role the commentator is speaking, the Germantown connection confirms the likelihood of some prejudice toward inclusion.

In cluster two, moderator Robert reads 1 Corinthians 13, a famous New Testament text which says this:

> If I speak in the tongues of mortals and angels, but do not have love, I am a noisy gong or a clanging cymbal. And if I have prophetic powers, and understand all mysteries and all knowledge, and if I have all faith, so as to move mountains, but do not have love, I am nothing. If I give away all my possessions, and if I hand over my body so that I may boast, but do not have love, I gain nothing.
>
> Love is patient; love is kind; love is not envious or boastful or arrogant or rude. It does not insist on its own way; it is not irritable or resentful; it does not rejoice in wrongdoing, but rejoices in the truth. It bears all things, believes all things, hopes all things, endures all things.
>
> Love never ends. But as for prophecies, they will come to an end; as for tongues, they will cease; as for knowledge, it will come to an end. For we know only in part, and we prophesy only in part. But when the complete comes, the partial will come to an end. When I was a child, I spoke like a child, I thought like a child, I reasoned like a child; when I became an adult, I put an end to childish ways. For now we see in a mirror, dimly, but then we will see face to face. Now I know only in part; then I will know fully, even as I have been fully known. And now faith, hope, and love abide, these three; and the greatest of these is love. [3]

This text includes a number of themes strikingly similar to Gadamer's emphases. There is the awareness of finitude, of recognition that "we know only in part," that "For now we see in a mirror, dimly." There is, in the description of all that love is, an implicit call to risk prejudices which is made nearly explicit in the insistence that love "does not insist on its own way."

After reading this text, with all its resonances, Robert asks delegates to "hold Paul's vision of love—to work with a deep sense of commitment, love for each other, Christ, and the peoplehood of which we are a part." As that conversation moves toward its conclusion, Robert tells delegates that they "can find the patience, endurance, and strength to hang in with each other. . . . in the faith that the Spirit is wise enough and large enough and patient enough to see us through." After calling delegates to remain in conversation, he reiterates that "faith in the Lord of the church will see us through." Invoking the "historic context" of the church, as he earlier puts it, Robert is assuring delegates that continuing to converse will place them in the stream of effective history which has produced them and will carry them forward.

Yet again in cluster three, Bradley, facilitator of cluster one and here asked to provide biblical commentary, says that

"As I've been thinking about this problem, I've been ranging back and forth over Scripture. This concern has been an issue for a long time. It's amazing to me how balanced Scripture is on some things. Take Matthew 18, which addresses church discipline. It also speaks of the one lost sheep who matters as much to the shepherd as the 99, says it would be better for the person who tempts someone to err to have a millstone hung round his neck. Then the gospel of John pictures a Jesus full of grace and truth. It's freeing that we can't possibly measure up to Jesus, but we must also reflect as a body on how we are to measure up to the fullness of grace and truth in relation to the gay and lesbian issue.

Bradley places the Franconia discussions squarely in the context of the Bible, moving back and forth between biblical texts and the present discussion to show how the Bible informs and holds potential to shape the latter.

But if the Bible functions in the conversation as source of effective history, as a key source of preunderstandings held in common, the prejudices it produces are not uniform. This is no doubt partly because the Bible itself is multivocal[4]—as is Mennonite effective history—and thus shapes commonalities in which can be discerned inherent tensions.

Preferring to let the Scripture he eventually reads speak primarily for itself rather than explicitly to apply it, Bradley's prejudices are in this instance not clearly articulated. In contrast, Robert grounds in Scripture the third-way prejudice that maintaining relationships between persons of contradictory prejudices is primary. And Harlan, who nowhere clearly calls for the third-way holding of prejudices in tension but uses such words as "welcome" and "accepting," may even lean toward inclusion.

Meanwhile for other participants in the conversation, very different prejudices flow from the Bible. It is clear to Hiram (C2) that the Bible requires holding an exclusivist stance.

"First Corinthians 5 says what we *must* do: if there is a homosexual in the church, we must get him out. We *must* expel him from the church. We're not doing that here. If Franconia Conference accepts the statement, folks here at the Franconia congregation will leave. We must expel from the church."

Likewise Elvin bases his exclusivism on the Bible, according to which the sin of homosexuality is "not small; it's the most serious of all! Romans 1 says it's one of the worst things, God gave over the homosexual reprobates. It can damn you to hell, no other issue is so serious."

At least two learnings can be gleaned from the diversity of prejudices produced by the same Bible. First, supported is Gadamer's contention that when they are products of the same effective history, different prejudices will be intelligible even if not shared. Though different, such prejudices emerge from what *is* shared. This is why no one in any conversation indicates having any problem grasping the importance of connecting a given prejudice with those strands of effective history the Bible helps produce or symbolize, including that network of understandings about community, the body of Christ, right relationship, grace, sin, and so forth traceable to the Bible. Participants may disagree on what prejudices the Bible most fully supports, but to all it makes sense to validate prejudices in relation to the Bible. Particularly Robert highlights the tensions both made legible by and evident in biblical effective history itself as he prays,

> "Dear God. . . . We wrestle now with issues of faith, with how we relate to those with a different understanding of faith. How do we wed grace and truth, live with the integrity of Scripture *and* love those who differ from our understandings of Scripture?"

Second, that different prejudices can arise from a shared effective history provides some response to those critics of Gadamer who contend that his view of history and tradition is overly dependent on a "single 'mainstream' tradition," as Eagleton puts it. Eagleton argues that "History for Gadamer is not a place of struggle, discontinuity and exclusion but a 'continuing chain,' an ever-flowing river, almost, one might say, a club of the like-minded" (1983, 72-73). Depending on what Gadamerian emphases one cites, Eagleton's view seems supportable. Certainly such quintessential Gadamerian phrases as "Deep common accord" (1976, 7); or "determined by the old that has already taken possessions of us (9); or "Only the support of familiar and common understanding" (15) do seem to open him to Eagleton's charges.

However, what Eagleton seems to understress is that Gadamer rarely makes statements about sameness except to link them with difference. Thus what is determined by the old "is our expectation and our readiness to hear the new," and what the support of common understanding makes possible is "the venture into the alien, the lifting up of something out of the alien, and thus the broadening and enriching of our own experience of the world."

Gadamer himself refutes the uniformity of history Eagleton attributes to him, insisting that far from holding cultures static in a "closed horizon," history "which exists in the form of tradition is always in motion." He underscores his conviction that "The historical movement of human life consists in the fact that it is never absolutely bound to any one standpoint, and hence can never have a truly closed horizon. Horizons change for a person who is moving" (1994a, 304). In a statement pertinent to a church-related study, he emphasizes that "The tradition is not something rigid; it is not fixed once and for all. . . . Even the church must deal with a living tradition and a continual conversation with this tradition" (2000, 49).

What Gadamer wants to convey, and it is hard to see how Eagleton would oppose this, is that yes, "struggle, discontinuity and exclusion" exist, but they can only register against the backdrop of what is held in common. Gadamer would say to Eagleton, as he once said to Derrida, that "Whoever opens his mouth wants to be understood; otherwise, one would neither speak nor write" (1989, 55). However much discontinuity there may be in the world, Eagleton presumably wants to be understood as he speaks in it; that which is sufficiently common, familiar, old to allow Eagleton to be legible even to one who disagrees with him is what Gadamer is intent on highlighting.

And that is what is highlighted as well in the Franconia conversations. Here persons are conversing amid intense conflict; as Robert (C2) observes, "In my lifetime I have never seen emotions higher than on this issue." There is much discontinuity and struggle amid the threat of literal exclusion. Still there is a bedrock of commonality which allows participants to make sense of ways they differ. That is what Gadamer affirms through effective history: it is active when combatants can at least discern what it is they are battling over.

GOODWILL HIGHLIGHTING OF PREJUDICES AS YOURS AND MINE

A theme running through the above comments on effective history is that it is what allows awareness of, enlargement by, or openness to the alienness, newness, or otherness of the other. That leads naturally to the next analytic category, which is goodwill highlighting of prejudices as yours and mine. Clearly this overarching category encompasses a number of subcategories which deserve to be treated one by one if not necessarily in order.

To begin with middle first and deepen a discussion begun in chapter one, *prejudices*, as Gadamer puts it, "constitute the initial directedness of our whole ability to experience" (1976, 9). Meanwhile Margolis, speaking from his perspective generally compatible with if not identical to Gadamer's, asserts that

> thinking is "prejudiced," tacitly constituted, impenetrably preformed, endogenously limited, "interested," perspectived, artifactually rational, variable, culturally "constructed," alterable merely by being exercised, at once cognitively restrictive and enabling. . . . (1995, 163)

This seems a rough paraphrase of what Gadamer means by prejudice and might for my purposes be further refined by highlighting such adjectives as "interested" and "perspectived," which are themselves strikingly similar to Gadamer's "initial directedness." Both the contribution of Gadamer's view of prejudices and the challenge of applying it is evident when summarized in this way. The contribution involves Gadamer's ability so persuasively to articulate the historical embeddedness, formation, and "prejudiced-ness" of all thought that he has been recognized as one of the major intellectual figures of the century. Making the case that there is no escape from prejudice may be increasingly commonplace amid the contemporary postmodern and interpretive turns,[5] yet precisely the fact that Gadamer has helped nurture these turns underscores the size of his accomplishment.

However, here also is where a challenge of applying Gadamer comes into view. If Gadamer's concerns encompass and address a century's worth of the largest of intellectual and philosophical issues, it is understandable—and inescapable—that his attention has been less focused on details of application. Gadamer offers a paucity of guidance regarding what prejudices *are* once he has made the central case that they involve the "initial directedness of our whole ability to experience," that they are, as Margolis puts it, "interested," or "perspectival." Prejudices point one way and not another way. Their primary inescapable quality appears to be that they are arrow-like. Thus when a prejudice is present something pointed—slanted, biased—is discerned.

That is why throughout this study such terms and phrases as viewpoint, stance, directedness, perspective, preconception, angle of vision, prejudgment, foreshaping, and more all function as rough synonyms of prejudice. What else might a prejudice be? Is it an attitude? An opinion? Gadamer does not spell out the details. However, it appears that though attitudes or opinions will surely accompany or be enabled by prejudices, a prejudice is deeper. *A prejudice is a trajectory my thinking and vision follow in perceiving the world.* This happens at a fundamental and not fully conscious level that precedes and even preforms my forming of attitudes or opinions. But if attitudes or opinions are shallower than prejudices, they are also markers of prejudices, indicators of the underlying directions of the prejudices which have formed their aim.

Thus the arrow-like quality of prejudice hopefully does clearly emerge even as some fuzziness persists and functions as one limitation of the research and an example of an application challenge. In this study, the arrow is pursued, then, through the characterizing of prejudices as in, out, and third way and seeing each as pointing in a different direction in relation to the question of Germantown inclusion. What aspect of these prejudices might be labeled attitude or opinion? To what extent do the prejudices function as an angle of vision those experiencing it have been grasped by before they become aware it? These are finer-grained distinctions than Gadamerian tools seem able to make; thus the study proceeds on the assumption that all such levels of "arrowness" are potentially involved and implicate each other.

Turning next to the labeling of prejudices as *yours and mine,* against those who worry that Gadamer cares only about what is same, Gadamer emphasizes the "potentiality for being other [*Andersseins*] that lies beyond every coming to agreement about what is common" (1989a, 26). The "yours and mine" part of the category is aimed at foregrounding this concern for "being other."

A pertinent issue here is how the "otherness" of what is yours becomes evident in contrast to what is mine. Do I first experience myself as having a prejudice, then see that this prejudice is different than yours? Or do I not even become aware of my own prejudice until it clashes with yours? As is often the case with such specific questions, the precise answer is difficult to find in Gadamer, but he does offer clues. Significantly, and in terms that go to the very core of Gadamer's thought and thus will be quoted at some length, Gadamer notes that

> We say, for instance, that understanding and misunderstanding take place between I and thou. But the formulation "I and thou" already betrays an enormous alienation. There is nothing like an "I and thou" at all—there is neither the I nor the thou as isolated, substantial realities. I may say "thou" and I may refer to myself over against a thou, but a common under-

standing [*Verständigung*] always precedes these situations. We all know that to say "thou" to someone presupposes a deep common accord [*tiefes Einverständis*]. Something enduring is already present when this word is spoken. When we try to reach agreement on a matter on which we have different opinions, this deeper factor always comes into play, even if we are seldom aware of it. (1976, 7-8)

Then, having made his famous comment that "Prejudices are biases of our openness to the world," Gadamer stresses that

this formulation certainly does not mean that we are enclosed in a wall of prejudices and only let through the narrow portals those things that can produce a pass saying, "Nothing new will be said here." Instead we welcome just that guest who promises something new to our curiosity. But how do we know that the guest whom we admit is one who has something *new* to say to us? Is not our expectation and our readiness to hear the new also necessarily determined by the old that has already taken possession of us? (9)

Playing a variation on this theme of the relationship between old and new, Gadamer goes on:

There is always a world already interpreted, already organized in its basic relations, into which experience steps as something new, upsetting what has led to our expectations and undergoing reorganization itself in the upheaval. Misunderstanding and strangeness are not the first factors, so that avoiding misunderstanding can be regarded as the specific task of hermeneutics. Just the reverse is the case. Only the support of the familiar and common understanding makes possible the venture into the alien, the lifting up of something out of the alien, and thus the broadening and enrichment of our own experience of the world. (15)

What Gadamer seems to envision here, as applied to my concern for identifying prejudices as yours and mine, is a situation in which each person dwells regularly in the vast world of what is familiar but finds the familiar interrupted, arrested, unsettled by the alien. My prejudices are the directed angle within which I experience the familiar. Thus for instance it might seem perfectly familiar, perfectly commonplace to me to experience the world as structured in such a way that of course a church which affirms homosexuality cannot be supported—perhaps the more likely prejudice, given how recently homosexuality has become an issue of contention. To the extent a prejudice and my view of the world are seamless, I will be unaware of the directedness of my thought.

However, when *your* prejudice comes into view, its contrast with what is familiar to me may allow me to know this "guest whom we admit is one who has something *new* to say to us." Now I can see you *have* a prejudice. In turn I may see that if your stance has a certain quality of directedness, mine does as well, the arrow of my understanding being pointed differently than yours. I come to realize that I may conceptualize myself as an "I" in contrast to your "thou," even though, as Gadamer stresses, we are united in an underlayer of commonality long before we can draw such a distinction.

It is hard, in light of Gadamerian comments quoted above, to specify more precisely how persons come to see themselves as holding contrasting prejudices, as being, in effect, an I and thou. What *can* be said is this: first, particularly in the clash of prejudices the distinctions are brought into awareness. Second, amid all Gadamer's stress on commonality, clarifying the distinctions, valuing them, affirming them in their differentness is another Gadamerian move which allows us to recognize and affirm the newness of this guest we now welcome into our understanding.

And that welcome leads to *good will*, the third aspect of this category. Ever and again Gadamer portrays my relationship to newness as one of welcome, of showing hospitality to the guest—or of extending good will toward it. He insists that understanding requires good will and that this entails not "identifying the weaknesses of what another person says to prove that one is always right, but one seeks instead as far as possible to strengthen the other's viewpoint so that what the other person has to say becomes illuminating" (1989b, 55).

As usual Gadamer does not spell out the exact markers of good will to be sought, say, in lived conversation. What *is* clear is that unless I approach your prejudice with openness to its potential validity, its potential ability to teach me something new and valuable—as I anticipate its completeness—I have not approached it with good will.

Good will is crucial to making Gadamerian the category of *good-will highlighting of prejudices as yours and mine*. If good will is changed to antagonism, as it is in the next chapter, the category marks failure rather than success. However, with good will added, the highlighting of differences, of whatever it is that sets us apart—in other words, your prejudices in contrast to mine—is a move in Gadamerian conversation.

What is seen when the Franconia conversations are viewed through this category? Harvey (C1), for one, highlights the prejudices in play when he comments that in his congregation,

> "We have both extremes—of those who want a proposal stronger for GMC, others who if the proposal were stronger for GMC would find it difficult to maintain fellowship. Others wonder, why are we even discussing this? We're a loving people. The bottom line is that our congregation found the proposal a good compromise. We're willing to support the position for now."

Here Harvey is pointing to the three prejudices which emerge as key throughout the conversations: inclusion, exclusion, third way.

Andrew (C1) defines his own prejudice in the direction of inclusion when he notes,

> "I can accept the proposal reluctantly, but with frustration and sadness. I ask forgiveness for maybe not being a peacemaker. If we really believe we are sinners in common, then here we're being hypocritical. Why is this sin singled out and others not? This bothers me. I don't know why, but I can't keep quiet. I'm so upset."

However, what conversational moves are characterizable as a *goodwill* highlighting of prejudices is a tricky matter. Throughout the conversations prejudices are frequently highlighted, but, as I will elaborate later, this is rarely done simply to sharpen the matters at issue so as to allow the differing views to enlarge each other. Rather, the distinctions are made to set one's own prejudice in motion against another. Harvey and Andrew do highlight their own prejudices for inclusion on the way toward explaining their pragmatic willingness to be enlarged by the third way, but even their moves are only marginally Gadamerian if their statements of reluctance are given weight.

As will be seen, here begins the trail leading to the conclusion that evidence for the Gadamerian character of the Franconia conversations is modest and overwhelmed by counter-evidence. Highlighting prejudices with good will rather than to prove one is right is rare indeed in the conversations.

This seems not sufficient cause to dismiss Gadamer's emphasis here. Gadamer himself provides a powerful example of what he calls for when he describes Heidegger's ability to highlight with good will the distinction between Heidegger's and Aristotle's prejudices by following "the principle put forward in Plato's 'the Sophist,' that one should make the dialogical opponent stronger. . ." (1997a, 10). In addition, I suggest in my analysis of the third-way statement itself (see below), that there the evidence for goodwill highlighting of prejudices is considerable.

Nevertheless, a question which will haunt this book and never be fully resolved on the basis of the evidence is whether conversations which do not live up to Gadamer undercut Gadamer—or simply show that not all conversations are genuine. If replication of this study in relation to many different data sets were undertaken, it might be significant conversational success would be noted. This would help validate the descriptive potential of Gadamer's hermeneutics. On the other hand, if failure proved regularly to be the outcome of conversations studied, this would underscore those key questions, introduced above, related to whether Gadamer is normative or descriptive: can Gadamer's hermeneutics be considered "worldly," congruent with actual as opposed to idealized conversation? Does Gadamer cling to a normative ideal unsupportable by data?

I will return often to consideration of such questions. Here let me again simply underscore my prejudice that even as I conclude the Franconia conversations provide only modest evidence of Gadamer's descriptive validity, insights ensue. There is valuable work to be done with tools that permit assessing conversation as successful or failed.

AWARENESS OF FINITUDE

"In relying on its critical method," Gadamer argues, "historical objectivism conceals the fact that the historical consciousness is itself situated in the web of historical effects" (1994a, 300). There is no escaping these historical effects, or effective history, because the very thinking through which I analyze the historical is itself a product of that which I analyze. This has a bearing on the very undertaking in which I am here involved; if Gadamer is correct, then I am myself, a member of the same Franconia Conference whose conversations I analyze, embedded in and produced by what I study. My goal, as Gadamer views it, should not then be to transcend this situation but at most to become aware of it. As Gadamer stresses,

> To acquire an awareness of a situation is . . . always a task of peculiar difficulty. The very idea of a situation means that we are not standing outside it and hence are unable to have any objective knowledge of it. We always find ourselves in a situation, and throwing light on it is a task that is never entirely fin-

ished. This is also true of the hermeneutic situation—i.e. the situation in which we find ourselves with regard to the tradition that we are trying to understand. The illumination of this situation—reflection on effective history—can never be completely achieved; yet the fact that it cannot be completed is due not to a deficiency in reflection but to the essence of the historical beings that we are. To be historically means that knowledge of oneself can never be complete. All self-knowledge arises from what is historically pregiven, what with Hegel we call "substance," because it underlies all subjective intentions and actions, and hence both prescribes and limits every possibility for understanding any tradition whatsoever in its historical alterity. (301-302)

Elsewhere and as introduced above, Gadamer asks, "Is not our expectation and our readiness to hear the new also necessarily determined by the old that has already taken possession of us?" (1976, 9). What Gadamer is saying is both that our embeddedness in history is inescapable and that it is precisely through this embeddedness that we are able to open ourselves to the new. What we were is what enables us to move toward what we are becoming.

Here Gadamer makes clear our human finitude—and the paradox that it is through our embracing of finitude that we are enabled truly to grow. "Real experience," he affirms, "is that whereby man becomes aware of his finiteness. In it are discovered the limits of the power and the knowledge of his planning reason." Gadamer explains that anyone aware of being situated in history gains "the insight that all the expectation and planning of finite beings is finite and limited. Genuine experience is experience of one's own historicity" (1994a, 357). As Gadamer says in conversation with Derrida, "I believe I am not very far from Derrida when I stress that one never knows in advance what one will find oneself to be" (1989b, 57).

Awareness of finitude, then, is another appropriate category for interpreting the Franconia conversations. Several delegates appear to demonstrate such awareness. Leonard (C1) says that "we experience the brokenness of so many lives. This convinces me I'm a sinner saved by grace, with so much broken too." Grace (as explained in chapter 2) is that gift of God through which God forgives and makes acceptable the sinner and through which God offers the power to transform one's life. Awareness of the need for grace is thus roughly synonymous with awareness of finitude in that it indicates a sense of not yet being fully whole or complete but rather needing the completion which comes from God.

Julia (C1) prays in awareness of finitude as well as shaped by effective history when through her "mote in our own eye" she unintentionally reverses—while maintaining the meaning of—the Bible's injunction not to try to take the speck or mote out of another's eye when one has a log in one's own:

> "Dear God, we all acknowledge our sin and blindness. We acknowledge again our own need for grace. Work with us here and in the Conference to acknowledge that not one of us is without a mote in our own eye."

Robert (C2) prays, "When we are limited in our wisdom, we pray especially for yours." Similarly Bradley (C3) thanks God "that we don't have to know it all, because only when that which is perfect comes will we understand all. So you come to us tonight amid our inadequacy and even brokenness."

Leon's focus in cluster three is not on finitude but on responding to criticism of Charles, a congregational member. However, Leon acknowledges finitude in vocabulary which is strikingly Gadamerian when he notes that "Robert is human, not complete; as is true of us all, he recognizes that his anger as expressed was inappropriate." James points to finitude in terms visibly shaped by biblical and Mennonite effective history when, focusing on the need "to wrestle" and to remember that not all judgment calls will be perfect, he says,

> "We are a brotherhood and sisterhood by nature. We don't snap our fingers and come to things easily. We have to wrestle. Discernment happens where two or three are gathered. Jesus said we have the power of binding and loosing; we have to make calls. He didn't say we'd call them all 100 percent."

OPENNESS

Closely related to finitude is the next category, *openness.* Gadamer defines his hermeneutics not as "an 'absolute' position but as a path of experiencing" with

> no higher principle than this: holding oneself open to the conversation. This means, however, constantly recognizing in advance the possibility that your partner is right, even recognizing the possible superiority of your partner. Is this too little? (1997a, 36)

Gadamer believes this path or "dialectic of experience has its proper fulfillment not in definitive knowledge but in the openness to experience that is made possible by experience itself" (1994a, 344).

All the previous categories are implicated in openness, and indeed there is no obvious dividing line between them and openness. If I am aware of my finitude as one situated in rather than empowered to transcend the effective history which has produced me, and if I enter conversation with another in that spirit of good will which recognizes that another's prejudices may be of value equal to or superior to mine, I am open to that person's perspectives.

When a delegate suggests that the Franconia third-way proposal is unfair to Germantown because it puts no time limit on how long Germantown will be under the discipline of associate membership, Leon (C3) responds that "The document, while *open-ended*, gives the sense that there is *more we can learn from each other* and what appropriate occasions there can be for joint study and worship" (emphasis added).

Such an attitude that through openness there is more to be learned from each other is what Gadamer is advocating, but explicit evidence of it is rare in the conversations. Interestingly, as can be discerned in the conversational quotes already offered under finitude, the most significant evidence of openness emerges in relation to God and prayer.

Openness through prayer

Harlan (C1) asks God to help delegates "all to be sensitive so we might hear very carefully what you might be saying to us." Julia (C1), prays to God "to open our hands to each other." Robert (C2) says that "It's easy to disagree, to separate, harder to remain in contact face-to-face, committed to each other, in the faith that the Spirit is wise enough and large enough and patient enough to see us through." He prays that God's message be "vested in us with wisdom, understanding, openness, to find our way amid this issue of our time." Bradley (C3) prays, "We gather this evening, kind Father, to seek your face and to listen to you and learn and share a measure of the understandings and experiences we have." Leopold (C3) prays "that the Spirit might move in our midst. Help us find peace, to reflect on who you are. Help the church to find faith, to listen intently to what you are saying to the church."

A theme repeatedly evident here is that of God as the one through whom openness is achieved. Prayer has no direct analogue in Gadamer, thus it is a stretch to apply Gadamer to it, and others will need to decide whether the links I make are persuasive. Yet it does seem that the role prayer plays here is arguably Gadamerian. It is Gadamerian because the "default setting" of the praying person is to be, precisely, open to that which is larger than what is finitely human.

Such a view has roots traceable to the early Anabaptists. As Dyck observes, crucial to them was the concept and experience of "the new birth," which involved that process whereby finite and sinful persons opened themselves to the "enabling power" (1995, 52) of God to be "progressively renewed through faith working in love" (54). Praying as a form of being open to the transforming power of God's grace is one key way the Christian participates in the process of becoming a new or (in Gadamerian terms) larger person.

A model prayer well-known to Mennonites is that of Jesus who, facing crucifixion, yearns for the kinder destiny he is requesting by asking God to "remove this cup from me." But quickly Jesus continues, "yet, not what I want, but what you want" (Mark 14:36). Such a prayer connects with the strong Mennonite valuing of *Gelassenheit*, of humility, of yieldedness or surrender to God, of "humble trust" as Marcus G. Smucker (1990, 718) puts it—or openness.

Then when prayer, with such strong connotations of openness, occurs in a public setting, it can be argued that God becomes a mediator in the group's conversations. As in each other's presence and hearing delegates open themselves to God—speaking to each other even while aiming the talk at God—God functions as a kind of relayer of indirect openness *between* delegates. Thus it should come as no surprise that some of the more notable evidences of openness in the Franconia conversations emerge in the language of prayer.

Openness through play

Perhaps one important analogue of prayer is play. What is play? For one thing it is a form of dancing; Gadamer notes that *spiel*, the German word for play, "originally meant 'dance.'" In a key passage, Gadamer also says that

> play itself contains its own, even sacred, seriousness. Yet, in playing, all those purposive relations that determine active and caring existence have not simply disappeared, but are curiously suspended. The player himself knows that play is only play and that it exists in a world determined by the seriousness of purposes. But he does not know this in such as way that, as a player, he actually *intends* this relation to seriousness. Play fulfills its purpose only if the player loses himself in play. Seriousness is not merely something that calls us away from play; rather, seriousness in playing is necessary to make the play wholly play. Someone who doesn't take the game seriously is a spoilsport. The mode of being of play does not allow

the player to behave toward play as if toward an object. The player knows very well what play is, and that what he is doing is "only a game"; but he does not know exactly what he "knows" in knowing that. (1994a, 103)

Note that Gadamer does not mean to convey by play merely the notion of lighthearted, fun-filled frolicking, though that meaning too may be pertinent, but rather is emphasizing something that "contains its own, even sacred, seriousness." Gadamer adds that "the play is not to be understood as something a person does." This leads to the conclusion that there is a *primacy of play over the consciousness of the player. . ."* (104). "The structure of play," Gadamer claims, "absorbs the player into itself, and thus frees him from the burden of taking the initiative, which constitutes the actual strain of existence" (105). Such emphases suggest that care must be taken not to equate Gadamer's play with frolic so much as with what "absorbs the player into itself." Thus even combative interaction, such as the Franconia conversations typically were, hold at least the potential to exemplify, in their own solemn way, Gadamerian play.

But there is something curious about play. Play directs itself and is structured by the goal of fulfilling a goal, yet that fulfilling is not itself finally the purpose of play. Rather, play exists for the sake of play or, as Gadamer puts it, to "self-present" itself. The player's behavior is shaped by the tasks of play, but "the 'meaning' of these goals does not in fact depend on their being achieved. Rather, in spending oneself on the task of the game, one is in fact playing oneself out" (108).

Let me note three implications of play. First, a goal—whatever presenting issue initiates either play or conversation as play—is needed. Second, however, the goal in the end sets in motion dynamics that transcend it, as the playing of play becomes the ultimate goal. Third, the players must consciously know the goal of the play and their contribution toward achieving it but must simultaneously open themselves to the rhythm of the play in such a way that they are being played by play as much as playing it.

Such implications of play significantly shape Gadamer's view of the hermeneutic process and of conversation. A crucial form of openness *is* to be willing to play, to be possessed by what is other than the self, to accept that "One must lose oneself to find oneself" (Gadamer, 1989, 57). Here the Christian interpreter cannot help noting the debt Gadamer owes Jesus, who is quoted as saying, "For those who want to save their life will lose it, and those who lose their life for my sake will find it" (Matt. 16:25).

In the Franconia conversations, prayer becomes a means by which participants are called to relinquish their initiative—to lose their lives to find them—and enter a play of conversation understood as unfolding in and through God's presence. Here Gadamer's implicit pointing toward the divine through describing play as "sacred seriousness" becomes an explicit interaction with God, who is viewed as a kind of playing field in which the entire game unfolds.

Participants can be seen as daring to open themselves to the risks of playing this particular high-stakes game with each other because God will move the game in a direction the participants can trust. This is evident in Robert's quoting of 1 Corinthians 13, which says that "For now we see in a mirror, dimly, but then we will see face to face. Now I know only in part; then I will know fully, even as I have been fully known." Awareness of finitude and openness to the other in love can be risked *because* through God completeness will ultimately be found.

In addition to the God-oriented exchanges, there is one intriguing interchange which seems nearly—and only nearly!—to exemplify play. Nelson and Annie exchange these statements:

Nelson: "Yes, I'm with spelling out more clearly a strong statement. Give a time limit, draw a line in the sand. I guess my position is not in conflict here tonight. I'm not sure how to express grace. To cut them off is like shunning. That's wrong. Even if what they're doing is sin. It's wise to keep fellowship. I have high regard for the people on the committee. They recommend keeping the dialogue going and leave room for God's grace to have an effect on Germantown."

Annie says she has questions about why Paul would write on issues of maintaining food laws and so forth as he did if he did not mean to say that we should not judge those who are outside the church, but we must judge those inside and break fellowship with violators.

Nelson: "I know Jesus ate with sinners."

Annie: "Not Christians, he didn't. They weren't Christians yet. Once you're in the church and unrepentant, then you're to put them out, that will give them a shock, maybe make them shape up. Otherwise you love them into hell."

Nelson: "I'm not proposing that; the statement says that it's sin."

Rosalyn: "To the public, we're seen as accepting homosexuality."

Nelson: "The Conference statement is strong, right?"

Annie: "The statement is strong, but Germantown doesn't accept it."

Nelson: "We don't accept Germantown's stance, we'll keep dialoguing. Would you not let a person from Germantown in your presence?"

Annie: "Those at Germantown who disagree with what Germantown is doing should go to other churches; they shouldn't stay there in a church with unrepentant practicing homosexuals. How can God's blessing be there?"

Nelson: "I don't mean to get off-track—"

Annie: "We argue every Sunday in Sunday school; we're not really at each other!"

Group laughter.

Nelson: "I've spoken to two persons in leadership, both have sons who have acknowledged homosexuality, both have expressed to their sons their disapproval of their living in sin—and both also continue to love and fellowship with them."

Annie: "That's a parent's job."

Nelson: "The church should be like that."

Annie: "The church is not a parent."

Nelson: "Is the love of a parent different than the love of a church, of the brotherhood?"

Annie: "It's different—"

Tobi: "If I as their pastor could just jump in on these two Sunday school debaters"—laughter—"the Conference position is clear. . . ."

Now I do not contend that the spirit of this interchange does more than hint at a Gadamerian tone. Annie's aim appears to be to brook no opposition to her own passionately-held stance. Nelson's moves, though couched in more open language, seem not intended to promote his own readiness to grow through contact with Annie's prejudices. And yet. . . . A kind of play or dance emerges here, a military dance, a rat-tat-tat-of-rifles-firing kind of dance—but there is a rhythm, a sense of timing, a sense of almost-playful dance-step matching dance-step here, that points in a Gadamerian direction. The participants themselves seem to recognize this with several rounds of the laughter that so commonly accompanies playing and dancing.

Highlighted is also the difficulty, as will be explored later, of ever quite pinning down what is going on in such individuals and how their readiness to change or lack of it is to be evaluated. Nevertheless, the clues at least seem to hint at the possibility that slight shifts in perspective have taken place.

Remember, for Gadamer success does not finally require *agreement*; rather, it takes place whenever those in conversation experience a fusion of horizons such that they can in some way glimpse what the other sees. Annie and Nelson show little evidence of doing this. They do not indicate ability to grasp what the other is seeing. However, as they dance back and forth across each other's turf even in disagreement, and amid laughter, they are at least in the same game and in this small way point illustratively to Gadamerian play and the fact that the play does not require marching in lockstep but only on the same field.

However, with the exception of the Annie-Nelson near-playing and the God-oriented ingredients, evidence of Franconia playing is sparse. The participants on all sides are too determined to preserve the truth they see through their initial stances to risk losing such truths through openness to play. They do not trust that if they do yield to play, the fuller truth that emerges will be worth the potential loss of the truths they at the outset hold so dear.[6]

RISKING PREJUDICES IN RELATIONSHIP

And the risks of playing the conversational game are precisely what need to be addressed next. Although, as will be seen, I needed to modify it, initially I labeled this category *risking my prejudices*. Gadamer contends we begin to understand "when something addresses us," but for us to be thus addressed requires "the fundamental suspension of our own prejudices. But all suspension of judgments and hence, a fortiori, of prejudices, has the logical structure of a *question*" (1994a, 299). It is through seeing that all prejudices can be questioned or put in question that we are enabled to risk our prejudices. The essence of such risking is precisely to open ourselves to the power of the question "to open up possibilities and keep them open."

But Gadamer's view here is rich and nuanced. A prejudice has not been risked if "it is simply set aside and the text or the other person accepted as valid in its place." Gadamer is not saying that the way I risk my prejudice is by seeing it from the outset as something I must transcend or too-easily give up in submission to another's prejudice. Going that route is to make the error of any objectivism which "forgets its own historicity" (299). There is no transcending prejudices, so to risk a prejudice is by no means to rise above it. It is rather to handle prejudice in such a way that I move precisely through its resources to insights larger than those it initially offered me.

Gadamer makes the perhaps impossible but creative demand
that I at the very same time risk a prejudice and ensure that it is
"given full play" (299). He appears to be saying that I must simultaneously proceed on faith that I am correct and that I am not. Risking
prejudices is a difficult dance indeed. I must ever and again and at
the very same time trust in my own historically-situated vision as
the only way I can see anything at all even as I remind myself of how
finite and in need of enlargement my vision is.

If Gadamer is correct, this helps explain why Franconia evidence of a unilateral act of risking prejudices is slim: I do not in a
simple and isolated act risk a prejudice; rather, I do so through engaging with others in mutual and complex juggling acts. My original projection was that risking prejudices was perhaps the key category through which to seek instances of Gadamerian conversational
success. What I was at that point missing was the ineradicable tension and dynamism woven into Gadamer's understanding of what
it means to risk a prejudice. Once I sought risk in the form of prejudices placed in dynamic tension and consequently changed my category to *risking prejudices in relationship*, much more data became pertinent. The key move here is to shift from evaluating prejudices only
in isolation to examining how they may be risked as they rub against
and perhaps at rare (at least in these conversations) moments fuse
with one another there in the interactive tensions of a living conversation.

Several aspects of this category can be discerned as Gadamer
and the data are placed in conversation in this category. In addition,
problems of application, one having to do with focus on relationships as relationship, the other with performance versus talk, arise.
Let me first detail some of the many instances in which the category
of risking prejudices in relationship is pertinent, then comment on
the subcategories and problems.

Robert (C2) provides one of the clearer portrayals of the category. As he summarizes the third-way proposal, he is also providing
a rough definition of prejudices in relationship.

> "To summarize the proposal as presented to you: it is to affirm
> and reaffirm the position on sexuality expressed in the Confer-
> ence and churchwide statements. It's clear in the proposal here,
> the suggestion is not that the beliefs in the Conference have
> changed. Noted further is the understanding that German-
> town is not in conformity with statements of the churchwide
> body and Conference. The attempt is to recognize on the one
> hand that GMC is not in compliance with Conference, and on

the other an attempt to maintain some sort of relationship. That I see as the thrust of the proposal."

Later he reiterates that the question delegates face is this: "Can we simultaneously affirm the Franconia position and that Germantown is not in compliance, yet retain the relationship as spelled out here?" He also asserts that "The official Conference stance is clear. Homosexuality is a sin. Germantown is not in compliance. So we're testing, what relationship should we have?" And he clarifies,

"Conference is standing by its position that Germantown is not in compliance. Germantown recognizes that. There is full recognition of that. The question is simply, what is the way to relate? Full acceptance is out. Some will be troubled if the relationship is not fully cut. This is a way in between."

Here is Ronald's summary:

"I guess I hear Germantown say they want to be in relationship to Conference. In light of the differences, the committee is trying to say how they might get along despite differences. Germantown wants full membership, but how to proceed? The idea is to exercise some action, some discipline, yet keep open the door to relating while not to full membership. I see it as really not a compromise. It's pretty clear where Conference is at, but we're saying, "We still want you to be in relationship here."

Robert's statement appears more clearly to maintain the distinctions between the Franconia and Germantown positions. Flatly he notes that Franconia defines Germantown as out of compliance and that Germantown fully concurs. The lines are sharply drawn. The challenge then becomes obvious: if both sides disagree and agree that they disagree, what are the relational options? Again Robert starkly observes that some will only be satisfied with full inclusion and some only with full exclusion. The third way aims to be "in between."

Ronald's statement has many affinities with Robert's. He too notes that the challenge is to find a way between different positions. But Ronald seems more concerned to "sell" the third way as a means for maintaining relationship with Germantown without weakening the Franconia position: "I see it as really not a compromise." Ronald's statement seems less able than Robert's to envision an outcome in which starkly opposing positions together contribute to a third option potentially larger than either.

Beyond differences of nuance, however, and based on comments such as Robert's, Ronald's, and other similar ones, I propose that, at the most general level, risking prejudices in relationship pertains whenever two factors are simultaneously present. First, the integrity of different prejudices is maintained. Second, without dissolving either prejudice, both are held in tension, are placed in relational contact with each other. But what are the features of prejudices in relationship that entail risk?

Presence

Presence is the first feature.

> Who has not had the experience—especially before the other whom we want to persuade—of how the reasons that one had for one's own view, and even the reasons that speak against one's own view rush into words. (Gadamer, 1989a, 26)

What Gadamer wants to stress here is that it is the sheer encounter with the other that brings our views to words. He goes on to claim that "The mere presence of the other before whom we stand helps us to break up our own bias and narrowness, even before he opens his mouth to make a reply" (1989a, 26). This is a succinct description of the minimal requirement for risking prejudice in relationship, which is simply to show up, to stand before the other, to be present, to be in at least the relationship of standing face-to-face with the other.

The issue of presence connects with the earlier discussion of how prejudices relate as yours and mine. Gadamer notes that "interpretive distance," that which allows distinguishing of what is so familiar that it recedes into background from what is new, is "an important hermeneutical element." He cites as an example "the encounter between persons who try to find a common ground in conversation" and argues that

> Every encounter of this kind allows us to become conscious of our own preconceptions in matters which seemed so self-evident to oneself that one could not even notice one's naive process of assuming that the other person's conception was the same as one's own, which generated misunderstanding. (1997, 45)

Presence is simultaneously distance. This is because inherent in the very presence of the other is the possibility that the distance between us will call forth awareness that what had seemed to be given may not after all be. That is why the words may rush. And that is why presence involves risk: it stirs recognition that each of us has a view which is potentially other, not as seamlessly same as we may have without really thinking thought. Thus suddenly it is frighteningly possible to imagine thinking *other than* what until now was safely beyond the need for pondering, testing, and maybe changing.

By the standard of presence and the distance it entails, the Franconia conversations are replete with risk. Robert (C2) understands this when he notes that "it's easy to disagree, harder to remain in contact face-to-face." Regardless of their prejudices—including the perspective that homosexuality is so self-evidently wrong that there should be no need for discussion of whether to exclude any congregation which violates this historic position—those conversing are present to each other.

Here is a slice of the Annie-Nelson interchange analyzed earlier with a strong linkage to presence.

> Nelson: "We don't accept Germantown's stance, we'll keep dialoguing. Would you not let a person from Germantown in your presence?"
>
> Annie: "Those at Germantown who disagree with what Germantown is doing should go to other churches; they shouldn't stay there in a church with unrepentant practicing homosexuals."

Nelson appears to value presence and to promote it as a means for maintaining relationship even between persons who disagree. Annie, in contrast, appears to equate only agreement and presence. If persons disagree, they should remove themselves from the presence of those with whom they experience the disagreement. Whatever her reasons for thinking those who disagree should cease to be present, Annie appears to see presence as charged with power, perhaps even the power to foster change which Gadamer sees it as having. An interesting twist here is that presence is an issue at two levels. Even as Nelson and Annie clash over whether homosexuals or persons from Germantown should be in the presence of those who reject their views, Nelson and Annie are present to each other.

Gadamer does not provide the fine-grained analytic tools that might allow precise measurement of how the risk of presence has enlarged the participants. But this at least can be observed: Nelson and Annie and the rest have accepted the risk implicit in the very acknowledgment that the other *is* other, not same. And this inherently demonstrates that even what may seem to some self-evident can, after all, be called into question. This questionability is itself key to Gadamer, who says that "The real power of the hermeneutic consciousness is our ability to see what is questionable" (1976, 13).

In the Franconia conversations, the delegates have through presence stepped into questionability. Even if some continue to insist on the self-evidentness or superiority of their prejudice, these participants have allowed presence to reveal that their stance is one among a range of options, rather than a truth whose validity is so secure its questionability is not even discerned or discernible.

Journey

For Gadamer the very existence of questionability, of the potential to enter the process of question and answer in relation to the object of understanding, initiates a *journey*. Gadamer repeatedly stresses that "we understand in a *different* way, *if we understand at all*" (1994a, 296-297). There is no understanding without movement, without traveling. If after encountering the other my understanding remains the same, I have understood nothing. Gadamer believes every true effort to understand "is only a step on a path that never ends." When one "accepts the blow, the thrust" of what one seeks to understand, one sets in motion a journey that continues ever on (1989b, 57).

Bradley (C1) explicitly accepts a comparable view: "We are on a journey of faithfulness," he tells the delegates, because "all are committed to God's grace faithfully as believers seeking a right relationship with God and one another." Bradley also says that "I encourage people to stay with the process—process is the important part—rather than get hung up on something." Process in this context is a synonym for journey. Bradley is asking delegates to accept the blow or thrust of what they are discussing, to risk being changed by it.

This is a theme to which Bradley continually returns. Later he comments that

> "this represents a discussion about how we read the Bible. If there's been anything good about the last two years, hopefully it was that we read the Bible and didn't focus on proof texts. Yet we still don't come out at the same place. I think of Willard Swartley's book on *Slavery, Sabbath, War, and Women* [cited several times in this study], or whatever the exact title is. Christians have wavered all over the place for centuries, then sometimes still differ. I have a feeling this is another such process; it takes time."

Robert (C2) identifies the task as being "to come together to address each other, to find a way to proceed amid deep and difficult issues." Journey is implied in the quest to move through difficult issues in search of a way to proceed. And presence, "to come together," is identified as a starting point for the journey. James (C3) also implies a journey or process, which unfolds as thrust by thrust the quest for understanding proceeds, when he says that "We don't snap our fingers and come to things easily. We have to wrestle."

Seth offers the most wholehearted support for viewing prejudices in relationship as a journey which should be granted freedom to lead where it will.

> "I cannot foresee a relationship building in strength between GMC and FC in this approach. It's contrary to the Spirit of Christ. It infers mistrust—not trust that Germantown will go the way they feel the Spirit of God leading them. It would appeal to me if FC said, 'We trust you, we believe you follow Christ as much as we do, whether we agree with you or not, the community is ready to walk with you where the journey leads.' "

The journey aspect of prejudices in relationship is sensed as well by Franconia delegates who resist the third way precisely because it permits continuing movement. Earl, who leans toward exclusion, explains that

> "we feel the need to just be protecting ourselves all the time in an indecisive place. So I think it's just wearing to go on and on. It's like a husband and wife on the verge of a divorce who just can't get one, and they're just waiting and wishing it was over. So I hope we'll get something more clear to be worked with."

Earl is at this moment present to those with whom he disagrees and is thus temporarily fulfilling at least that aspect of Gadamerian conversation. But he wants as soon as possible to cease being in this "indecisive place" where "it's just wearing to go on and on" and where, he implies, presence among those with whom he disagrees is being needlessly called for. Using the striking image of husband and wife ready to divorce but unable to complete the act, he calls for the matter to be resolved so presence and journeying can cease and the divorce—the wanted severing of relationships—be completed.

Meanwhile Marcus's problem is that journey is inherent in the third way, and he in this situation interprets openness to journeying as negative. He wants not an outcome which allows processing to continue but one in which the journey is halted by clarity.

Jay says that

> "As I read this statement, on page 40 something jumped out: 'We have seen in the past, division over numerous issues

which became acceptable at a later time. We did not wish to propagate that pattern. The committee searched for a way to affirm and support the churchwide position and still maintain a relationship with Germantown that would avoid the schism and brokenness of some past decisions.' Maybe I'm interpreting it wrong, but I support Morris Derstine, and I've been in dialogue with him through e-mail, and this is really a concern to me. Is FC someday going to accept this ministry style? I'm the youngest person here, I'm twenty-eight—"

With Marcus and others, Jay worries that the third way offers too much dynamism, too much potential for the journey to unfold beyond the instabilities he perceives in the attempt to hold prejudices in relationship. As will be discussed (chapter 4), because Jay believes that his prejudice represents an already-completed truth which will be betrayed by any enlargement, journey for him is negative. But the point here is not so much how Jay evaluates the journey as that he and others do see that placing prejudices in relationship sets journeying in motion.

Growth

Growth, the product of journeying some delegates fear, deserves attention in its own right as a risk-involving feature of prejudices in relationship. However, it appears in at least two forms, one more Gadamerian, one perhaps less so.

Our growth. Saul (C2), wants to affirm the prejudices held in relationship by the third-way statement. "FC stands strong yet allows us to continue to have opportunity to need each other, to discern what we're needing to find our way on." Here also there is an implied call for presence, "to continue to have opportunity to need each other. . . ." Saul's juxtaposition of the need for each other of those with differing prejudices and awareness that the journey is not completed is a pointing toward the possibility that mutual enlargement of prejudices can take place as participants maintain relationship. The focus is on "my" or "our" potential for growth.

Larry (C1) comments,

"I know why I support the proposal, not the particulars. Because of who we are, we want the ministries of [our congregation] eventually tested by Conference. We don't want to lose the relationship, we need the discipline, we need all churches in relationship even if we disagree. We want all churches to speak forth what they understand. I plead for that for Germantown."

Later Leonard adds, "We're pleading for an opportunity to dialogue in Conference and remain in relationship for what we can all learn from each other." Leonard is passionate about the learning which can emerge for all participants if they expose themselves to risk by maintaining prejudices in relationship. Again the speaker's own self is included among those able to benefit from growth.

Their growth. However, assessing how Franconia participants handle growth is a tricky matter. On close inspection, it turns out that discerning who is wanting the growth of whom is a very murky business indeed. In the above quotes it does seem Leonard is implicating himself, and those who share his prejudice, in openness to growth. However, even there his implicit intent may be to call those who disagree with him toward growth; if so, he is not actually risking prejudices but calling others to do so. This appears to become explicit as he continues that he supports the proposal partly because "People wrote it trying to help those most against homosexuality still see the value of relationship." Here Leonard wants those who disagree with him to do the growing as they accept his prejudice in favor of relationship.

After making clear that he considers homosexuality sin, Nelson asserts that

> "To cut them off is like shunning. That's wrong. Even if what they're doing is sin. It's wise to keep fellowship. I have high regard for the people on the committee. They recommend keeping the dialogue going and leave room for God's grace to have an effect on Germantown."

Nelson's stance exemplifies the trickiness of the analysis here. Based on Nelson's openness to the presence entailed by relationship, he is prepared to risk enlargement of the prejudice toward exclusion his opposition to homosexuality would otherwise entail. However, another reason he is prepared to support the third way is not to risk his own stance—but in the hope that through maintaining relationship Germantown's stance will be enlarged. Here again it appears to be *the other* who is to do the growing.

Dan takes a somewhat similar position, contending that

> "No one is perfect in the church. The mission is more to offer grace than to judge; the goal should be to extend grace by bringing together both the fact that the Conference has a stand and a decision not to cut GMC off immediately."

By noting that all in the church are imperfect, Dan moves toward a stand that all are in need of growth. However, his support for not cutting off GMC "immediately" suggests an alignment with Nelson's view that maintaining relationship is intended partly as a means to incite the other toward growth.

As I understand Gadamer, a risk is taken primarily to the extent that participants are open to their own growth. Thus the move toward growth is Gadamerian *when it entails my or our receptivity to change and growth*. The move to enlarge the other, to ask another to grow, is on the other hand potentially a move *away* from Gadamer. In the Franconia conversations, the two moves become thoroughly intertwined, making it possible partly but not fully to distinguish them.

Talk versus performance

This difficulty of distinguishing when growth is risk-taking and when not leads to consideration of a significant problem in applying Gadamer to the Franconia conversations: *talking about* growth or risking of prejudices is not the same as *performing* it. The Gadamerian analysis of the Franconia conversations I have performed throughout this chapter has yielded, I think, findings which exemplify the value of viewing conversation through Gadamerian lenses. However, still elusive after all that work is straightforward, conclusive evidence that actual risking of prejudices has taken place. *Where* the risking is to be sought is hopefully considerably clearer than it was before my analysis; *that* it has taken place is not so clear.

What in the Franconia conversations might constitute performance? The key criterion, I believe, is whether any initial prejudice has grown as a result of engagement with some other prejudice. Thus if either exclusivists or inclusivists lean from their respective sides more toward each other or the third way than they initially did, while integrating this leaning with their original perspectives, this might constitute one form of evidence that their prejudices have been enlarged. This means that enlargement of prejudice in the FC conversations is not automatically support for prejudices in relationship—or the third way—but whether this support represents movement from an initial stance.

A concern that could be raised here is that some growth may not be good. What if, for example, certain of the adherents of the FC conversations are viewed by others as evil? What if the inclusivists see the exclusivists as intolerant homophobes, the exclusivists see the inclusivists as those *fin de siecle* libertines who can be expected to emerge during a culture's death throes, and both see the third-way adherents as wishy-washy compromisers unable to stand for the right? Such concerns deserve the further attention they are given in chapter 5. Here let it simply be noted that amid the worries this may raise, the Gadamerian bias remains to risk remaining too ready to learn from the other rather than to risk too quickly leaving the conversation.

In light, then, of this continuing concern to seek change in views as form of performing Gadamerian conversation, it may well be that third-way supporters were initially exclusivist or inclusivist, in which case their current stance is evidence of prejudices risked. But what of those whose initial prejudice is toward the third way? Third-way prejudice is trickiest to analyze, because it inherently stands for risking of prejudices. However, the third-way danger is calling other prejudices but not its own to be placed at risk.

Thus potentially the bulk of the calls for the third way are themselves counter-examples of Gadamerian conversation. Awareness of finitude, openness, and calls for growth are all possibly means for imposing third-way prejudice rather than genuinely performing enlargement of prejudices. Paradoxically, those who most passionately espouse the third way and who through such talk sound the most Gadamerian, may be no more Gadamerian at the level of performance than the harshest exclusivist whose closure contradicts Gadamerian precepts.

Yet if it is the case that Gadamerian-sounding talk is not necessarily Gadamerian performance, how is performance to be identified? At least two factors must be considered: first, it seems access to longitudinal change (Warner, 1991) may be needed. There may need to be some means for tracking what prejudice a participant in a conversation initially holds and how it changes over time. Gadamer's thought seems to assume a kind of longitudinal narrative in which a character in the story can say, "Once I was blind, but now I see. That is how I saw then; this is what I see now." Second (though this is agenda fraught with problems, as will be seen), it seems that in some cases there may need to be some means of access to "author" intent or introspective condition; otherwise it can be unclear whether a speaker is actually risking prejudices or reaffirming prejudices already held.

Both factors are explored at greater length in chapter 5. But it is not necessary to detail all considerations to observe that neither condition is satisfactorily met through the available data. In theory the conversations could have provided longitudinal cues; participants could have uttered remarks describing this or that move from earlier blindness to new vision. None did. And not even in theory was access to intent likely to be gained; the study is of conversations as they publicly unfold, not of participants prepared to grant access to internal states.

Relationship for its own sake

In the category of prejudices in relationship, a second problem in applying Gadamer emerges. Gadamerian analysis seeks evidence of commitment to relationship, and this makes all the Franconia talk about relationship seem intrinsically Gadamerian. However, the key distinction in the Gadamerian concern with relationship is that it unfolds as participants in conversation relate not so much to each other as to the subject matter around which they are gathered. The picture here is of persons led by the nudges of the subject matter rather than by whatever relational warmths, coldnesses, trusts, mistrusts they feel for each other as persons. Given that distinction, there are Franconia conversational elements which resist rather than align themselves with Gadamer.

Carol (C2) provides one of the clearer examples when she summarizes the sense of the conversation to that point as pragmatic support for the third way because it is

> "the one hope holding the 'family' together. We must listen to all among us. Germantown is a good example of diversity. We want to accept people where they are, not cut relationship."

Included are comments which may lean toward readiness to risk for the sake of enlargement, but the emphasis is on maintaining the "family" relationship. The focus of concern is not on maintaining a right relationship with the subject matter but on keeping the family intact. James likewise stresses that "the relationship between brothers and sisters is crucial."

Milton (C3) provides another human-relationships-drenched example.

> "What James asked, what is love, is key. It's hard to talk about in the abstract. So I want to tell a family story to bring it down to earth, make it concrete. My sister came out in 82, or 81. When she did the family had a choice. I remember her telling me that her stepdad told her, "Don't bring that trash into the house. That was the initial reaction. My reaction—I was out of the house by then—was, how do I meet this? I was already an assistant pastor, in L.A. I met with my sister and asked her whether she would like help changing. The grace of God could heal her. "No," she said. So there was nothing I could do. Okay. She went her way, I went mine. For two-three years I came to

realize, we hadn't talked. I hadn't been deliberate, but it was like I had shunned her. Yet I was thinking, what does this mean. If I'm not talking to her, it's like shunning. What does it mean to love her, to be in relationship with her, yet hold onto the convictions I have still?

"So I wrote her a letter.

"'I want you to know I love you,' I told her. 'Your lifestyle doesn't change my love.'

"That started up our relationship again. I never preached to her about her condition, though she knew where I stood. We were not cut off.

"Years later—about two years ago—she contacted me. She was happy, in the church, no drugs, her life turned around. I can't help thinking that if it were not for the letter telling her 'I love you,' and regaining relationship—with disagreements but not shunning—there might be very negative dynamics to this day.

"As I read the document, the key question, assuming convictions about what is right and what is wrong can be maintained with integrity, is how do you still love? Assuming discipline and not falling into the trap of pluralism and wishy-washy thinking—given that, how do we relate in a loving way to people who are maybe in involved in a destructive lifestyle? My sister's situation was very destructive. Grace was involved in turning her around. I had to learn how to hold my convictions yet not change my loving and being in relationship with her. Can Germantown be loved by Conference while FC keeps its convictions? With that perspective, I see the third way as possible."

Above I explore that aspect of prejudices-in-relationship which involves seeking growth of the other. Some of Milton's concerns fall under that rubric, as he talks of grace "involved in turning her around" from a "destructive lifestyle." In addition, however, Milton wants to make the point that being able to say, "I love you" amid disagreements, preserving the relationship for its own sake—apart from its links to the subject matter—is crucial.

This stress on relationship for the sake of relationship itself is one Gadamerian analysis has difficulty addressing. It seems clearly to play a role in these conversations and to have a bearing on the totality of what emerges from them. This may be an aspect of the data which requires attention it cannot properly receive from philosophical hermeneutics. Here (as detailed in chapter 5) another problem in applying Gadamer emerges.

ANALYZING THE THIRD-WAY STATEMENT

The above problems do pose significant challenges in applying Gadamer to the Franconia conversations and underline the limits of what I have been able to learn, particularly regarding whether prejudices have in fact been risked. Thus it is noteworthy that there is one additional source of data that may yield more promising results. This is the third-way statement which, as introduced in chapter 1, emerged from several years of conversations between Conference and Germantown representatives, was ultimately signed by both, and is reproduced in full in Appendix C. It was considered so critical to the unfolding discussions that it was printed in the spring 1997 program booklet for delegates (Miller et al, 1997) and was a key springboard for the delegate discussions analyzed in this book.

The third-way statement itself, though not at this point in its development an actual conversation so much as the record of what earlier conversation produced, deserves attention in its own right, for two reasons. First, it was introduced in full into cluster one and thus officially made part of that conversation. Second, it is accompanied by documents in which those who drafted the statement provide some access to their original prejudices and intent, thus permitting some longitudinal evaluation. These documents as well were made part of the conversations by being introduced, at least in part, to delegates in several clusters.

Thus I turn now to analysis of what can be learned from viewing specifically this data through Gadamerian categories. To the best of my knowledge, no Franconia leaders or writers of the statement operate knowingly in a Gadamerian framework. Yet as I hope to demonstrate, the statement is amenable to Gadamerian interpretation, offering an illustration of how Gadamerian theory may actually be practiced and what fruits it may yield. This is not to claim that the only viable or perhaps even preferable way of analyzing the statement is through Gadamerian lenses; obviously other ways of approaching this product of a Christian conversation could include theological or biblical evaluation, to name just a few of many potential interpretive grids. Nevertheless, I hope at least to show that a Gadamerian assessment usefully highlights significant aspects of the document.

EFFECTIVE HISTORY PRODUCING COMMONALITY

Ingredients of Mennonite effective history (detailed in chapter 2) are indelibly engraved on the third-way statement. The Bible plays a central role. The cruciality of maintaining both the *right* and *fellow-*

ship aspects of right fellowship in the body of Christ is clear. The effects of the Purdue 87 statement remain in the background but inevitably have helped shape the context, limits, and spaces in which the statement unfolds.

Immediately after introducing the issue of Germantown acceptance of gay and lesbian members as the impetus for the statement, its framers say,

> This initiated a two-year discernment process. Through it, Christ has revealed to us that GMC and other FMC congregations have substantial unity of faith and purpose. Christ has also given us a clearer understanding that serious areas of disagreement remain unresolved.

Throughout the statement are scattered phrases concerning Christ, God, the Holy Spirit, the gospel, New Testament citations. Here the statement framers show they are rooted in common ground. Even as they disagree over how to live in a world brought into being by biblical and Christian language and beliefs, they converse with each other in the terms provided by that world.

GOODWILL HIGHLIGHTING OF PREJUDICES AS YOURS AND MINE

The statement painstakingly highlights and documents which prejudices belong to whom. "GMC and its supporters in FMC," it is said,

> focus on the unity and prefer that GMC be restored to full membership. Those who see GMC's position as a threat to unity prefer that FMC's relationship with GMC be completely terminated. Many others find themselves seeking a "third way."

Here in bold relief are the three prejudices in play. The statement elaborates:

> Full inclusion or complete exclusion need little explanation. But we offer a "third way" for consideration by the delegates. This third way seeks to embody Christ's call to maintain both unity and purity of faith. It suggests a GMC-FMC relationship that recognizes both the integrity of GMC's faith journey and the faithful concerns of a majority of FMC congregations that believe GMC errs in one important aspect of faith.

Later further detail is added:

> Yet these differences are not inconsequential. GMC, affirming the earlier FMC call to be "a people of invitation," welcomes

persons of faith and commitment to Jesus Christ including some who are living with a partner of the same gender. GMC believes it would be unfaithful and destructive to revoke the membership of persons who actively contribute to its spiritual life. On the other hand, the majority of FMC congregations believe it would be unfaithful to continue to sanction membership for people who are gay and lesbian.

The prejudices are laid out cleanly, concisely, carefully, exemplifying Gadamer's vision of a genuine interchange of prejudices in which, with good will, conversation partners clarify differences and seek to see strengths in the position of the other. Why each prejudice is held is described respectfully, persuasively, allowing holders of any prejudice described the possibility, if open, of understanding the appeal of the other stances.

AWARENESS OF FINITUDE

"In a spirit of brokenness," says the statement, "we pray for God's mercy and for the Holy Spirit to enable us to pursue healing and holiness in our relationship." Participants define themselves as "sinners in common." If they do not quite rise to the level of a well-developed theme, here at least are meaningful hints of awareness of finitude.

OPENNESS

Both Conference and GMC affirm the importance of our relationship. GMC values the nurture, resources, and mutual accountability that can come from a body bound together with a common purpose of growing in faithfulness to Christ and the gospel. FMC recognizes the continued enrichment of the urban challenge that GMC offers and acknowledges that many aspects of GMC's vision may serve the larger body as we enter the twenty-first century. We have many rich gifts to benefit one another. In this light, the differences between GMC and FMC may seem small.

Here explicit language affirming openness to the other is not used, but an implicit openness seems evident in the readiness to value the visions and contributions of the other. Supporting this conclusion is the fact that the participants are intending to walk their talk; these affirmations of each other arise in the context of pledging to walk with each other in openness to the other's potential to offer enlargement.

Risking Prejudices in Relationship

> Persons from both sides of the issue wish to respect the conviction of those who, out of conscience, hold a different position. Both share a concern for faithfulness, authority of the Scriptures, holiness, and holy living. In this apparent impasse, GMC takes inspiration from Paul's counsel to an equally divided Roman church to welcome those who are "weak in faith" but "not to doubtful disputations" (Rom. 14:1). Though, as sinners in common, we may not agree who is the "weaker" party, we can seek a relationship that does not center on disputation. . . .
>
> We recognize that this association does not fully satisfy the deepest concerns of GMC or other FMC congregations. Yet we desire that FMC and GMC will together experience more fully God's intention for the church of Jesus Christ through this relationship. In it, we recognize opportunities for some mutual accountability and growth, while not ignoring the important difference that exists concerning homosexuality. May the Spirit of God guide us to welcome one another respectfully while putting behind us distracting disputations.

Discernible here are factors I have identified as accompanying prejudices in relationship, including presence, journey, growth. The commitment to *presence* is one of the most inescapable features of the statement. The very reason for being of the statement is intrinsically to encourage the participants to remain in each other's presence. Thus they agree to accept the key risk posed by presence, which is that it keeps ever before those who differ the questionability of their own prejudices.

With clear gaze the statement framers are acknowledging that they differ and even with good will allowing each other to give persuasive reasons for why they differ. Then they are agreeing to remain respectfully in each other's presence. This is a courageous move for all involved. Rather than resist the possibility of being changed by the other through cutting themselves off from the other, they agree to the persistent risk posed by remaining in relationship.

Readiness to *journey*, to recognize that participants are on a path whose destination remains an open issue, is somewhat evident in the statement. Among the terms Germantown agrees to is "continuing to search the Scriptures, welcome counsel, and maintain a teachable spirit on issues of sexuality." To be teachable, amid continuing (not static) searching of Scriptures and readiness to receive counsel, is to remain open to further learning, further movement. Here is an agreement to journey. The statement concludes with the mutual acknowledgement that through agreeing to relationship, the participants "recognize opportunities for some mutual accountability and growth, while not ignoring the important difference that exists concerning homosexuality." The journey is hedged; not all destinations are fully available. But some growth, some traveling from initial stance to whatever lies beyond it, is encouraged and welcomed.

Both forms—ours and theirs—of the potential for growth associated with retaining relationship are evident. On the Franconia side, not to be minimized is the explicit admission that the third way "allows GMC to discern and pursue ministry in its context." Although the statement hastens to stress that the third way also "acknowledges FMC's firm and continuing opposition to including gay and lesbian people in congregational membership," the initial move is dramatic when viewed in context. Franconia has historically opposed accepting gays and lesbians into homosexual membership and continues to do so in the statement itself. Nevertheless, and this is key, Franconia's commitment to relationship with Germantown is so strong it will permit a carefully-qualified exception. In this way, despite hedges, Franconia explicitly accepts its own growth as a conference prepared to include at least one dissenting congregation.

Meanwhile Germantown is prepared to live with numerous forces asking it to move beyond its current stance. From one angle, this is hardly growth; Germantown can be viewed as submitting to restrictions, to contraction, instead. But if growth is defined as a readiness to remain present to others on a journey which may change one, growth *is* taking place, and who is to predict what the outcome of this Germantown willingness to continue growing might be.

The question of *performance versus talk* takes much different shape in the third-way statement as compared to the cluster conversations. In the clusters, I concluded, talk outweighs performance in relation to risking prejudices in relationship, or if there is performance, it tends not to be accessible to the research as structured. The third-way statement, in contrast, *is* performance. The participants are performing their talk in the very act of talking it.

But if risking is defined as including a longitudinal element, such that performance is difficult to discern except when movement from here to there is verified, does the statement live up to this test? Even on the face of it, it appears to. Included in the statement are the longitudinal cues that show movement, as when mention is made of past dynamics, past positions held by both sides, the "apparent impasse" which the statement aims to address.

There is also supportive data external to though connected with the statement. In the delegate book in which the third-way statement appears, and printed immediately before the statement, are two reports on the process which led to the statement, one from Franconia (Miller, 1987), one from Germantown (Germantown Mennonite Church's Process, 1997). The Franconia report does not detail the conflicting prejudices but indicates the Franconia "commitment to the resolution of the apparent impasse." Clearly, based on the third-way statement, Franconia's contribution to impasse was the initial stance that no congregation could accept practicing gay and lesbian members and retain Franconia affiliation.

Germantown's contribution to the impasse is spelled out: "It became evident that Germantown could not disrupt the structure and unity of the congregation by banning certain participating and contributing persons from membership." The Germantown version of its stance is that "We remain unable to bar from church membership persons in whom we have witnessed the work of the Holy Spirit." Such comments make clear the initial stances with which each party entered the discussions two years before, providing longitudinal access to the unfolding process.

The reports then document how risking of such stances took place. Franconia notes that once the impasse became clear, its committee "began to focus on 'a third way' or to ask the question, 'how can we, Franconia Conference and Germantown congregation, continue to relate with integrity from our adverse positions on one issue?'" Then the report continues,

> We have seen in the past, division over numerous issues which became acceptable at a later time. We did not wish to propagate that pattern. The committee searched for a way to affirm and support the churchwide position and still maintain a relationship with Germantown that would avoid the schism and brokenness of some past decisions.

The report concludes with comment on what Franconia intends the third-way statement to be. It is "an attempt to be faithful and compassionate, to acknowledge our differences and similarities, and to admit our limited wisdom and understanding as we anticipate the continued call of God to follow Him."

The Franconia report details a process of risking which unfolds in what could be viewed as remarkably Gadamerian terms. Goodwill highlighting of prejudices as yours and mine takes place as Germantown's stance is charitably described even as it is contrasted with Franconia's. Awareness of finitude, of "limited wisdom and understanding," is evident. The commitment to prejudices in relationship, to "maintain a relationship with Germantown," is strong. The journey motif appears in the "continued call of God to follow Him" and in the awareness that one may journey from what seems right at one point in time to future enlarged perspectives: "division over numerous issues which became acceptable at a later time."

The Germantown readiness to risk is not quite so explicit; Germantown does not so clearly move from an initial stance to a demonstrably different stance. Nevertheless, Germantown indicates willingness to accept the risk of enlargement through the persistent commitment to maintain relationship with Franconia and through the openness to the other demonstrated in the report of "coming to understand that our severest critics are honestly concerned for our spiritual welfare and about faithfulness to the good news of Christ as much as we are."

Interestingly, the focus on *relationship* for its own sake which I detected in the cluster conversations seems de-emphasized in the third-way statement and subsidiary reports. As quotes from the statement have shown, the stress on relationship remains strong, but the Gadamerian view of a relationship set in motion not only for its own sake but also as a common gathering around the subject matter is at least partly present. Among key reasons the relationship is to be maintained is that "We have many rich gifts to benefit one another." And the framers note their "desire that FMC and GMC will together experience more fully God's intention for the church of Jesus Christ through this relationship."

If the subject matter is limited to homosexuality and whether to include or exclude those who differ, both parties partly accept the claims of the subject matter yet also partly place limits on what openness they will tolerate. But the subject matter may also be defined as the gospel, in which case there is strong evidence that the participants have agreed to allow its questions to continue setting the agenda of the conversation.

Two aspects of the statement and reports point to problems in applying Gadamer. First, despite the lack of strong emphasis on relationship for its own sake, relational concerns are raised here:

> Our recent history reflects that GMC has felt betrayed by the Conference in its selective attention regarding the congregation's faithfulness to Conference actions. On the other hand, the Conference has felt betrayed by GMC for moving in a direction that did not have the Conference's full sanction. Out of

this brokenness of our communication, trust, and social isolation, we seek to find unity of purpose and spirit.

In this quote the feelings of people as people, not merely as interpreters of subject matter, come into view. Particularly in the Germantown supplementary report, relational factors emerge as well. Writers of that report speak of "feeling angry, hurt, and despondent," then describe how "through a renewed focus on worship, we regained our emotional equilibrium." They note that as their committee and Franconia's began in 1995 the discussions that led to the third-way statement, they "appreciated the level of candor and vulnerability on everyone's part and began to feel heard." As will be elaborated later, Gadamer undertheorizes such concerns as emotions, betrayal, trust, social isolation, vulnerability.

Second, the mention of "full sanction" is a reminder that the conversation being reported on and conducted through the statement does not, in relation to power, unfold in a pristine Gadamerian context. As chapter 6 explores, the Gadamerian view of genuine conversation entails the absence of constraints imposed by power imbalance. Here power parity clearly does not exist. One side has power to impose an outcome on another. Roughly a third of the statement is devoted to making this clear. This material details the terms of the third way for Germantown, which include accepting nonvoting associate member status, acknowledging that its position is inconsistent with Franconia's and not attempting to persuade others otherwise, accepting the power of Franconia to credential or not credential Germantown pastors as Franconia sees fit.

Meanwhile Germantown has its own power. Germantown possesses, for example, whatever power may be present in such options as assenting to the Franconia terms and in what spirit (gracious or sore losing being yet additional forms of power with varying consequences) or choosing eventually, perhaps, the route of dissent, which as history shows may have its own power over time to turn tables.

Although I believe the insights gained above by bracketing power remain valid, power tends to cloud matters when viewed through Gadamerian lenses. And whenever power intrudes as an inescapable issue, challenges of applying Gadamer will with equal inescapability become evident. But the problems of applying Gadamer to power are mostly a story to be told later. Now it is time to turn to what can be learned from applying Gadamer negatively, from asking what may be seen if one looks for how participants in a conversation fail to live up to Gadamerian ideals.

FOUR CHAPTER

FRACTURED DANCE: CHARACTERISTICS OF NON-GADAMERIAN CONVERSATION

Robert Sokolowski contends that "It is important to discuss not only the positive side of interpretation but also the negative"; he believes that "the failures are as interesting and as important as the successes, because they define the borders of success" (1997, 230).

INTRODUCING CONVERSATION FAILURES

Sokolowski offers an intriguing list of potential failures of Gadamerian conversation. First, a speaker may be too immature to engage in genuine conversation; he notes, for instance, that "if a child starts crying during a discussion, the cries are not necessarily . . . a move in the conversation." The point here is simply to take into account, as part of setting the parameters of genuine conversation, the possibility that some "interlocutors" simply may be incapable of genuine conversation (230).

Second, a speaker may change the subject because the initial subject is too disturbing. Third, despite goodwill intent to contribute to genuine conversation, a speaker's contribution may be confused. Fourth, regardless of appearances, a speaker's actual intent may be to deceive. Fifth, a speaker may refuse to change, remaining "stubborn and soaked—opinionated—in his convictions." Sixth, a speaker's contributions may be Gadamerian but may partly fail due to inability to be an equal partner, as evidenced in being too overbearing or too submissive (230-231).

Sokolowski's fifth failure, refusing to change, will be picked up in my own category of closure, and the sixth, relating to lack of power parity, in my category of coercion. However, the other failures are strikingly difficult to employ as research tools. This points again to the challenge of operationalizing Gadamerian categories. It suggests also the likelihood, as elaborated in both chapter 1 and the next, that Gadamerian thought ought primarily be seen as inspiring research conducted with more formal tools than Gadamer himself provides; or for energizing Gadamerian interpretive criticism rather than more methodologically systematic studies.

Yet if Sokolowski's failure categories (along with Gadamer's thought) are difficult to apply, they emphasize the value of seeking instances of failure. Without entirely avoiding the application challenges Sokolowski faces, I have attempted to reduce theory/application gap by allowing the data itself to play a key role in producing instances of failure.

Here is my own list of potential failures culled from asking what shadow or counter-hermeneutics, Gadamerian theory turned inside-out, might look like: (1) effective history producing commonality; (2) antagonistic highlighting of prejudices as yours and mine; (3) certitude; (4) closure; (5) severing prejudices; (6) coercion. As noted in Appendix B, this list emerged from applying earlier categories to the conversations, then allowing the data to provide cues for eliminating, modifying, or sharpening the categories.

As I prepare to analyze the conversations according to these categories of failure, let me offer three preliminary comments. First, discussions of Gadamerian theory will be less detailed here than in relation to Gadamerian categories of success. This is because much of what needs to be addressed is simply how what has already in many cases been addressed at length fails to be achieved.

Second, clearly many of the failures I identify pertain to those who hold exclusivist prejudices. This is predictable; it is in the very nature of the exclusivist stance to strive for closure, certitude, victory of right over wrong. As will be addressed more fully in the next chapter, there is an inherent conflict between this prejudice and the Gadamerian vision. The other prejudices are not exempt from failure. However, for a variety of reasons they are in this chapter rarely in focus. Two reasons particularly deserve mention. One is that to the extent those holding the inclusivist or third-way prejudices fail to engage in genuine conversation, their failure tends to involve lack of openness in performance rather than absence of it in talk. Such failure is addressed in the previous chapter.

Another reason failure of these prejudice-holders is not emphasized in the next pages is that the situations of the exclusivists on the one hand and inclusionists or third-way adherents on the other is not symmetrical. The exclusivists are in the majority and hold the power (which, as will be seen, they eventually exercise) to enforce their own prejudice. This means those who hold alternate prejudices risk having their own stances forcibly violated—placing them in a different situation than those in the majority. This suggests that, in evaluating how those with and without coercive power manage their prejudices, some means for addressing perturbations of power are necessary. Whether and how Gadamerian tools might permit accounting for power are among key matters pondered in chapter 6.

Third, I have needed to make decisions regarding how to enact Gadamerian precepts in my evaluation of conversational failures. How do I myself engage with good will stances which I judge not in accord with Gadamer's—and my—prejudices? This has not been an easy matter, plunging me as it does into the same riddles I seek to probe. I have tried to find a strategy enabling me both to highlight my own prejudices and seek their enlargement.

This has led me to mobilize my Gadamerian prejudices in this chapter as critical tools. Thus here I model my conviction that to be Gadamerian is not to eradicate what makes me different but to value it as that arrow of directedness through which I initially view the world. This means, I think, that I need not pull punches in assessing how, from my vantage point, the Franconia participants fail to practice Gadamerian conversation. If Gadamerian thought is viewed as a whole, then the totality of any Gadamerian communicative transaction must show ultimate evidence of good will, but clarifying distinctions between one prejudice and another, even sharply, need not in itself be evidence that good will is finally lacking.

Certainly, however, good will must at some point emerge. Thus in chapter 5, particularly under the heading "The Relationship of Openness and Truth," I aim appreciatively to examine ways those whose prejudices (as described below) may differ from mine and Gadamer's nevertheless bring into the open and invite enlargement of my and Gadamer's viewpoints.

THE CATEGORIES OF FAILURE

EFFECTIVE HISTORY PRODUCING COMMONALITY

Undoubtedly the first category of effective history producing commonality is anomalous. Something seems amiss; what is this category, identified also in the previous chapter as a characteristic of successful Gadamerian, doing here?

The answer is that it is included largely for symbolic purposes but is no less important as a result. As I have aimed to make clear in any number of ways throughout this study, among the strongest prejudices guiding it is the bias that even amid the sharpest of differences an irreducible layer of commonality can be discerned. That prejudice has hopefully been enlarged, transformed, often even chastened during the course of my research, but it remains to the end an aspect of my own "initial directedness," my own particular perspectival "openness to the world." Placing this category here underscores my and Gadamer's conviction that even where failure to converse in Gadamerian terms is judged to have occurred, always some measure of success accompanies the failure. Always in the very act of failing to understand each other, participants in conversation continue to experience the We that enables their meeting sufficiently to fail.

The case for this position is made at so many other points that I will not repeat it at length here, nor will I again seek to apply this category to the data in this chapter. That work has already been done and reported on (particularly in chapter 3). The goal here is simply to symbolize that amid all the failures addressed below, there are always levels of commonality undergirding the conversation. Below is a We in battle, a We riven by misunderstandings, tensions, hardnesses of position which cut against the grain of the openness Gadamer sees as the *sine qua non* of genuine conversation, but a We nevertheless.

ANTAGONISTIC HIGHLIGHTING
OF PREJUDICES AS YOURS AND MINE

In the previous chapter, I discussed goodwill highlighting of prejudices as yours and mine. There I noted the value, in Gadamerian terms, of this move. It allows assessing differences of positions yet seeks to bring out the strength of the other stance. This helps set in motion the mutual growth Gadamer seeks. In this way, Gadamer believes, true understanding is nurtured, because it is only as I assume the potential superiority of another's position that I allow it to make claims on my initial stance and potentially to change it.

Here my focus is on the same move turned in the opposite direction. An important failure of genuine conversation takes place when the opponent's position is weakened, minimized, ridiculed, cast in the worst possible light. An *antagonistic*, combative, oppositional—rather than goodwill—highlighting of differences takes place. Then predictably the impetus to learn from interaction with the other is minimized—and combat against or severing from that terrible thing with which one differs is encouraged.

The Franconia conversations are replete with this antagonistic as opposed to goodwill move. Raymond's (C2) is among the most striking.

> "I want to affirm Conference leadership's courage in facing the challenging issue of GMC. The process has been good. But look at page 44, that's a big mistake, compromising with sin. A huge mistake. If we open the door one-half inch it's only a matter of time before we've swung wide open the door for our children and grandchildren. History shows how it works. You leaders need to place the church solidly on God's Word. We're not dealing here with something minor, like the covering. We're dealing with *sin*. When is the church itself separated from God? I believe deeply that if Franconia is not solid on God's Word, it will leave our children and grandchildren in a living hell. You think it's a problem now? Think ten or fifteen years. Then it's not just Germantown, it's widespread, and who will have the courage to take this back? This living nightmare?"

Note that this willingness to cast the other's position in negative light is undergirded and enabled by closure and certitude, as pointed out under discussion of these categories.

Note also that Raymond does make what appears to be a gesture of good will: "I want to affirm the Conference leadership's courage in facing the challenging issue of GMC. The process has been good." However, this does not appear to be good will of the variety called for by Gadamer. An ineradicable ingredient of Gadamerian good will is the readiness to "anticipate the completeness" of the other's position, to open oneself to its persuasive force and consequently to consider some modification of one's own position. The remainder of Raymond's comments indicates that his good will is aimed toward the Conference *to the extent* that the Conference stance confirms his own position.[1]

Moving on, Raymond notes that according to the proposal, "Germantown believes it would be unfaithful to revoke the membership" of those who are gay and lesbian.

> We're responding with not even a smack on the hands. We say we have these sexual standards. But what Germantown is wanting is like allowing any sin—say if I'm a womanizer— and wanting the church to say I can be a member. Okay? There's one main difference between the Mennonite church

and a cult. God's Word. If you stand on the word, you're the church, if you don't you're a cult.

Raymond aims in a variety of ways to portray the Germantown situation as negatively as possible. If the door to compromise with Germantown is pushed open, he warns, the future for children and grandchildren will be terrible, a living hell, a living nightmare. Germantown is affirming sin, there can be no question about that, in taking the stand it has. Germantown is like a cult in deviating from the word of God on which Franconia must firmly stand if it is not itself to be a cult—with cult radiating images of Jim Jones and Heaven's Gate. Germantown is like a womanizer, or adulterer, he implies. And surely, he assumes, no one would quibble with the sinfulness of *that*. But whereas the womanizer would be disciplined, Germantown receives "not even a smack on the hands."

After several others take conversational turns, Raymond is back. Now he compares opening the door to homosexuality to opening it to polygamy:

"Imagine you open the door that much to polygamy. Soon your grandchildren have five wives. You open the door, that's the way things go. We see how society is going. And the only hope for society is the church. Especially the Mennonite church, where we're holding the line. Without hope like the church, society is completely empty."

By the time Raymond is done, opening the door to Germantown opens the door to the collapse of society itself. Without the church society is empty, and if Germantown is accepted, the church needed to sustain society will itself collapse. Through such comments Raymond succeeds in highlighting his own prejudices and contrasting them with the prejudices with which he disagrees. It is important to note that this in itself could be potentially a move toward successful Gadamerian conversation. If there were evidence that Gadamerian goodwill accompanied Raymond's management of his prejudice, then to that extent Raymond would be engaged in Gadamerian conversation. What particularly turns Raymond's comments into examples of failure is his *antagonistic* highlighting of prejudices, which places him in a mode of affirming his views against opposing views rather than seeing alternate perspectives as resources for growth of his own.

Morris (C3) also is taken with the adultery comparison.

"If I decide I want to minister to adulterers, who run around with other women than their wives, I can see them as no longer broken. Ridiculous, right? But it's what happens when every congregation says what goes and what doesn't."

Open the door to Germantown, and adultery runs rampant. He also suspects the issue isn't just homosexuality: "Plus in the literature I see, they're talking now about bisexuality, but how can you be bisexual and monogamous?" All boundaries begin to collapse unless Germantown is excluded.[2]

Marcus connects homosexuality with desire to rape and even, in an implicitly threatening move, dares associate this imagined rape with the wife of Willis, moderator of the meeting and one of the writers of the third-way statement.

> "But do we still call desire sin? It's like saying it's okay to desire, to burn with lust. It's like if I have a desire, Willis, to violently rape your wife, and not saying that desire is sin. Of course it's sin, I need to be saved from my own terrible urges."

The picture is of gruesome urges held barely in check by the sanity of the Conference but soon to be unleashed by the licentiousness Germantown is already introducing. Again failure is evident not in the actual positions taken but rather in the absence of clues that opposing positions are treated, with goodwill, as potentially providing the resources of completeness or truth.

Not only Gadamer but also the effective history of Mennonites who once prized the openness of humility seems far away. Here and below the nineteenth-century readiness, for example, of John Brenneman to "be convinced . . . that he is in error" (1863, 4, cited in Liechty), seems to have been overwhelmed by the need to discern what is right rather than to seek the "common mind" Liechty sees as having once been the goal humility enabled (1980, 17). The rightness of the fellowship trumps the fellowship itself.

CLOSURE

Annie (C2) thinks that the third-way statement is flawed because it calls for ongoing ambiguity she wants no part of.

> "It seems like we're gutless wonders. Either tell them they're okay or not okay. Vote one way or the other. We're just postponing an event that has to be dealt with unless we just want to pass it on to future generations."

Gadamer calls for openness, openness to change, to growth, to the mystery of what may be yet to come. For Annie, such openness is to be fought. Annie wants nothing to do with a statement that "has no teeth, it's wishy-washy." Annie wants *closure*. She wants the matter resolved now, decided now, closed now.

Elvin (C2) quickly backs Annie up. "I think too there should be a time limit. In a year or two there might be practicing gays and lesbians at GMC but no way to address it while they practiced. Set a time limit, they're trying to soft pedal." Again what is feared is the potential openness or dynamism of the third way. By holding opposing prejudices in tension, Elvin fears, matters which should be closed now are allowed to remain open, undecided.

Hiram (C2) and Robert (C2) have a pertinent interchange. Robert has a few turns earlier explained the third way as an "attempt . . . to recognize on the one hand that GMC is not in compliance with Conference, and on the other an attempt to maintain some sort of relationship." Hiram is dubious:

> "I appreciate the work the committee did on this, I like the position the Conference takes, but our general members do not see the matter how you say it here, Robert. The public out there is not sure that's the Conference position. The proposal here is not acceptable to them. They're not sure that what you say is where Franconia is."
>
> Robert: "So it needs to be stronger—"
>
> Hiram: "Absolutely. People see it as Franconia accepting Germantown's position. That's not what Conference is doing, but that's how people see it."

How exactly to view Hiram's stance here, given that he claims partly to speak for himself but also partly for others is unclear. An additional complication (elaborated below) is that his statement appears to include features of good will: "I appreciate. . . ." However, the trend, at least, of his concern is to move the statement nearer to closure.

Robert's Gadamerian espousal of openness and the anti-Gadamerian preference for closure of the other participants clash in a fascinating C2 interchange between Robert, Warren, Hiram, and Annie.

> Hiram: "Germantown says it can't expel sinners because of the Spirit. Are they saying you can be a practicing homosexual *and* have the Spirit? Is that possible as you understand Scripture?"
>
> Robert: "I understand their view as that persons in covenantal relationships show evidence of the fruits of the Spirit—their test for the Spirit's presence."

Hiram: "Do you understand the Scripture as allowing that to be possible? I'm hitting *you* now."

Robert: "Let me put it this way, I'm not perfect but I hope I have a little evidence of the Holy Spirit. So we're all capable of being sinners *and* having the Holy Spirit. Sin and the Spirit is part of all of us."

Warren: "I want your opinion. Are you saying that if homosexuals practice and get married, do they have the Holy Spirit in them?"

Robert: "They're saying—"

Warren: "No, you."

Robert: "I'm saying all of us have a combination of sin and the Holy Spirit."

Warren: "No, *your* opinion. Sins and homosexual sins are not on the same level. If homosexuals are married, do they have the Holy Spirit?"

Robert: "I'd like to stick to the question: are any of us without sin? Are any of us saying we don't have the Holy Spirit?"

Annie: "The question is asking others to accept sin. Why can't I have my favorite sin? I don't know when the Holy Spirit comes and goes. But I know Germantown wants that sin. They don't even see it as sin, so they don't have to deal with it. Franconia *does* see it as sin."

Warren: "When we *have* sinned, with Christ working in us we repent and are forgiven. Here there is no repentance. That's what I'm struggling with."

Robert: "I'm hearing the conversation, and David is recording and will report it. I'm wanting to stay on the proposal. I'm not afraid to state my position, but the focus is on FC and GMC. The official Conference stance is clear. Homosexuality is a sin. Germantown is not in compliance. So we're testing, what relationship should we have?"

Robert champions awareness of finitude and the openness it brings; he is willing to be on a journey in which it is possible for two seemingly contradictory qualities—having sin and the Holy Spirit—to rub against each other with unpredictable results. Robert also attempts a *goodwill* highlighting of Germantown's stance. The others highlight their stance as well, as when Warren suggests homosexual marriage is worse than generic sin, which is why the question can be raised whether homosexuals who marry can "have the Holy Spirit." However, the latter highlighting is *antagonistic*. Here that antagonism intertwines with eagerness for unambiguous closure: one can be either a sinner *or* have the Holy Spirit; one cannot embody both.

CERTITUDE

Why is closure not only so important for but so acceptable to some of the Franconia participants? Because they are certain they are right. Far from showing Gadamerian awareness of finitude, they believe they can transcend finitude to know right and wrong. They would almost surely disagree with viewing their prejudices *as* prejudices. Prejudice for Gadamer is inextricably tied to finitude; by definition a prejudice is one limited perspective on what is larger than the prejudice can ever comprehend; it is one "bias of our openness to the world."

Some Franconia participants believe it is possible to see the world, reality, truth as they are—rather than only perspectivally. For many of these affirmers of certitude, the key guarantor of their access to truth is the Bible. The comprehensive story of how they view the Bible is beyond the scope of this study. However, it should be noted that a common exclusivist view is that the Bible is the inspired and possibly inerrant word of God whose meaning is plain and to be obeyed. (As cited in chapter 2, Kaufman and Driedger report survey results indicating that 75 percent of Mennonites and related groups hold roughly this view; 1991, 70.)

Both certitude and the view of the Bible which undergirds it is present in a comment made by Hiram (C2). Now Hiram, as quoted above, had first supported the Franconia position, though noting his concern that others would not be able to. Here Hiram, if he was on the fence earlier, gets entirely off it:

> "First Corinthians 5 says what we *must* do: if there is a homosexual in the church, we must get him out. We *must* expel him from the church. We're not doing that here. If Franconia Conference accepts the statement, folks here at the Franconia congregation will leave. We must expel from the church."

Here also an application challenge again emerges. Hiram's initial and earlier-cited affirmation of the third way does appear to include effort to show good will, but it is unclear (as chapter 5 elaborates) whether it is Gadamerian good will or how such a question might be answered. To complicate matters further, might Hiram be seen as experiencing growth by having engaged the views of the exclusivists so thoroughly that he too has now moved from earlier readiness to support the third way to new readiness to become an exclusivist? Then from which direction should we evaluate evidence of good will? What is good will in a situation where movement toward one prejudice is simultaneously movement against another?

Deferring further comment on that question to chapter's end, we return to Rosalyn (C2), who agrees with Hiram. "And further— if we allow them in, we're guilty of the same sin."

"Right," concurs Hiram. "It's a very serious matter."

There can be few clearer examples of certitude than these "must"-filled statements. But additional examples of certitude are not lacking. When one delegate says that though homosexuality is a concern, but "it's one small issue" among many, Elvin is appalled: "But it's not small; it's the most serious of all! Romans 1 says it's one of the worst things, God gave over the homosexual reprobates. It can damn you to hell, no other issue is so serious."

Marcus (C3) turns the discussion in the direction of philosophi-cal bases for certitude:

> "As we talk about this, there are two bases for truth: either plu-ralism or objectivism. Pluralism keeps us all working together until we agree. Objectivism says there's right and wrong. Plu-ralism says there's no right or wrong, just keep working at it. Many congregations are trying to firm up, to become objec-tive. But Conference is into pluralism, into "That's your opin-ion." You take a poll, you come up with ten wrong opinions. Saying all have the truth, that's just majority rule. . . ."

Based on the certitude of objective truth, Marcus can say, "Is being gay or lesbian a sin? Yes." Later we will see that Gadamer sup-ports nothing so un-nuanced as what Marcus defines as pluralism, yet clearly Gadamer affirms neither objectivism as Marcus defines it nor certitude. Marcus's position forces a halt to the ongoing open-ness to truth from many perspectives demanded by Gadamerian conversation.

Because my Gadamerian bias calls for openness to the charac-teristics of failed conversation wherever they may be present, even among inclusionists who may themselves in their own way be un-willing to grow, I would prefer to be able to offer significant evi-dence, based on the data, that this study is not biased against the ex-clusionists. Yet unfortunately for the quest, if perhaps happily for the inclusionist or third-way adherents of C1, based on the data the best it appears can be done to be evenhanded is simply to note that in addition to the largely exclusivist certitude so far reported, there *may* also be some tendencies toward certitude among holders of in-clusivist or third-way prejudices, particularly in cluster one. There, without notable exceptions, participants mutually contribute to the dominant trend of the discussion, which is that the third-way statement is flawed and needs to be moved, if in any direction, toward further inclusion. And a few C1 statements, such as this one, seem to incline toward certitude, yet if so a certitude complexified by readiness simultaneously to affirm the prejudice that homosexuality is sin and a prejudice toward inclusion:

> "At the personal level I say, yes, homosexuality is a sin, however, I still can open my arms to those sinners; other sinners open their arms to me. There's no reason to put GMC on associate member status, to exclude these persons from membership in congregations."

However, because the primary concern of the C1 participants is to seek some viable form of accommodation with Franconia, the comments typically do not take the tone of assured position statements so much as mutual and somewhat tentative pondering regarding what may prove acceptable. Here is an example that emerges as a response to the comment just quoted:

> "I agree with Ted, but the bottom line consists of community. Is there a way to maintain fellowship in our body of congregations? This seems to me at present the only way. If we give a complete blessing to Germantown, this will cause a split. If we broke with GMC, this would also create a heavy burden for some of us. In that respect, I'm a pragmatist—this is the only way we'll hold the brothers and sisters together. If this is what it takes, I support it, even if personally I disagree."

If there is certitude here, it appears to be that maintaining fellowship takes priority, but such certitude is tempered by the speaker's acknowledgment or readiness for the sake of the community to place at risk a bias toward inclusion. Such a tempered stand is not uncommon in C1, where repeatedly the trend toward inclusion is modified by the quest for an outcome that enables continued membership in Franconia.

That readiness to bend principles to maintain fellowship seems a form of risking prejudices. Thus even in the act of seeking examples of certitude in C1, I incline toward the conclusion that if perhaps partly due to circumstantial pressures, C1 participants are among those less likely to be demonstrably locked into certitude.

SEVERING PREJUDICES

A key failure to perform Gadamerian conversation is present in the emphatic determination of many to sever the relationship between opposing prejudices. For Gadamer genuine conversation does not rely on agreement; it is possible to disagree, to challenge, even perhaps to oppose the other's position yet participate in a genuine interchange, provided that in some way participants remain in contact with and potentially enlargeable by each other. Some in Franconia want to violate even this basic Gadamerian condition for "good" conversation.

Annie (C2) says that "Those at Germantown who disagree with what Germantown is doing should go to other churches; they shouldn't stay there in a church with unrepentant practicing homosexuals. How can God's blessing be there?" The very act of maintaining relationship is for Annie unacceptable.

Morris (C3) concurs. He points out that in relation to Illinois Conference, where other congregations were subject to a discipline that placed them on associate membership status, one person defined the meaning of associate as having "to do with inclusion. My understanding of associate is that it's a very inclusive term. For me, they're people *I associate with*. That raises questions for me" (emphasis added). Later Morris makes clear why questions are raised: "If we all agree on a position but we have a congregation that disagrees, I have a problem. If all agree on the statement of homosexuality but Germantown disagrees, yet I have to be in association with Germantown, I have problem." The problem for Morris is remaining in relationship with someone with whom he so fundamentally disagrees. He wants the relationship severed.

Marcus (C3) continues the theme. "If you have some other definition of sin, *what kind of relationship* can we have? If we can't agree on something as basic as that?" (emphasis added). Later, criticizing the third-way statement, Marcus elaborates:

> "It seems a good bit is said about walking together. It says division is unacceptable, we want to 'still *maintain a relationship* with Germantown that would avoid the schism here. . . .' I wrote 'impossible' after that" (emphasis added).

Accepting then refusing presence and its questions

As noted in the previous chapter, such exclusivists do initially accept the risk of *presence*. This moves them provisionally toward Gadamerian conversation. They are present in these discussions. They are to that extent and to this point contributing to a Gadamerian thrust. However, their goal is counter to their current provisional performance. They may temporarily be willing to accept being present among those with whom they disagree, but their aim is to sever the relationship and thus end exposure to the risks of presence.

In addition, even as they remain provisionally present before the hoped-for cutoff of relationship, they simultaneously fight to minimize the risk that the presence of those with whom they differ will lead to the questionability of their own stance. Stanley Deetz describes one block to Gadamerian conversation as "naturalization," in which "one view of the subject matter is frozen as the way the thing is" (1990, 236). To put it in more Gadamerian terms, naturalization is refusing to accept the *questionability* of something.

Some participants want to sever the relationship to evade the questionability of their stance. Warren says that "we're not making it the issue, Germantown is; Germantown is who has brought it to us." And Lorraine complains that "It's not very charitable, for Germantown to want to have people living in sin. Why don't they leave instead of stirring up a hornet's nest? How loving is it, really, what they're doing?" For Warren and Lorraine, there would be nothing in their stance to question if it were not for Germantown's insistence on questioning. They oppose the third-way promotion of an ongoing relationship with Germantown which will continue to raise irritatingly the questionability of what they are convinced should never be questionable.

Severing relationship unless they grow

There is strong feeling among some participants that severing relationship is a tool or weapon for attempting to promote the growth of Germantown. In the previous chapter I noted examples of calls for relationship apparently motivated by hope that maintaining relationship would change the other. Here, in contrast, I look at calls for severing relationship which have the same aim.

Kenny says,

> "I have a young daughter. I've been taught that to reprimand a child is to love the child more. I don't enjoy it, it doesn't feel good, it's not easy. But I do it because I love her. I see reprimand as greater love than the third option."

When Julie asks, "You don't see this as a reprimand?" Kenny responds,

> "What the document says Franconia feels, is that important or not? This will state how important this is to Conference. If this is accepted, that will say how important sin is. That's not better for Germantown, but calling sin sin."

Kenny is saying that if the third way is accepted, this will show what a weak view of sin the Conference has, and operating from this view will not be as helpful to Germantown as "calling sin sin." Since the statement actually does call homosexuality sin, what Kenny appears to want is ratification of the seriousness of the sin by cutting relationship with Germantown. This is the reprimand that will show Germantown love and help Germantown grow as Kenny thinks a reprimanded daughter will grow.

James asks, "Are those at Germantown unbelievers?"

Wilbert responds, "If they don't maintain the faith, we must consider that. For the sake of what Christ called love. Christ was not always 'loving' in a fuzzy way when he reproved error." Again the definition of love involves severing relationship. Such love may help Germantown see its error and grow. It should be obvious by now that this position tends not to fit Gadamarian conversation.

COERCION

Strongly implicit and at times explicit in the Franconia discussions whenever they turn to severing relationship is the threat of coercion. As probed at various points in my study, this is a troublesome category in relation to Gadamerian theory. In the next chapter I explore why it is possible to see coercion as implicitly non-Gadamerian. Here let me briefly anticipate that discussion by noting that the thrust of much of what Gadamer says about true conversation requires that it unfold without constraints, so that all may be free to respond on its own terms to the claims of the subject matter to which they seek to open themselves, rather than under external compulsion.

This suggests that the presence of coercion is a failure of Gadamerian conversation evident not only implicitly in the Franconia conversations but sometimes explicitly. Particularly Raymond makes the threat inescapable:

> "I think if the leaders at Germantown don't do what Franconia says, their licenses for ministry should be revoked. We're not a country club, we're the church of the living God, they should do it his way or be on their own. It shouldn't be a choice for them how they think best."

When Robert makes sure he has heard correctly—"You want a clearcut statement: either change or out"—Raymond agrees. "Yes," he says, "two-year probation was good, we need to love and all that, but at a certain point, we're compromising."

Comments of Raymond's cited earlier fit here as well: "Germantown believes it would be unfaithful to revoke the membership" of those who are gay and lesbian. "We're responding with not even a smack on the hands." Raymond wants Germantown's hands smacked—surely a coercive move under the circumstances. Drawing an analogy with parenting, Kenny (quoted earlier), calls for reprimanding Germantown, saying, "I have a young daughter. I've been taught that to reprimand a child is to love the child more." Reprimand here functions coercively, with Germantown being pictured as the bad child of parent Franconia which must be called back into line from its wayward ways.

Such statements point to the fact that the potential for coercion shapes (or distorts) the entire set of conversations. The conversations are a stage in a process delegates know will probably at some later point be resolved through majority vote. Raymond and all other participants know some official coercion is inevitable; even if the third way carries, it includes sanctions of Germantown. Here Raymond explicitly aligns himself with the power of these sanctions to coerce. And here major constraints on the potential of the conversation to unfold freely and according to the self-guiding play of the conversation come sharply into view.

Mixed Failure and Success

There is an additional ungainly, messy category in the Franconia conversations I call *mixed failure and success*. I discuss it on the failure side of the ledger because I note it particularly in a few participants who in general contributed in the failure categories. However, the matter truly is messy and complex, because it may be in this category that Gadamerian success unfolds. Particularly Rosalyn helps generate this category when she has this interchange with Jim:

> Rosalyn: "Robert, I understand Germantown, my son went there. I understand a lot of good has come out of it, I don't want to lose that."
> Robert: "That speaks to the intent of the proposal."
> Rosalyn: "But if they would remove membership of practicing homosexuals as sinful, we don't know what that would do to the rest of the congregation."

Rosalyn seems undeniably conflicted or troubled. She does not want to lose the good of Germantown, of which she is personally aware through her son. She has elsewhere made clear that she is inclined toward exclusivism, because she is too certain homosexuality is sin to see how it can be right to compromise with Germantown's view of homosexuality. But here she is worried. She senses exclusion may create damage she does not want brought about. Through her worry she demonstrates at least partial openness to the other, partial willingness to risk considering the possibility that she can be enlarged by and not only be in permanent and resolute conflict with the other. Thus here, if in a small way, may be an example of the willingness to move from an initial stance which Gadamer is seeking.

Note also that amid rejecting the third way, Marcus makes sure to quote the document accurately. Even though he then adds, "I wrote 'impossible' after that," he does take pains also to explain that "I don't want to be rude here. I'm concerned about the brothers and sisters at Germantown." This hints at openness, readiness at least to take at least one or two steps of good will toward the other's stance. Then there is the case of Hiram, who may in showing good will toward one position turn against another; there seems no good way to evaluate this except as an ungainly mixture of success and failure.

And here, in such messiness not easily analyzed, is an appropriate transition to the next chapters. There I aim to enter squarely the untidiness of any attempt to apply Gadamer and to ask when the mess is attributable to difficulties in Gadamerian application and when the reality that life *is* a mess not easily reduced to system and pattern is precisely what Gadamer's emphases help shine forth.

CHAPTER FIVE

AWKWARD DANCE: COMPLEXITIES AND AMBIGUITIES OF APPPLYING GADAMER

Here a key task of this study must be performed as I wrestle with the question of challenges involved in applying Gadamer. In the previous two chapters I have intended, whatever my level of success, more to practice than to theorize about applying Gadamer. I have aimed not to be overly troubled by whether my practice is fully congruent with theory. Rather, drawing on Gadamer's own commitment to the priority of practice over theory, I have assumed that precisely through practice can much of whatever is theoretically valuable emerge.

Here, in contrast, I want to worry about those points at which application and theory do become disjoined. Here I want to investigate complexities, ambiguities, tensions that seem to emerge when the data and Gadamerian thought and categories are brought into interaction. My focus in this chapter is on problems and challenges that have become evident through the effort to apply Gadamer.

Among questions to be faced when challenges arise are these: where does the tension between the data and Gadamer rise too high to ignore? When there is tension, what does this mean? Does it mean Gadamer is inapplicable? That Gadamer is applicable at one level but not at another? That Gadamerian prejudices must at points be risked and enlarged? Areas of problem or challenge which below receive particular emphasis in relation to such questions include the subject matter, effective history, ambiguity, conversation, and truth.

THE SUBJECT MATTER

As mentioned in the Appendix B description of my decision to turn from the subject matter as a category of analysis, there are questions to be raised regarding the applicability of Gadamer's concept of the subject matter. Gadamer's vision of the subject matter seems to me highly compelling; that is why in these pages it appears so often, both explicitly and implicitly, as that which justifies, guides, and rewards my openness to what I seek to understand. As Deetz notes, for Gadamer "The genuine conversation is hermeneutically shown to be a special interaction among two persons and the subject matter before them" (1990, 231). Deetz sees in this foregrounding and empowering of the subject matter a crucial contribution: through it Gadamer moves from a view of communication as reproductive to an understanding of its productive possibilities.

Drawing on Gadamer's own comparing of conversation guided by the subject matter with the appreciator of art guided by what the art, in its greatness, calls forth, Deetz says, "The conversation has the character of progressively opening the prejudicial certainty of each individual to question." Then, making the link with art, Deetz immediately adds, "A truly great work might call one's very way of life into question" (231). And genuine conversation, he means to convey, likewise has the ability to call one's life into question.

With Deetz and with Gadamer, I myself am inspired by this understanding of conversation as guided by the subject matter like great art guides its own interpretation, and I play various variations on this theme of appreciation in chapter 6. I can imagine instances of such conversation. Here is one which, as noted in the frontmatter, has played a critical behind-the-scenes-role in inspiring this book. This is why it also appears as a sort of epigraph on page 4.

Some time ago and far up north, the conversation at a table of Mennonites turned to homosexuality. A farmer bluntly insisted the church must affirm its traditional stance or forever lose its way.

One woman said to me, "Isn't homosexuality an issue down your way?"

Someone else said, "Yes, at Germantown, isn't it?"

Suddenly it hit them. Years ago I was pastor at Germantown Mennonite Church.

"Uh, end of discussion," the woman said, "no offense."

"No," I said, "Let's work at this."

So we did. I described my thinking and stressed to the farmer that though we differed, I thought the issue was so complicated the body of Christ needed all our stances, and his could help mine grow.

I cannot explain exactly what happened. I can only say I genuinely believed the farmer had things to teach me. He reciprocated. Eventually, tears in his eyes, he said, "Maybe it really *is* true that we need each other. It scares me, but that means I need you." He drew my own tears. We still did not fully agree, but now we not only abstractly but truly experienced being knitted together as two whose perspectives had been guided in new directions by mutual openness to the subject matter before us.

Such an anecdote helps explain why valuing the power of the subject matter continues to be among my prejudices. But it is also that: an anecdote. And therein lies the problem, at least in relation to the Franconia data, of applying the subject matter. I have been largely able to discern only anecdotal support for my understanding of how Gadamer envisions the workings of the subject matter.

There *is* some evidence, reported in the chapter 3 analysis of the third-way statement, that those who framed that document can be viewed as allowing the subject matter to possess them. Under the impetus of the presenting issue of homosexuality, they opened themselves to the gospel and its complex mix of calls for Christians to discern what is right for the community while doing so in a spirit of love and relational integrity. Precisely their openness to the subject matter appears implicated in their ability to reach a position enacting and pointing to the possibility of genuine conversation between contrasting prejudices. This achievement stands out against the backdrop of the eventual decision of Franconia and its delegates (see next chapter) to accept instead failure genuinely to converse.

However, except for this notable exception (and as explained in Appendix B), I abandoned categories for assessing whether the conversations were guided by the subject matter because the subject of the conversations was generally so rigidly predetermined I could not see how this category could do more than confirm the obvious. I continue to think the category would not be useful for analyzing the bulk of the Franconia conversations but also have difficulty being sure why. Is it because truly the conversations were governed by predetermined subject matter, so the free workings of subject matter could not be identified? Is it because, with the possible exception of the third-way statement, no moments comparable to the one I believe I experienced up north took place? Or is it because even if such moments took place they could never, or only with difficulty, be discernible to a researcher?

A guarded yes to all three questions, I conclude, helps explain the challenge: first, the foreordained structure of the Franconia conversations added a layer of difficulty to discernment of the workings of the subject matter. Second, given the chapter 4 report on the many observable conversational failures, it is unsurprising that this data set would shed little light on the real-world positive incarnation of Gadamer's vision. Third, I find it a challenge to envision how the anecdotal sense I had of experiencing the workings of the subject matter could be translated into research methodology.

This probably points partly to my limitations but also to a problematic aspect of applying Gadamer. Tellingly, Deetz himself moves quickly from sketching the normative aspects of the Gadamerian ideal to describing "blockages" to "genuine conversation." His very last sentence notes that "Implicit in this is a research agenda to carefully describe these blocked interactions and an instructional agenda to enable participants to overcome them" (241). Deetz makes no mention of how research might validate the positive workings of the subject matter. This suggests there remains quite a gap between vision, incarnation, and researchability.

DELIMITING EFFECTIVE HISTORY

As noted in my chapter 2 discussion of effective history, properly limiting the scope and focus of effective history in the attempt to apply the concept to a particular range of data is a significant challenge. My chapter 2 discussion addressed a range of matters argued to be ingredients of the Franconia effective history. My goal was to allow the data to set the parameters of what I addressed as effectively history. Although this appears a defensible move, as I aimed there to support, it may also be an attempt to provide boundaries to the concept of effective history where there may be none. This does point to a significant challenge of applying Gadamer. The concept is itself heuristically fruitful: it did inspire a variety of insights I at least consider productive. However, applying it appears to entail practicing an art rather than replicable research methodology.

Let me examine the implications of that challenge more closely through interaction first with the question of silence, then with Fred Kniss.

EFFECTIVE HISTORY WHEN THE DATA ARE SILENT

If the scope of effective history is limited by what the data addresses, this raises the question of what to do with aspects of effective history that may be pertinent yet remain potentially hidden—at least until somehow teased out—by silence in the data regarding them. A case in point is the historic Mennonite peace position. Mennonites have a five-centuries-old heritage of seeking to articulate and live out pacifist principles rooted in Jesus' admonitions to "Love your enemy, and do good to those who persecute you." Indeed the Mennonite effective history which has helped produce my horizons of understanding is undoubtedly implicated in my attraction toward Gadamer's emphasis on risking my prejudices to be enlarged by the questions posed by the prejudices of the other—who is perhaps even the enemy.

Based at least on surface markers, pacifism remains core agenda in the Mennonite church. This is attested to by the regular appearance of peace-related stories, such as *Peace was in Their Hearts* (Anderson, 1996), a Mennonite publication which presents reflections of one thousand World War II conscientious objectors, some of them Mennonite; sociohistorical analyses (Driedger and Kraybill, 1994); dissertations (such as Stutzman, 1993); or books intentionally aiming to argue for the nonnegotiability of a pacifist core (Weaver, 2000). What a community teaches its children is a clue to its values. Thus also significant is the regular production of curricular resources for children which promote the peace position, such as *But Why Don't We Go to War?* (Landis, 1993).[1]

One important Mennonite contemporary controversy, perhaps only second in intensity to that surrounding homosexuality,[2] is whether persons can be Mennonite and also serve in the military. Here the shaping power of a Mennonite pacifist horizon is evident. One side believes it impossible to be pacifist and serve in the military. The other side believes it possible to be *moving* toward pacifism yet continue at least for a time in the military while the journey is made.

In light of such examples of the Mennonite propensity to place pacifism at the center of denominational identity and discussion, it is fascinating and noteworthy what explicit role pacifism plays in the Franconia conversations: no discernible impact is evident. In the entire round of conversations, peace is mentioned twice. Once one speaker says, "I can accept the proposal reluctantly, but with frustration and sadness. I ask forgiveness for maybe not being a peacemaker." And once in a prayer a moderator mentions "peace" among a list of gifts he asks God to grant. Given that this exhausts the explicit mentions of peace, these seem the exceptions that prove the rule. Otherwise regarding peace there is only silence. As the participants battle, none pause explicitly to say, "But how can we, whose peace tradition calls us again and again to love our enemies, do this to each other?"

It can be speculated that the tensions in the Mennonite valuing of right fellowship (leading sometimes to valuing right over fellowship, as addressed in chapter 2) are playing a role here. Perhaps in this case *right* does become so pre-eminent that the pacifist concern for fellowship, or maintenance of relationship even with the enemy, is repressed. However, it is difficult to derive clear guidance from Gadamer here. As elaborated below in relation to another example, this points to the challenge of applying effective history amid silence.

EFFECTIVE HISTORY AND THE MACROLEVEL

As noted in chapter 2, due particularly to silence of the data regarding other levels of potential analysis, the focus of my application is on the local, on what Kniss, a sociological analyst of Mennonite patterns of cultural conflict, has termed the "microlevel" (1997, 15). Such a narrow definition of research scope is by no means unusual. As Kniss notes, "Studies of intrareligious conflict have tended to view religious groups as closed systems. Thus, explanations of internal events like conflict do not attend to the larger historical or cultural context" (14).

However, Kniss is convinced there is much to be learned from analyzing "the intersection between culture or religion and processes of social change." Based on his own studies of twentieth-century Mennonite patterns of microlevel intragroup conflict and its interaction with macrolevel cultural and historical forces, Kniss concludes that against their own common self-perception, "Traditional Mennonite communities, far from providing a shelter from the storm, spawned internal tempests of their own that *drew power from external winds of change*" (3; emphasis added). Later Kniss stresses again that

> Mennonites may have viewed themselves as separate from the world and resistant to change, but the chronological and thematic patterns of cultural conflict among Mennonites . . . contradicts such a self-understanding. Both the timing and the content of cultural conflicts were influenced by internal organizational and ideological change and by events and changes in the broader American culture. (133)

On a related note, J. Howard Kauffman and Leo Driedger have been convinced enough of the mutual interaction of Mennonite (and related) denominations and the larger culture to produce a book (1991) reporting their analysis of data derived from surveying thousands of Mennonites. Among their key concerns has been to assess the impact on Mennonites of such macrolevel cultural forces as modernization, secularization, pluralism, and more.

These and other studies of Mennonites persuasively make the case that Mennonite dynamics, including by extension those identifiable in Franconia Conference, do not unfold in pristine isolation from the larger culture. Rather, they are the product of constant and intricate transactions with that macrolevel. Thus it seems North American and Western cultural dynamics are a significant aspect of that effective history which can be argued to have produced the Franconia conversations.

. In principle this certainly appears congruent with Gadamer's description of effective history, which he stresses has to do with the fact that no consciousness is objective. Rather all consciousness, including "historical consciousness is itself situated in the web of historical effects" (1994a, 300).

However, what in practice is the researcher to do with Gadamer's view of effective history? Here the challenge of application does seem to rise. Gadamer is not proposing a set of criteria for identifying what ingredients of effective history have "effected" what aspects of consciousness or knowledge or a given conversation. Rather, Gadamer is pursuing the crucial but broader and more philosophical task of showing that we think always in a "situation." And "The very idea of a situation means that we are not standing outside it and hence are unable to have any objective knowledge of it" (301). Gadamer wants us to understand that "*To be historically means that knowledge of oneself can never be complete.*" This is because such knowledge "arises from what is historically pregiven. . ." (302).

What Gadamer seems clearly to provide is the *principle* that humans are situated beings whose present knowledges are not to be seen as founded on transcendent access to the world but as effects of the ongoing flow of history. What Gadamer does not provide is a detailed gameplan for isolating what currents of history have produced what effects. In fact, a crucial aspect of Gadamer's position here is that "the power of effective history does not depend on its being recognized" (301) and that the "illumination of this situation—reflection on effective history—can never be achieved . . . due not to a deficiency in reflection but to the essence of the historical being that we are" (302).

Is there almost a move here to define virtually any historical-contextual features as effective history? And if so, if everything is effective history, then in applying the concept can one isolate given features of effective history? In addition "illumination of . . . effective history . . . can never be achieved. . . ." Amid such murk, what is the researcher attempting to apply Gadamer to do? There are undoubtedly a number of alternatives worth testing, but my conclusion in relation to my study has been that the most viable path has the following features.

First, in the absence of criteria for pursuing an explicitly Gadamerian delimitation of scope, the data itself have provided at least a provisional source of that delimitation. To attempt, for instance, to link the microlevel to the macrolevel through Gadamer in the absence of explicit links with the data or theoretical guidance from Gadamer would have been to risk pursuing potentially productive yet ultimately non-Gadamerian insights.

As will be elaborated in relation to conversation, nearly any investigations, whether of effective history or other matters, may be argued to be in the *spirit* of Gadamerian hermeneutics. But many such explorations will require additional guidance from other theories and thus are unlikely to proceed in purely Gadamerian terms. This is *not* to say it is invalid to do broadly Gadamerian research that pursues micro/macro links (or the implications of pacifism) through mediating theories other than provided by Gadamer. Kniss, for instance, cites Griswold (1987) as providing theory through which to link "ideas" and "macrolevel structures or processes" by "defining a proper explanation as one which refers to the social and cultural context and the interaction of object and context" (Kniss, 1997, 117). But this is a Griswoldian and not a Gadamerian point. That in turn is *my* point: only at a broader level is such research Gadamerian.

Second, the very fact that Gadamerian thought appears to provide here no clear trail should be flagged as confirming the challenge of applying Gadamer in relation to effective history.

Third, the fact that in the absence of such Gadamerian guidance this study does not claim fully to analyze levels of the Franconia conversations regarding which the data is silent, such as pacifism or the macrolevel, is a limitation of the research. It is also, according to Gadamer, a limitation of human thought itself which no researcher can ever fully surmount.

MANAGING AMBIGUITY

In chapter 3 I suggested that Gadamer on the one hand provides some resources for rich handling of ambiguity. His insistence that *nothing* has been understood until it is applied to the particular opens floodgates of ambiguity; meanings or truths are no longer fixed (if they ever were) and potentially universal. Rather, they shift, ambiguously, with every effort to understand any viewpoint different than my own.

But as seems so often the case with Gadamer, this is a rather abstract or philosophic handling of ambiguity. If the goal is to pull out the tangled threads of ambiguity present in living conversation, then Gadamer risks repressing or downplaying ambiguity. That leads to the challenges of application which are my focus here (whereas in the next chapter I make related comments focused on power).

An example: as I introduced in chapter 4, Hiram's initial affirmation of the third way does appear to include effort to show goodwill. "I appreciate the work the committee did. . . . I like the position the Conference takes," Hiram says. Then later Hiram makes clear just how different from the third-way position his own conclusions are: "First Corinthians 5 says what we *must* do: if there is a homosexual in the church, we must get him out. We *must* expel him from the church." The problem of application is lack of clarity regarding what type of good will is present. Is this Gadamerian good will, which anticipates the completeness or truth of an opposing prejudice as part of the process of understanding it? Or is this good will employed as rhetorical strategy to identify with the Conference while actually aiming to deepen divisions between the Conference and the speaker?

In addition, is it possible that someone like Hiram (or any of us) may be caught in such complex crosscurrents that a goodwill effort to understand one position may unintentionally set us against another? What to do if a whole host of opposing positions begin to make claims on us?

The Burkean reader will recognize that underlying the above alternatives to Gadamerian analysis is the thought of rhetorician Kenneth Burke, who has much to say about *identification* and *division* (particularly in 1969). For Burke there is a dialectical tension, embedded in the heart of language, between that which divides speakers and draws them together. The two aspects of communication entail each other and are never to be found except in combination with the other. Thus all communication is inherently ambiguous.

Burke's perspective here and elsewhere provides resources for handling ambiguity which appear to elude Gadamer. Arabella Lyon (n.d.), a literary theorist who learns from Gadamer yet finally moves toward Burke's capacity for exposing and perhaps even celebrating ambiguity, underscores Burke's ability to theorize ambiguities and complexities of the clashing and intertwining motives, strategies, and deceptions animating all communication.

This is no Burkean study, but Burke's nimble managing of ambiguity, and the contrast with Gadamerian tendencies, deserves brief attention as a way of exploring what it is that Gadamer does not do. Burke's style is evident in his theorizing of identification and division. As Burke sees the matter (such as in 1969, 19-46), the ubiquity of division drives speakers to seek means to overcome division. A key way they work at this is through rhetoric, through those communicative practices whereby they strive to build bridges across alienating rifts. This process of building bridges is what Burke terms identification, and identification is Burke's key term for rhetoric. Thus whenever human thought and communication addresses whatever it is that divides humans or whatever it is that draws them back together, it is for Burke rhetorical.

This rhetoric of identification must always keep in mind the two poles in which it operates and which are always present in the other. Such rhetoric remembers that the need for identification is entailed by division. "We need never," Burke notes, "deny the presence of strife, enmity, faction as a characteristic motive of rhetorical expression." So central is the division which makes identification a necessary strategy that Burke sees rhetoric as focusing on it, as involving the individual "in conflict with other individuals or groups," as "concerned with the state of Babel after the Fall" (1969, 23).

The very presence of a call for identification, or the very effort to identify, as in Hiram's case, is evidence of the division the rhetoric of identification aims to overcome. This is why again and again rhetoric has to do with a speaker's showing how she connects with, is like, identifies with an audience; or with how a group's interests are compatible with the interests of another group the rhetorician wishes his audience to identify with; or with why the nation should identify with its leader's wish to do this or that.

And this is precisely why even a cursory Burkean analysis of Hiram's efforts to identify with the Conference quickly generates a vision of an ambiguous dance between identification and division in which one points to other and vice-versa. Such analysis may be pertinent as well in relation to the category of mixed failure and success noted at the end of the previous chapter. Mixtures are what Burke expects; for every conversational move emphasizing this position, Burke anticipates a related but contrasting move toward that position. This approach is congruent with the conflict felt by Thelma, who sees no alternative but to exclude Germantown yet mourns the potential loss of the good she associates with Germantown.

The nimbleness in relation to such data of the Burkean handling of ambiguity underscores the potential stiffness of a Gadamerian approach, which can lead to forcing some ambiguities into categories too rigid or abstract appropriately to contain them. This suggests that any student of conversation wishing to highlight those aspects of communication which "are the tangled webs we weave when first we practice to deceive" will find not Gadamer[3] but the chaos-comfortable Burke the more likely of the two theorists to inspire results that enter rather than straighten the tangle.[4]

Then why not have pursued a Burkean rather than a Gadamerian study? Because if Burke offers resources Gadamer does not, Gadamer also offers resources Burke does not. For Burke all communication is in constant motion, a slippery eel never to be pinned down or a shapeshifter transforming itself into something else the moment you think you have caught it. Such agility allows Burke to unveil the chaotic glories of the ceaseless play of ultimately uncharacterizable conversation. It also makes it a challenge to slow down the action long enough to study it before it is gone. And it makes it difficult to imagine what relatively stable We Burke enables.

Gadamer seems less nimble than Burke but precisely through editing the film of life less manically provides fuller access to some important scenes. Thus for instance Gadamer does posit a more stable deep common accord rather than an identification which quickly transforms into division. Through this move Gadamer allows one more effectively than Burke, who deconstructs commonality the moment he finds it, to linger with and feel one's way into the possibilities of the threads that link a We together.

CONVERSATION

It may seem nearly outrageous to raise at this juncture Gadamer's applicability to conversation. How can I ask questions of this nature after having spent the bulk of this study engaged precisely in the task of applying Gadamer to conversation?

Whether appropriately or misguidedly, my decision to work at theory of application to conversation after attempting its practice was deliberate. I knew in advance that questions could be raised about such applicability; as I will shortly address, Williams (1995) is, for example, among those who doubt that Gadamer and analysis of conversations is a fruitful blend. Nevertheless, I concluded that here the proof would be in the pudding: what I could learn by trying to apply Gadamer and possibly failing would outweigh what I could learn by not making the attempt on grounds that it was impossible.

So what *have* I learned? And what have I learned specifically by theorizing in relation to an attempt already made?

APPLICATION CHALLENGES
RELATED TO RESEARCH AND METHODOLOGY

Some of my conclusions were foreshadowed earlier; it will come as no surprise that one learning has to do with the difficulty of generating through Gadamer any sort of systematic method. Williams' own study was inspired precisely by her assessment, which I have indicated I share, that Gadamer's "perspective is anti-method and has a strong bias toward historical written texts." Foreshadowing my own assessment of Gadamer's view of method, Williams contends that "The central difficulty for the speech communication scholar interested in Gadamerian hermeneutics is Gadamer's concern that his work not be taken as a 'method.'" Williams cites Gadamer's insistence (1994a, xxxiii) that his hermeneutics is not "a methodology . . . but an attempt to understand," and she notes Hekman's (1986, 95) view that to see Gadamer as believing "that the social sciences need a distinctive 'method'. . . . is the antithesis of Gadamer's approach" (Williams, 1995, 4).

Then Williams surveys the difficulties of applying Gadamer to empirical research; indeed, she notes, "I know of no empirical research which specifically labels itself as 'Gadamerian.'" This is why, she explains, when the focus of research falls on communication praxis, the "theoretical concepts alone" provided by Gadamer "will not be satisfactory" (6-7).

Convinced a direct application of Gadamer is impossible or virtually so, Williams turns to Garfinkel. She judges that "Garfinkel's ethnomethodology is problematic for the speech communication scholar because of his refusal to engage in theoretical discussions" (1995, 2). But Garfinkel "focuses on the description and analysis of actual discourse which seems to be absent from Gadamer's approach" (13). Williams believes that integration of Gadamer's theory and Garfinkel's methodological guidance can provide a creative "ethnomethodology of speaking informed by Gadamer's philosophical hermeneutics" (14).

The outcome is a creative and heuristically valuable one. Williams points out one fruitful direction to be traveled by those who want to analyze conversation using a theoretical underpinning which is—at least as Williams sees it—informed by and compatible with Gadamer while evading the inapplicability of Gadamer's thought.

Although I have learned much from Williams' project, I question whether even she provides a roadmap for research labeled Gadamerian. By accepting the inspiration provided by Gadamer's vision but implementing it through Garfinkel, she generates an approach to research which is in its implementation, if not inspiration, more "Garfinkelian" than Gadamerian. Thus even after Williams' pathbreaking effort, it may be that there remains no research which is both Gadamerian and empirical. Certainly I do not claim that title for my work, which is itself qualitative rather than empirical. The point here is not to judge rank qualitative versus empirical research but rather simply to note the difficulty of pursuing research which is both Gadamerian to the core and conducted with quantitative, experimental, or microanalytic aims.

On the other hand, suppose research is defined more qualitatively. Take Babbie's descriptions of field research, in which "social phenomena in their natural settings are directly observed" (1995, 279-304). Field data are then assessed through a search for themes which do recur, but at a relatively informal level, as identified through the interpretive work of a researcher who interweaves "observation, data processing, and analysis" (303). Something like this is what Marcia Witten (1992) attempts (as noted in Appendix A) and what I as well have been aiming to do.

Or suppose research is defined as interpretive analysis (as in the various forms of rhetorical analysis described by Hart, 1990), whereby the researcher examines a situation, event—or series of Franconia conversations—with the intent of analyzing, interpreting, articulating the richness of what is studied. Here the aim is production of added insight as yielded through whatever lens—in this case Gadamerian—the researcher employs for gazing meaningfully at the data. The applicability of Gadamer will rise when definitions of research move in the direction of interpretive and often, in this case, normative criticism, or "the art of developing and then using critical probes, which are nothing more than intelligent and specific questions to be asked of a given text" (Hart, 54).

Hopefully this book is one of the puddings which provides the proof that such methods yield insight. Another may be the dissertation of Jeffrey Frances Bullock (1996), who develops through Gadamer an interpretive method for studying sermons. Bullock aims to develop for preaching the "hermeneutical underpinnings to fully justify the move from what Gadamer calls *Erlebnis* to *Ehrfahrung*, from making an argument to facilitating an experience" (10). Bullock contends that a preacher so informed will "embody the recognition that it is through talk, question and answer, and genuine dialogue that 'the preaching of the Word of God *is* the Word of God" (149). He then employs a method comparable to my own as he sets up several specific sermon texts to be analyzed and commented on, a procedure which involves correlating units of text with Gadamerian emphases, examining congruities and incongruities, and enlarging his and our understandings of text and Gadamer by so placing them in dialogue.

IMPLICATIONS OF A NON-MEDIATED APPLICATION OF GADAMER

Now if some qualitative or interpretive forms of research are the primary potential candidates for the Gadamerian label, then they are, it seems to me, to be conducted through categories derived directly from Gadamer, rather through mediating categories such as those provided by Garfinkel or comparable scholars. Moves toward applying Gadamer through operationalizations provided by non-Gadamerians can be heuristically valuable. I simply question and have tried to avoid the assumption that such research finally remains Gadamerian—other than by inspiration, important though that can be. My goal has been to go as far as is reasonable in applying categories drawn either directly from Gadamer or derived explicitly (not the case with Garfinkel) from Gadamer by commentators seeking to extend his thought.

Such an attempt to apply Gadamer through Gadamer forces careful consideration of this related question: *is Gadamer applicable primarily to research based on written texts or also to the study of conversation?* Establishing that Gadamer may be applicable in some forms of qualitative analysis does not substantiate his applicability to conversation itself. Because Gadamer is so regularly interpreted as focusing primarily on written texts, and I am thus applying him against the grain of a common tendency, I will justify at some length my conclusion that Gadamer's thought gives conversation a major and even originary role.

That Gadamer is applicable *only* or primarily to written texts is the conclusion reached by Williams, who judges that philosophical hermeneutics is so thoroughly text-biased that application to conversation is not a viable stretch. As Williams sees the matter, Gadamer's handling of the hermeneutics of texts versus conversations is downright muddled. Gadamer never makes up his mind whether he is finally giving priority to living transaction between individuals in conversation or the more static relationship of text as read and understood by interpreter. She points out (1992) that even though Gadamer recognizes those dimensions of tradition passed down and communicated orally, he "always prefers the written text." Even "more significant," she thinks, is the fact that "Gadamer's writings display a tendency to explicate even his ideas about conversation in textually biased ways" (4).

Citing Gadamer's position that "Writing has the methodological advantage of presenting the hermeneutical problem in all its purity, detached from everything psychological" (Gadamer, 1994a, 392) Williams argues that this is a stance which "seems to undergird his entire project." She points to "The implicit assumption here . . . that oral speech is somehow polluted by psychological forces. . ." (4). She concludes that scholars interested in applying Gadamer's hermeneutics will want "to recognize that Gadamer's hermeneutics might be limited by an incomplete treatment of conversation" (6).

I do not reject Williams' conclusions as without foundation. Here I detect an example of the Gadamerian precept that knowledge and insight are perspectival; thus whenever the spotlight shines here, something there is darkened, shadowed, remains concealed. What Williams sees as she turns the spotlight of her perspectives on Gadamer's textual bias *is* an aspect of that thing called philosophical hermeneutics. However, I suggest that through my viewpoint, which reverses the angle from which matters are observed, a different though complementary set of insights is gleaned. It is possible to make the case (see below) that to *some* extent—making allowances for enlargement of my stance by the validity of many of Williams' observations of textual bias—conversation for Gadamer provides the model for interpreting texts, rather than texts providing the prism through which to refract conversations.

What then is observed when the spotlight brightens rather than darkens the role for Gadamer of conversation? Let me highlight first those Gadamerian statements that seem to support the importance of conversation, then explore those facets of philosophical hermeneutics which shift when priority is given to conversation, both in general and as observed in Franconia.

CONVERSATION AS ARCHETYPAL MODEL

The outline of Gadamer's position on conversation as well as the ambivalent handling of text versus conversation, which Williams rightly detects, is present in this Gadamerian clarification of his stand, in which he defines the "hermeneutic universe" as including

> everything intelligible. Since it brings this whole breadth into play, it forces the interpreter to play with his own prejudices at stake. These are the winnings of reflection that accrue from practice, and practice alone. The philologist's world of experience and his "Being-toward-the-text" that I have foregrounded

are only an example and a field of illustration for the hermeneutic experience that is woven into the whole of human practice. In it, clearly, understanding what is written is especially important, but writing is only a late and therefore secondary phenomenon. In truth hermeneutic experience extends as far as does reasonable beings' openness to dialogue. (1994a, 568)

Note the many levels of emphasis at play here. On the one hand, Gadamer does point to the "especially important" role of writing in human experience. On the other hand, he labels writing a "secondary phenomenon." He claims that hermeneutics encompasses "everything intelligible," then makes sure to include its applicability to that conversation defined as "reasonable beings' openness to dialogue." At a minimum, this passage appears to make inescapable Gadamer's own conclusion that his hermeneutics applies not only to texts but also to conversation.

There is more, however. Consider these words, which emerge as Gadamer is turning to the crucial task of elucidating the linguistic character of the hermeneutic experience, and which wrap some of the key Gadamerian themes into one concise summary organized around the topic of conversation:

We say that we "conduct" a conversation, but the more genuine a conversation is, the less its conduct lies in the will of either partner. Thus a genuine conversation is never the one that we wanted to conduct. Rather, it is generally more correct to say that we fall into conversation, or even that we become involved in it. The way one word follows another, with the conversation taking its own twists and reaching its own conclusion, may well be conducted in some way, but the partners conversing are far less the leaders than the led. No one knows in advance what will "come out" of a conversation. Understanding or its failure is like an event that happens to us. Thus we can say that something was a good conversation or that it was ill fated. All this shows that a conversation has a spirit of its own, and that the language in which it is conducted bears its own truth in it—i.e. that it allows something to "emerge" which henceforth exists. (1994a, 383)

Of the many elements of this passage which could be fruitfully explored, at least two shine forth. One is that here Gadamer does confirm the normativity of his view of conversation, which can be more—or less—"genuine." The other is the archetypal role genuine conversation plays. *Before* Gadamer details the implications of language for textual interpretation, he invokes conversation as the model from which his hermeneutics of texts derives. Then he explicitly states that "Everything we have said characterizing the situation of two people coming to an understanding has a genuine application to hermeneutics, which is concerned with *understanding texts*" (285).

It may be important to pause here a moment to note again the validity of Williams' contention that Gadamer is ambivalent about the priority of conversations versus texts. Earlier I noted Gadamer's extension of hermeneutics to cover *all* dialogue; here, in the very act of valorizing conversation, Gadamer defines hermeneutics in relation to texts. Thus it seems some textual bias in Gadamer is inescapable.

Nevertheless the importance for Gadamer of conversation as paradigm also seems clear. Consider more comments on the relationship between text and conversation. Gadamer describes his hermeneutics as trying "to examine the hermeneutical phenomenon through the model of conversation between two persons" (1994a, 378). In speaking of "Text and Interpretation" in an interchange with Derrida, Gadamer turns *first* to conversation. He stresses that "The ability to understand is a fundamental endowment of man, one that sustains his communal life with others and, above all, takes place by way of language and the partnership of conversation" (1989a, 22). It is through envisioning persons as speaking that he emphasizes how crucial it is "to expose oneself and to risk oneself" as part of becoming "involved with someone" (26).

Such statements seem to confirm that, in and despite Gadamer's ambivalence, conversation plays a key role. What is perhaps too easily missed by focus on Gadamer's ambivalence or textual bias is how consistently he justifies the "hermeneutic conversation" on the basis of the "real conversation," with the "real" conversation being precisely that: the literal, actual conversation which precedes any attempt to theorize the textual conversation (1994a, 388).

Gadamer's textual bias results not so much from minimizing "real" conversation as from viewing his project as setting in motion a real conversation with texts. Gadamer wants the "primacy of conversation" to set the stage for how texts are understood; he wants to restore to hermeneutics the conversational play of "question and answer, giving and taking, talking at cross purposes and seeing each other's point"; precisely this, he asserts, "is the task of hermeneutics." Moreover, he claims, he means here to offer "more than a metaphor," because the hermeneutic task is not simply to engage in a process which is like conversation but to restore to the text that "original communication of meaning" from which it springs by bringing it "back out of the alienation in which it finds itself and into the living present of conversation, which is always fundamentally realized in question and answer" (1994a, 368). As Kuang-Hsin Chen summarizes it, Gadamer wants to transform "the model of a text to a dialogue or conversation" (1987, 189).

Thus what any researcher seeking to apply Gadamer to conversation brings about is not some forcing of Gadamer into a stance alien to him, but simply a reversal of Gadamer's direction, which in a sense returns him home to the source of his concerns and insights. Gadamer argues from conversation to application in texts; the student of conversation needs to move from Gadamer's application in texts back to the vision of conversational dynamics which inspires that application in the first place. The need to make this move emphasizes again that Gadamer does primarily apply his hermeneutics to texts. On the other hand, the fact that, at least as I contend, the move can be taken suggests that philosophical hermeneutics can be made applicable to conversation.

As part of making the argument, I turn now to examining specific issues that must be addressed when applying Gadamer to conversation and to showing how viewing Gadamer from this angle spotlights his perspective on and valuing of "real" conversation—even as it continues to unveil problems of application. Among matters to be addressed are author intention and whether Gadamer is anti-psychological and anti-relational.

APPLYING GADAMER IN RELATION TO AUTHOR INTENTION

Intention seems to emerge from the Franconia conversations as an issue—and also, undeniably, as a can of energetically wriggling worms. Intention is integrally intertwined with the question of whether (as explored in chapter 3) the characteristic of Gadamerian conversation I have identified as prejudices in relationship is actually performed or instead simply called for or discussed. I concluded in chapter 3 that, except for the production of the third-way Franconia statement offered to delegates for discussion as the proposed Conference resolution of the Germantown issue, evidence supporting risking of prejudices through performance of prejudices in relationship was sparse. Repeatedly numerous delegates called for the risking of prejudices by holding different prejudices in relationship, but in so doing they were affirming rather than risking their own (typically) third-way prejudice.

Intention emerges here as an issue because some conversational turns may be categorized very differently depending on how intention is handled. Take Harlan's (C1) prayer:

> "Dear God, since we don't want to quarrel over differences of opinion we may have, give us a special measure of your love and grace to talk together and seek how we might be your church. Help us all to be sensitive so we might hear very carefully what you might be saying to us. In Jesus name, Amen."

Harlan and moderator Bradley make other attempts in cluster one to focus on process, openness, dialogue. Similar attempts are made in cluster two and cluster three by moderators Willis and Robert. In cluster two Leopold, who has earlier demonstrated third-way prejudice, prays that God will

> "help us to find a way. Bring us to a firm stand on your word regarding Germantown and your kingdom. Thank you for your presence, which each of us have experienced, as we continue to love, to listen, to seek to follow you."

What are Harlan, Leopold, or the moderators doing when they pray for or encourage openness? Are they aiming in a warm, wise, calm mode to open the group, themselves included, to risking prejudices? Or are they superficially promoting such risking but actually pressuring those who want to dispute over homosexuality to see this as an inappropriate quarrel to be resolved by acceptance of the third-way position? How are such questions to be addressed?

One approach might be to seek evidence in the external conversational record. However, at least in this set of data, that record seems to provide no definite evidence to indicate when openness is being performed and when it becomes paradoxically a closed prejudice which others are to adopt and which its holders have no *intention* of enlarging. Then what alternative evidence may be pursued? It is at this point that access to intention seems needed. Lacking knowledge of intent, a student of such a conversation is left with an incomplete analysis. That raises the question being addressed here: does application of Gadamer to conversation permit consideration of intent?

On first glance, the answer appears negative. Devaluing of intention is inherent in Gadamer's insistence that any true conversation or hermeneutic process is guided by the subject matter. As Linge notes, what is at stake is "not the personality or worldview of the author, but the fundamental concern that motivates the text. . ." (1976, xxi). Against Schleirmacher, who saw interpretation as involving an attempt to re-enter the mind of the author, Gadamer insists that "The real meaning of a text, as it speaks to the interpreter, does not depend on the contingencies of the author and his original audience." In each new age or setting, stresses Gadamer, the prejudices held by the interpreters in this new site, rather than those of the original author, will provide the entry point into the meaning of a text. Thus "Not just occasionally but always, the meaning of a text goes beyond its author" (1994a, 296). All meaning is handed down "in relation to the understanding I—and not in reconstructing the originally intending I" (473).

This rejection of author intent is no minor theme in Gadamer; it lies at the heart of his thought: not the author, not the human subject, but the subject matter itself takes priority and makes the pertinent claims. There can be no evading the force of Gadamer's view here: when philosophical hermeneutics is applied to texts, treating intention as a primary consideration is precluded.

However, the matter is more complicated than a first glance suggests. At a number of points Gadamer specifically distinguishes between texts and conversations in treating intention. In perhaps his most recent comments on the issue, Gadamer notes the "need to clarify a question I have tried over and over again to think through: what role in the hermeneutic event [or process] does the intention of the author play?" But then Gadamer makes this key and fascinating distinction: worries about intention arise primarily in relation to texts; texts are what prompt the question of whether understanding takes place "if one just goes back to what the author had in mind" (1997a, 52). Gadamer is convinced there is no way to reconstruct the author intention behind a text, so his concern is how to set up the interplay of question and answer between the text and its interpreter, which restores to hermeneutics the quality of conversation in the absence of the originator of the conversation.

What then of intention in actual conversations? Here Gadamer answers differently:

> In the usages of everyday speaking, where it is not a matter of passing through the fixity of writtenness, I think it is clear: *One has to understand the other person's intention; one must understand what the other person is saying as he or she meant it.* The other person has not separated himself from himself, so to speak, into a written or whatever other form of fixed speech, and conveyed or delivered it to an unknown person, who perhaps distorts through misunderstanding, willful or involuntary, what is supposed to be understood. Even more, one is not separated physically or temporally from the person one is speaking to

and who is listening to what one says. (1997a, 52, emphasis added)

Gadamer proceeds to qualify his comments on intention even in relation to conversation, pointing out that understanding what the other person says involves grasping "something shared" in addition to "something meant" (53). So even in relation to conversation Gadamer does not give such priority to intention that his usual emphases on meaning as emerging from shared subject matter vanish. Nevertheless, Gadamer seems to permit or even to insist on consideration of intention in conversations; it is precisely because intention behind texts cannot be reconstructed that he discounts intention in the text-based "conversations" he means to set in motion through philosophical hermeneutics.

Does this then mean the Gadamer is applicable in relation to the intentions of Franconia participants? In theory, a positive answer seems possible. Research can be Gadamerian and consider intention. This allows for the possibility of investigating whether, for instance, Harlan, Bradley, Leopold, Robert or other *intend* to risk their prejudices or rather to call others to risk theirs. Knowing what they intend may then become an aspect of analyzing precisely what it is they are doing in certain conversational turns.

Gadamer's comments on intention in conversation might open the possibility that tools for gaining access to intention could include accounts and narratives (Burnett, 1991, 121-140), diaries and logs (Duck, 1991, 141-161), and retrospective self-reports (Mitts, Sprecher, and Cupach, 1991, 162-178). Because the application of such tools is beyond the scope of my exploratory research, I will not assess them in detail, but it should be noted that even with such help access to intention would be limited. All such tools are affected by "The biases and limitations of human judgment," which are "well documented" (Metts et al, 1991, 168).

Such tools also risk plunging the researcher of intention into the morass of questions concerning to what extent humans can know themselves and whether motivation is conscious or not. In addition, a host of other complex matters related to intention are significant if too large fully to pursue here. Arabella Lyon (n.d.) points to some of the problems, both in general and in relation to Gadamer. She notes on the one hand that Gadamer's dialogic hermeneutic, with its call for openness, requires risking of the interpreter's intentions (39). She notes on the other hand that Gadamer leaves unaddressed complexities of intention that move into view when, for instance, the possibility of intention as deliberate resistance to an interpretation which frees the interpreter to act is counterposed with intention only as what is risked by submission to text and other (36-40).

These are major concerns which suggest that as much as intention may seem needed for Gadamerian analysis of some aspects of conversation, the coast is not clear for using intention in this way. Thus it seems at best a stretch, requiring considerable additional and perhaps impossible-to-provide justification, to view Gadamer as well-suited to consideration of intention in conversation. And it has already been noted that it would be interpreting Gadamer against himself to see him as validating use of intention to interpret texts.

This in turn confirms what a challenge it is to identify when in fact participants in a conversation are risking their prejudices. Shifts in viewpoint may sometimes be inferred from shifts in conversational contributions, but the inferences will be shaky. Enlargement of prejudices may be confirmed by various forms of introspective self-reporting, but confidence in the accuracy and sincerity of such reporting can never be more than tentative. Thus to the extent intention is at issue, Gadamerian precepts remain valuable as guides to interpretive analysis of conversations, but the conclusions are likely more to resemble the creative speculations of the interpreter than the verified or verifiable outcomes of the scientist.

APPLYING GADAMER
TO PSYCHOLOGICAL AND RELATIONAL DYNAMICS

A series of of intriguing interchanges (noted also in chapter 3) in the conversations cast in bold type the question of whether Gadamer's thought is anti-psychologist and anti-relational. Yes, it largely is, I think, and this is a concern because, as indicated below, human relational dynamics affect conversation in ways Gadamer's thought leaves untheorized.

Take Nelson and Annie, members of the same congregation. They launch into debate regarding Nelson's tendency toward compromise in contrast to Annie's exclusivist passions. If their relational dynamics are simply bracketed, the move Gadamer might make, something is lost. Here, at sufficient length to show the context, are their pertinent turns, along with an interjection from Rosalyn and a significant comment on their interaction from Tobi, their pastor:

> Nelson: "I know Jesus ate with sinners."
> Annie: "Not Christians, he didn't. They weren't Christians yet. Once you're in the church and unrepentant, then you're to put them out, that will give them a shock, maybe make them shape up. Otherwise you love them into hell."

Nelson: "I'm not proposing that; the statement says that it's sin."

Rosalyn: "To the public, we're seen as accepting homosexuality."

Nelson: "The Conference statement is strong, right?"

Annie: "The statement is strong, but Germantown doesn't accept it."

Nelson: "We don't accept Germantown's stance; we'll keep dialoguing. Would you not let a person from Germantown in your presence?"

Annie: "Those at Germantown who disagree with what Germantown is doing should go to other churches; they shouldn't stay there in a church with unrepentant practicing homosexuals. How can God's blessing be there?"

Nelson: "I don't mean to get off-track—"

Annie: "We argue every Sunday in Sunday school; we're not really at each other!"

Group laughter.

Nelson: "I've spoken to two persons in leadership; both have sons who have acknowledged homosexuality, both have expressed to their sons their disapproval of their living in sin— and both also continue to love and fellowship with them."

Annie: "That's a parent's job."

Nelson: "The church should be like that."

Annie: "The church is not a parent."

Nelson: "Is the love of a parent different than the love of a church, of the brotherhood?"

Annie: "It's different—"

Tobi: "If I as their pastor could just jump in on these two Sunday school debaters"—laughter—"the Conference position is clear.'

What leaps out here is that Annie and Nelson are in relationships larger than the relationship they enter by gathering around this particular subject matter. This is important in light of Gadamer's devaluing of such relational dynamics. They have a history of arguing in Sunday school which leads Annie to say that regardless of their topical polarization, their relationship is unimpaired; they're "not really at each other." The group responds with laughter to this distinction Annie draws between their interactions about the subject and their relationship with each other.

Tobi supports this distinction, and again draws laughter, when he "as their pastor" asks to "just jump in on these two Sunday school debaters. . . ." Through this comment Tobi appears to be positioning himself as the benevolent but maybe slightly patronizing leader who wants to highlight the relational connections that bind positively together these "Sunday school debaters"—even as he races on to make his own point amid the relational position in which he has placed himself. As the laughter seems to indicate, Tobi's intervention adds a light touch amid the polarization of the debaters, suggesting that even as they disagree they maintain underlying relationships.

Other relational dynamics run through the conversations. Describing the process through which Franconia and Germantown representatives generated the third-way statement, Willis (C3), says that "It took a little while for our group to learn to function. Some didn't know each other well; it took time to learn how to work, to learn our personal views." Here it appears that personal and relational dynamics intertwine with and perhaps even precede the ability to be open to the subject matter.

Describing how Germantown has experienced the process of working with Franconia, Robert (C3) notes that

> "Germantown felt under discipline for three years, and that was a very heavy experience. But through it we learned that the concern of the larger Conference is an expression of caring and love from the Conference and a concern for truth. We've experienced a sense of love from Conference, anger as well, ups and downs. We've talked to persons here one on one, as well as other, through it growing in a sense of a deeper and meaningful relationship with each other."

Robert's comments include ingredients, such as the concern for truth, which Gadamerian thought addresses. But the talk of heaviness, caring, love, anger, ups and downs, and relationship is primarily relational. Robert Hariman (1987), who seeks to integrate the strengths of rhetoric and hermeneutics, would expect such ingredients. In Hariman's pertinent vision, *friendship* is a fruitful image for interpreting communication. This is because it promotes a view of conversation as entailing both discursive practices *and* the relational dynamics associated with friendship.

Hariman's emphasis helps clarify the importance of the fact that intertwined with the Franconia quest for understanding are feelings and attitudes of persons experiencing each other *as* persons, possibly partly through but also beneath and above the dictates of the subject matter. In chapter 3 I noted also such relational ingredients of the third-way and supplementary reports as emotions, betrayal, trust, social isolation, vulnerability.

Recall also that the above interchange with Annie and Nelson was analyzed from a different angle in the previous chapter as an example of dynamics tending toward dance or play. The fact that it appears here as well as an instance of relationality suggests that the two—play and relational factors—may intertwine. Important in enabling Annie and Nelson to engage in conversational play with each other is their prior relationship, as tellingly referred to in Annie's comment that "We argue every Sunday in Sunday school; we're not really at each other!" Play does not in this case simply emerge, full-blown, from joy in opening oneself to the subject matter; rather, a preceding, "every Sunday," relationship seems to enable the capacity in turn to play.

But to whatever extent play or other Gadamerian categories are preceded by relational dynamics, this may pose quite a problem for Gadamerian thought. Williams claims that Gadamer devalues whatever conversational dynamics have to do with *person* as opposed to subject matter. Indeed, as she notes (1995, 128), Gadamer himself says approvingly that "Writing has the methodological advantage of presenting the hermeneutical problem in all its purity, detached from everything psychological" (1994a, 392). As Williams sees it, "most communication scholars would view conversation as inherently relational," but on the other hand "for Gadamer the relationship is somewhat residual" (130).

As usual, Williams provides solid support for her case; there is no denying that Gadamer de-emphasizes person and self—which is lost in the moment of understanding (Gadamer, 1976, 51)—in favor of the conversation which plays its players rather than being played by them. The question is whether a Gadamer viewed as more applicable to conversation than Williams deems him remains so anti-self that he provides no tools for addressing such an interchange as Nelson's and Annie's.

Here, though I regret it, given my prejudice in favor of finding as broad a Gadamerian applicability as possible, I conclude Williams is correct. Though Gadamer himself apparently prefers not to validate this, his call for openness appears to entail such relational bonds of trust as Nelson and Annie seem to exemplify. Though their readiness to change in response to what they are hearing is not much in evidence, it seems likely that any ability they may find to open themselves to and hear the other appreciatively, "to expose oneself and risk oneself" (Gadamer, 1989, 26), will be affected by their prior relationship. Certainly Annie at least believes that this personal relationship provides a meaningful context for interpreting what she and

Nelson are saying to each other. Concern for maintaining appropriate relationships may also catalyze Annie's statement that "To the public, we're seen as accepting homosexuality."

Bradley in C1 seems as well to place the emphasis on relationships rather than openness to the subject matter when he stresses that "The *relationship* is central, not what we believe." Of course, as we have seen, emphasis on relationship emerged in Franconia as its own discernible prejudice, so from another angle Bradley can be interpreted as being guided by the subject matter, whether he intends to be or not.

However, no matter how Bradley is interpreted, his comments join Annie's in pointing toward a need to evaluate how human relationships affect conversation. Much though a Gadamerian might prefer to ignore or bracket such issues, in the Franconia conversations and documents relational dynamics are inescapable. This very inescapability underlines how few tools Gadamer offers for assessing the importance or even presence of personal or relational dynamics. What Gadamer values in conversation is the dynamism produced by the exchange between participants of question and answer; this is what he wants to bring back to life in textual interpretation. To the extent relationship is fostered by and contributes to such dynamism, relational factors do matter to him. But they seem mostly not to matter, except negatively—as an obstacle to the purity of conversation—when they do not directly impinge on the subject matter.

What Gadamer devalues in conversation is the person herself or himself. He is very explicit about this: "To understand what a person says is, as we saw, to come to an understanding about the subject matter, not to get inside another person and relive his experiences (*Erlebnisse*)" (1994a, 383).

Showing the inapplicability of Gadamer to psychological or relational analysis of conversations is not to demonstrate that his prioritizing of the subject matter is unproductive; it is through this very emphasis that Gadamer offers many of the original contributions that give his perspectives on conversation a fresh twist. Deetz is impressed that by this "reclaiming" of the subject matter Gadamer provides a key definition of "genuine conversation" which entails "enabling the other to present itself on its own terms and an appreciation of it for what it is" (1990, 233).

However, valuable though Gadamer's focus on *Die Sache* may be, the fact remains that to whatever extent conversations include psychological or relational dynamics, a Gadamerian analysis will obscure rather than bring them to the fore. This forces the critic interested in such ingredients to turn elsewhere in search of the required tools.

THE RELATIONSHIP OF OPENNESS AND TRUTH

Two significant and interrelated sets of issues having to do with truth are raised by the attempt to apply Gadamer to the Franconia conversations. First, how is the tension to be managed when the call is for growth in what another considers already complete? According to such a perspective, there is no need or room for such truth to grow. What is to be done with prejudice which cannot be enlarged without violating itself? Second, how does the first set of issues intersect with the criticism that Gadamer's position is relativistic?

MANAGING PREJUDICES VIOLATED BY ENLARGEMENT

Repeatedly some Franconia participants make clear they can find no way to be true to themselves *and* enter deeply into a conversation whose implicit goal includes their openness to change their position. "Congregations that take a more objective stand on the issues of truth and authority," says Wilbert (C3), "feel they have to compromise." Wilbert is signaling here the worry that those who talk of openness are forcing an unwelcome compromise on those who "take a more objective stand."

This worry arises because if truth is objective, there is little need to discuss it; one need only affirm it. But if truth is seen as needing discussion and open to change as a result, then it must not be objective. Thus for someone such as Wilbert, simply defining truth as something discussable is at the outset to affirm another set of prejudices against Wibert's. The Gadamerian deck is stacked against him.

Marcus puts the point powerfully enough that he deserves to be quoted at some length. The first paragraph was cited in chapter four in relation to certitude and sets the context. The second paragraph plows new ground and brings to the fore Marcus's perception of having his stance violated by those who insist on openness. Citing the third-way effort to mediate opposing positions, which states that "Out of this brokenness of our communication, trust, and social isolation, we seek to find unity of purpose and spirit," Marcus indicates that

> "I have a lot a feelings about that—how do I phrase it without getting shot—that in Conference the call is for a third way. As we talk about this, there are two bases for truth: either pluralism or objectivism. Pluralism keeps us all working together until we agree. Objectivism says there's right and wrong. Plu-

ralism says there's no right or wrong, just keep working at it. Many congregations are trying to firm, to become objective. But Conference is into pluralism; that's your opinion. You take a poll, you come up with ten wrong opinions. Saying all have the truth, that's just majority rule.

"What about congregations that are trying to narrow our doctrines? Do we have a future in the Conference? . . . A good point is related to page 20, the FMC statement. It says we have to distinguish between orientation and practice. Do we have to hold that? . . . Is being gay or lesbian a sin? Yes. We're dealing here with original sin. Or are we not permitted to teach that? The orthodox doctrine of original sin? We are in a condition of sin; it all stems from that. Saying all views count except excluding some who want them out, is that a third way? No. Unless you go the first way of putting them out, you deny some their way. You ask us to deny the first way—our way—to go the third way."

Through the clash with the prejudices of such Mennonites as Marcus and Wilbert, who believe their stances transcend prejudice to become truth itself, it becomes evident Gadamerian hermeneutics may itself constitute a set of prejudices to be handled carefully due to risk of self-refutation. Gadamer stresses that his thought "does not understand itself as an 'absolute' position. Its modesty consists in the fact that for it there is no higher principle than this: holding oneself open to the conversation" (1997, 36). However, Gadamer seems not fully to address the absoluteness of the position he takes by denying holding an absolute. He seems to draw a bit too near to the proverbial bind of declaring absolutely that he is no absolutist, of making nonnegotiable one modest principle which turns out not to be so modest after all. There is no proceeding in a Gadamerian direction if one does not hold "oneself open to the conversation."

Marcus, Wilbert, and others did begin to converse, but the terms of the discussion were such that they appear to have concluded, and with some reason, it seems, that they could only fight for rather than risk their prejudices. If they had to sacrifice their prejudices just to enter genuine conversation, their unwillingness to consider such risking seems quite understandable.

Thus much as I share and cheer on Gadamer's prejudice toward openness, much as seeking instances of its fulfillment has been a key inspiration, it seems to place problematic limits on precisely the unfettered conversations it means to encourage. It leaves inadequate room for conversation partners who believe the essential integrity of their prejudice will be violated by any compromise which moderates their initial stance. They hold the stance precisely because it is the one "right" stance required for them to be true to their community and their understanding of its doctrines; how then can they allow their stance to be enlarged? Meanwhile it seems Gadamer cannot accept their closure without violating the non-negotiable openness on which his conversation depends.[5]

Wilbert, Marcus, and those who share their prejudice must accept Gadamerian openness as the initial foundation for the conversation if the conversation is fully to unfold. Yet they cannot risk their prejudice for the sake of openness without violating it: "You ask us to deny the first way—our way—to go the third way." There seem to be two obvious ways to break the impasse: one or the other prejudice—openness or exclusion—must go. But for the Gadamerian, this outcome is losing by winning.

Is there any other way? I doubt there is any straightforward, unassailable formula for applying Gadamer reliably in such situations. This seems to be a rock on which many would-be conversations are destined to founder, and thus one to be squarely faced. This seems to point as well to the possibility that in such situations the resources of rhetoric, with its ability to manage ambiguities and conflicts where understanding is absent, should augment the resources of hermeneutics and its seeking of mutual understanding.

However, perhaps two modest midcourse corrections can yet be made to allow the Gadamerian ship to sustain serious yet not necessarily fatal damage when it strikes this rock.

Gadamerian openness to the closed

One correction can be made by the Gadamerians, and one has already been made by the "first-way" adherents, as addressed in the section that follows. The Gadamerian correction is this: perhaps genuine openness includes receptivity to the possibility that even closed positions can enlarge the prejudices of the ostensibly open-minded. Perhaps from their side the Franconia inclusivist or third-way prejudice-holders could have engaged in more genuinely open conversation had they not decided in advance that only openness to some form of inclusivism was acceptable. Perhaps if they had not foreclosed exclusion at the outset, their openness even to that which seemed to violate their own core assumptions would have promoted a more dynamic exchange with the exclusivists, leading to a fuller readiness of all sides in this conversational dance to be possessed by the subject matter rather than pre-determining what steps of their partners they would automatically override.

Of course this is a messy and possibly untenable route. Perhaps the inclusivists are no more ready to expand their inclusivity to include the closed than are the closed to violate their integrity through openness. Perhaps the impasse can no more be resolved from this side than the other. But at a minimum it appears that particularly those who advocate openness from the outset bear the burden of remaining open even when it hurts.

This relates to a concern that is often raised about the potential drift of Gadamer's thought, which is that it does not wrestle adequately with what is to be done when the other is evil or at least thought to be. Surely openness must cease in the face of neo-Nazi hate groups or the Ku Klux Klan, for example. This concern, which is linked as well with the worry (explored below under "Gadamer and relativism") that Gadamer lacks adequate accounts of truth and validity and so opens himself to relativism, does merit further attention. As I understand Gadamer, the concern can at least begin to be addressed as follows.

First, if Gadamer's core insistence on the anticipation of "completeness" is to be honored, then indeed some readiness to grow even through contact with what is potentially evil may need to be risked. Remembering that *understanding* need not finally entail *agreement*, if understanding requires the assumption that what is being interpreted is to be viewed as "the complete truth" (1994a, 294), then even to understand what is evil is at least temporarily to assume the possibility that here there is truth.

How can there be any merit in such a view? One answer is simply to restate Gadamer's contention regarding what it means to understand, which is that, like it or not, understanding requires the ability to grasp what is persuasive in the other's position. So long as the one seeking to understand cannot see how the other could conceivably hold that position, the assumption of truth has not been made and true understanding has not taken place.

What value there may be in seeking to understand even what is potentially evil may be evident in a story told by Will Campbell, a fiery civil rights fighter in the 1960s and a Baptist minister who sharply challenged his own denomination's racism. In *Brother to A Dragonfly*, Campbell tells of putting his life literally on the line for the civil rights struggle—then gradually, amid the battle, realizing that even the "enemy," the KKK, deserved a modicum of understanding. He tells of President Johnson's nationally televised warning to the Klan, in which Johnson says, "Get out of the Klan, and back into decent society while there is still time." Then he says this:

The closing five words must certainly have been heard by those in the Klan as a threat from an impending police state. And the President did not tell them just how they could get into the decent society of which he spoke, how they could break out of the cycle of milltown squalor, generations of poverty, a racist society presided over, not by a pitiful and powerless few people marching around a burning cross in a Carolina cow pasture, not by a Georgia farmer who didn't know his left hand from his right, but by those in the "decent society" to which the President referred, the mammas and the daddies of the young radicals who would soon go home to run the mills, the factories, the courthouses and legislative halls, the universities and churches and prisons they were then threatening to burn to the ground. (1977, 245)

As his book ends, Campbell's ability to understand the KKK does not equal affirmation; he is not remotely interested in *supporting* the Klan. But he is realizing that some of the "same social forces" that produced the Klan produced the African-American Watts riots and other unrest that might in that era have been deemed "politically correct" in contrast to the sheer evil motivating the KKK. As he grapples with what to do with the tragedies of race and class and violence tearing apart 1960s America, Campbell strikingly concludes that he was, in relation to the Klan, "learner more than I was teacher." Here is an implicit application of Gadamer that highlights the radicality of what following Gadamer may sometimes entail—and how much it may hurt (245-246).

The importance of this line of reasoning in relation to Franconia is this: there may be those on either side—including the otherwise seemingly open inclusivists tempted to view exclusivists as evil homophobes—inclined to demonize the other. But a "Campbellian" reading of Gadamer at least throws obstacles in the way. It appears to be difficult simultaneously to demonize and to be Gadamarian.

That still leaves unresolved one key concern, which is whether there is ever a way through Gadamer to place limits on openness for the sake of likewise limiting evil. My reading of Gadamer is that in fact there is no fail-safe means for appropriating Gadamer as an enabler of such limits, and that this is indeed another important challenge of applying Gadamer.

However, Gadamer is not entirely defenseless here. He has in fact put considerable effort into pondering moral agenda, as can be seen in *Hermeneutics, Religion, and Ethics*, a volume which though recently published records decades of his wrestlings with such matters. Scattered throughout is his continuing insistence that from the "conditionedness of our insight . . . follows neither the legitimacy of moral skepticism nor the exercise of political power in the form of technical manipulation of opinion." Drawing on Aristotle, he contends that "Family, society, and state determine the essential consitution of the human being, in that its ethos replenishes itself with varying contents" (1999, 35).

The ambiguity and riskiness of a dynamic process—which yields "varying contents" is in view here. Gadamer himself seems to recognize this, when he immediately adds that "Of course, no one knows how to predict what might become of humankind and all its forms of communal life." However, there is also the insistence that as our lives unfold within the ceaseless, age-old stream of effective history, we are being created as moral agents by the ethics embedded in that stream. This is why after acknowledging uncertainty about the future of communal life, Gadamer instantly adds, "yet this does not mean that everything is possible, that everything is directed by arbitrariness and caprice and can be determined by the powers that be. There are things that are naturally right" (35).

As such comments indicate and as my discussion below of relativism and the *sensus communis* elaborates, Gadamer does see truth as connected to what emerges as self-evident within the human community. This does not provide us with simple ethical formulas or leave Gadamer invulnerable to criticism but does suggest the possibility of saying that finally there may come a point where the benefits of openness are exhausted and the need to affirm the boundaries of the community becomes clear.

Presence as openness of the closed

Earlier I introduced the idea I want to elaborate here, which is that the "first-way" correction has already been made. I say this because the "first-way" participants remain at least rudimentary Gadamerians so long as they stay in the conversation. Their act of openness is to talk, to engage, to participate even in this dialogue they consider unnecessary and at points offensive. Remember these Gadamerian words: "The mere presence of the other before whom we stand helps us to break up our own bias and narrowness, even before he opens his mouth to make a reply" (Gadamer, 1989a, 26). Those who opt for exclusion are by definition closed. They want to close Franconia to homosexuals. And they want to close themselves off from corruption by other prejudices. Yet so long as they converse, they open themselves to the possibility of having their own bias and narrowness broken up even before the others open their mouths to reply.

This too is a difficult route. At least some of these closed ones undoubtedly want any such conversations as Franconia's to end as soon as possible, if they are permitted to begin at all, precisely because they understand the danger of being opened by the presence of the other. The worry that such openness will befall them seems evident in remarks by Marcus, who explains that those who share his exclusivist prejudice "feel the need to just be protecting ourselves all the time in an indecisive place. So I think it's just wearing to go on and on." Marcus, and those he sees as joining him, experiences his stance as under pressure, under an assault against which he requires protection. Thus going "on and on" is "wearing," and he wants as soon as possible to have the discomfort ended by ratification of his position. A call to openness is then understandably experienced as a threat, a continuation of an assault which can only be ended by closure.

Raymond (C2) also opposes any compromise due to the danger of being involuntarily changed. As noted in the previous chapter, he fears "compromising with sin" will be "A huge mistake. If we open the door one-half inch it's only a matter of time before we've swung wide open the door for our children and grandchildren," which in "ten or fifteen years" will lead to a "living nightmare."

Noting his youth and how long he might be forced to endure the consequences of change, Jay (C3) comments that "If God permits me to keep pasturing, I might outlive nearly all of you here, and it concerns me what church I'll live in. I and all my generation are concerned about that." Jay seems to be making two moves here. First, he can be read as saying that because he will be around so long yet, he wants to make sure inappropriate openness is not pursued. Second, he just may be making a threat: he is younger than most and thus will be in a position to lead the church in his own direction if the oldsters send it on the wrong path.

For such participants, any openness is fleeting and operates against their own preferences. But surely if there is any truth to Gadamer's view of the power of presence, the primary request that can be made of those who hold such perspectives *is* their presence. When they offer it as they do in Franconia, however reluctantly, they deserve credit for contributing their modest yet meaningful part to the Gadamerian quest for prejudices not only larger than theirs but larger as well than the prejudices held by the opponents whom they too through their presence influence.

Though I see hope for rescuing Gadamerian conversation from shipwreck through such corrections, the Franconia evidence suggests that the clash of openness with truths held to be already complete makes genuine multi-party conversation difficult. Here is one of the more serious obstacles to the conduct of Gadamerian conversation. Whenever the clash between openness and completed truth becomes severe enough, impasse may result and conversation in the Gadamerian mode may be derailed.

GADAMER AND RELATIVISM

This leads to the related and important question of whether Gadamer's thought is relativistic. If truly it is, then impasse when Gadamer confronts those who see their truth as certain seems likely. For this reason, it is important to assess whether Gadamerian conversation is foreclosed at the outset to all but those prepared to think and dialogue relativistically. If Gadamer *is* inescapably relativist, this in itself may be defensible—but it then seems unlikely that the views of Marcus, and the many other Franconia participants who share some version of his understanding of truth, can be incorporated into Gadamerian conversation. If so, Gadamerian conversation will prove attractive primarily to those whose prejudices are aligned with Gadamer's. Then prospects for a conversation which fosters valuing of *all* prejudices will be minimal. Then Gadamerian conversation may appeal mainly to Gadamerians.

However, if Gadamer's thought is not relativist, then hope rises for Gadamerian conversation that includes non-relativists. I see little likelihood that *any* form of Gadamerian thought will ever be fully squared with the ahistorical perspectives of those who unqualifiedly believe in their direct access to transcendent truth. My vision is not that Gadamerian perspectives and the absolutist or transcendental perspectives of those committed to closure and certitude can be fully integrated. Rather, my hope is to show that Gadamer does make significant moves toward those suspicious of relativism. He does so through his deep conviction that if *all* parties in a conversation genuinely open themselves to the truth seeking to call them toward itself, there in their midst truth will be made manifest. Now to the task of unpacking what this means and how Gadamer gets there.

How Gadamer avoids relativism

Certainly Gadamer is charged frequently with relativism or at least with an inadequate account of truth and validity.[6] In brief, his critics see him as giving too much priority either to the object of interpretations or to the interpretations themselves. In either case, the door is opened to a relativism in which any number of potential interpretations proliferate without there being means for adjudicating between them. By now it is surely evident why Gadamer is vulnerable to the charge; it seems no great stretch to move from Gadamer's emphasis on the non-negotiable historicity of human perception to relativism.

Gadamer's key response to the charge, as I understand it, is that as perspectival as his thought unabashedly is, it also posits the non-negotiability of there being perspectives on *something*. As I shall soon show, this something resists, questions, talks back, insists it is more than whatever a perceiver can initially or finally perceive. It is thus entitled to request an enlargement of the perceiver's vision. As Richard Bernstein puts it, for Gadamer there is, at the very heart of hermeneutics, "always something 'other' to which we are being responsive, that speaks to us and constrains us" (1987, 554-555).[7]

Before exploring its resistance, however, it is necessary to inquire what makes this thing visible or legible to us in the first place. Whatever this thing may be, there can be none of those radical separations between thing and perception which make relativism fully possible. Here the understanding of relativism, as Weinsheimer relates it to Gadamer's thought, is that it ensues when "the meaning of the fixed past is relative to a changing present" (1985, 225).

The idea is that relativism emerges when primarily the current conditions of knowing determine meaning. Envisioned here is an object which can be perceived from many different angles, relative to the perspective of the knower. But for Gadamer this relativized perceiving can only occur if it is possible to experience a getting-outside-of whatever is being cognized. This is a move Gadamer believes impossible, because for him thing and language are inextricably bound together; our only access to the thing *is* through language. Gadamer believes that

> Verbal experience of the world is "absolute." It transcends all the relative ways being is posited because it embraces all being-in-itself, in whatever relationships (relativities) it appears. Our verbal experience of the world is before everything that is recognized and is addressed as existing. (1994a, 450)

We can only know the world and whatever in it we seek to understand through being embedded in the language which makes the things on which our understanding focuses present for us. We can never be completely alienated from whatever things are made available to us by language because the very means by which we cognize them are the same means that made them available to us. Thus we do not know an objectified "world-in-itself" from which we can be severed and regarding which we can hold a variety of relativistic views. Rather, our cognition and what we cognize are inevitably joined: "the object of knowledge and statements is always already enclosed in the world horizon of language" (1994a, 450).

Linge stresses the extent to which Gadamer's view of language provides resources for eluding relativism. Gadamer views languages as open to each other. By learning a first language we gain a horizon through which to approach those other languages which can eventually enter and enlarge our own (Linge, 1976, xxxvi-xxxviii). Thus we do not experience a variety of discrete languages through which to set up, say, three different views of a thing and see each as providing a relative perspective.

If we were able to gain access to the thing outside language, it might be coherent to claim to be able to identify potential contradictions between the thing itself and the thing language presents and thus open the door to skeptical relativism, in which a thing may be one thing or another based entirely on how it is perceived. But since we cannot stand outside language, it is incoherent to "assume, as the skeptic does, that we are able to understand a language and still suppose that in understanding this language we misunderstand the world" (Steuber, 182). If language and world belong together, then "we can only coherently believe . . . that . . . our linguistically mediated beliefs accurately reflect, for the most part, the way the world is" (Wachterhauser, 1994, 153).

"As verbally constituted. . . ," contends Gadamer, every historical and linguistic "world is of itself always open to every possible insight and hence to every expansion of its own world picture, and is accordingly available to others" (1994a, 447). This understanding, Gadamer stresses, does not lead to the captivity in different languages which might "lead us into any kind of linguistic relativism." Gadamer states boldly and memorably his conviction that our linguistic and historical particularities, far from imprisoning us in incommensurable relativisms, have just the opposite effect: "Precisely through our finitude, the particularity of our being, which is evident even in the variety of languages, the infinite dialogue is opened in the direction of the truth we are" (1976, 16).

Such a comment seems at first glance murky but begins to open up when joined with the whole of Gadamer's thought. This particular statement emerges in the context of his discussion of prejudices,

where Gadamer is saying that we can see *only* through our prejudices and also stresses that through them we welcome as a guest
whatever is new—meaning, ultimately, *the entire world.*

Now the groundwork for exploring the resistance of this lin-
guistically-constituted thing has been laid. If the thing in question is
a text, then, says Gadamer, "the text itself still remains the first point
of relation over and against the questionability, arbitrariness, or at
least multiplicity of the possibilities of interpretation directed toward it" (1989a, 30). If the thing is, even more specially, a "literary
text," such as a poem, then it may "possess its own authenticity in itself," as it becomes a text which "surprises and overwhelms even
the poet" (42).

If the thing is art, then it serves as a powerful example of how
what is other can make a claim on us. Gadamer stands against the
aesthetic understanding of art, according to which humans claim the
power to stand in judgment over it, "to push it away from us once
again and to accept or reject it on our own terms." For Gadamer,
when we are in the right relationship with art, we experience that it
instead has "seized us" (1976, 4). "Beautiful things," such as art, "are
those whose value itself is evident" (Gadamer, 1994a, 477).

If the thing is what participants are seeking to understand in
the play of conversation, then "in the exchange of words, the thing
meant becomes more and more present" (1997, 22).[8] The thing becomes present more through its initiative than ours; when we understand something, "It has asserted itself and captivated us before
we can come to ourselves and be in a position to test the claim to
meaning that it makes." When what is meaningful captivates us, it
"really has something of the truth of play about it. In understanding
we are drawn into an event of truth and arrive, as it were, too late, if
we want to know what we are supposed to believe" (1994a, 490).

Weinsheimer summarizes powerfully the implications of
Gadamer's stance, noting that Gadamer is aiming to solve a problem wrestled with going back to Plato: "How can these many appearances be true? That is, how can they all be appearances of one
idea?" Gadamer believes "the beautiful offers an answer to these
questions." This is because "if something seems beautiful, it is. There
is no distinction between real and apparent beauty. . . . Beauty makes
itself immediately apparent." There is no realm of beauty behind
beauty which is more "real" than it; rather, in each appearance of
beauty, "beauty itself is present. . ." (257).

For Gadamer, what is true of beauty is true of being, which "is
indivisible from its historical manifestations." And this "Being pres-

ents itself in the light of words which reflect it as it truly is, just as beauty is revealed in what makes it beautiful." Then comes the crucial conclusion, which is that beauty is a "symbol of truth" which is "characterized by its being immediately apparent—that is, by its self-evidence" (Weinsheimer, 257).

There is a truth, Gadamer is saying, which cannot be proved, rationally decided, grasped by a knower who dominates the known. This truth validates itself, as great and beautiful art validates itself, and the appropriate response is not judgment but acceptance of the claim.

Implications of Gadamer's vision of communal truth

Here we reach the nub of the matter in relation to the question of whether Gadamer is a relativist. Finally the answer boils down to whether or not one shares Gadamer's faith. What Gadamer genuinely appears to believe is that in the play of question and answer, as set in motion by conversationalists who in openness to the subject matter place their prejudices at risk, truth emerges. Through such truth-seeking conversation—but only in it—the truth of the thing itself is unconcealed. If one shares this faith that through truth-seeking openness one arrives—though never fully and finally—at truth, then one cannot accuse Gadamer of relativism. Rather, one will want to join Gadamer in enlisting more and more participants in the conversation until truly all peoples have been included and are making their rich contribution toward conducting that "infinite dialogue" which sets us on the path toward "the truth that we are."

But suppose one lacks Gadamer's faith that the unveiling of truth happens in this way. Suppose one defines truth as emerging not from history, lived experience, the sensus communis, or "from custom and habituation." Suppose one sees truth as arriving through "autonomous reason" (which Christopher Smith, 1991, 181 opposes to hermeneutics), "universal norms" (Apel), or an ahistorical Word from the Lord. Suppose one sees Gadamer's faith in the power of open conversation more as mysticism than rigorous thought, or more as fallible human wisdom than that true word from God knowable through an inerrant Bible. Then one will seek in one way or another to rise above history and pronounce from outside it the truths shrouded by it. Then Gadamer's position may seem inescapably to trend toward a worrisome relativism.

In the world of Gadamer, there is transcendence, but it glimmers as that which is always and already incarnated in the world of flesh and blood and history; there is never Transcendent transcendence, or rather, if there is, it is fully knowable only to God and never to humans in their historied lives. This world *is* at least partly hospitable to many members of the Mennonite tradition and the Franconia conversations. As introduced in chapter 3, Robert (C2) quotes the apostle Paul, who in 1 Corinthians 13 prepares the way for openness to the finiteness and partiality of truth—as experienced in this life—when he says that "as for knowledge, it will come to an end. For now we know only in part; but when the complete comes, the partial will come to an end." Here a complete truth is also pointed to, but it is the truth of then, of beyond, of that mystery beyond history which, whatever it is, cannot be known *in* the historically-situated human condition.

The deja-vu likely to hit anyone who stumbles across these words after immersion in Gadamer makes it seem probable that Gadamer's hermeneutic is indebted directly or indirectly to this Pauline stream which through the Judeo-Christian river has so nurtured Western effective history. Gadamer and the Franconia conversations themselves share the "deep common accord" of being swept forward in unifying currents which have helped produce them both. Thus the set of Mennonites and the set of Gadamerians overlap; it is possible to belong to both and to share a view of history and God in which if there is an absolute perspective, it belongs to God.

In the world of Wilbert and Marcus, on the other hand, there is a Transcendence which shines into and enlightens human history before history can capture and corrupt it. It is possible in this world for the landscape to glow with the Truth of God radiating perhaps through but also always already beyond history, even the history of the Bible and church. Here there may be perspectives, but some viewpoints are clearly true and some not, and it is possible to know with certainty or nearly so which is which. From this perspective, Gadamer looks relativist. The sets of non-Gadamerians and Mennonites also overlap.

Even among those committed to Transcendence, however, there may be discerned at least glimpses of a perspective compatible with Gadamer. For example, Myron Augsburger, who has spent much of his life as a Mennonite evangelist committed to sharing a truth viewed as coming from God, appears ready in a quote reported in a popular Mennonite periodical to work at a Gadamerian anticipation of completeness. Wrestling at an urban leaders meeting with the challenges of contemporary pluralism, Augsburger says this: "If you want to be a missionary to people of another religion, you [should] study it so well that you could be tempted to join it. That's risky. . . .

Real evangelism means the difficult thing of interacting with your Brahmin, Hindu, Muslim neighbors" (Price, 2000, 7).

Here an evangelist, committed by definition to the mission of inviting others to value his prejudices, nevertheless emphasizes the value of entering theirs. Likely this is envisioned only partly a two-way street, since Augsburger adds that "Others will hear you better when they know you have heard them well" (7). This may suggest that the motivation includes hearing the other as much to earn being heard as to actually hear the other. Yet whatever Augsburger's response if pressed on this might be, the point is that a framework of questions suggested by Gadamer turns out to be pertinent even in thinking through the role of a Mennonite evangelist.

What then is the upshot of surveying the range of positions from that of Mennonites who accept their historical situatedness through Augsburger's complex joining of Transcendence and flexibility to the nearly ahistorical assurance of the views of Wilbert and Marcus? I conclude that Gadamer's views of conversation *will* tend toward congruence with settings where his understanding of truth is shared. There his hermeneutics can be applied as a *practice* experienced as valuable by those doing the playing because they feel kinship as well with the assumptions from which it flows.

The Myron Augsburger example suggests the importance of not quickly stereotyping what thinking is compatible with Gadamer, yet it at least appears safe to hazard that Gadamer's practical usefulness in a given setting is likely to decline to the extent definitions of truth contradict his. Likewise his applicability to practice in such a mixed setting as Franconia exemplifies, where the boundary between definitions of truth runs squarely through the middle of the participants, will be mixed. The problem in mixed settings is this: the fissures dividing participants in a mixed conversation before application of Gadamer are likely to be re-enacted in the very quest to carry out the application. The cluster conversations demonstrate the difficulty of continuing a conversation in such unresolved tensions.

This does not mean Gadamer is useless in such settings, for several reasons. First, given that, according to my analysis, the basic structure and goals of the Franconia conversations were shaped by their leaders in an implicitly Gadamerian direction, the value of Gadamer in such contexts seems evident. And certainly the third-way statement and its genesis, as described in chapter 3, model an effort to go as far as possible toward genuine Gadamerian conversation in the limitations imposed by the clash of two (at least) sets of non-negotiable prejudices.

Second, even in mixed settings whose participants hold contradictory and non-negotiable prejudices disallowing more than a marginal fusing of horizons, Gadamer's many guidelines for the conduct of genuinely dialogic conversation contribute to whatever enlargement, civility, and hearing of the other is possible amid the constraints.

Third, even where applicability through practice is limited, applicability at the level of theory may remain unfettered. As commentator on the Franconia conversations I myself, for instance, have at times applied Gadamerian theory to the discussions to generate insights which can remain fruitful even if some of the participants would, as we have seen, reject the validity of the practices or evaluations to which such theory can lead.

Fourth, and most importantly, the midcourse corrections suggested earlier will hopefully inspire those committed to Gadamerian openness to seek ways so thoroughly to radicalize this openness that it becomes openness *even to the closed* rather than an openness *closed to the closed.* Then to some extent theory and practice may fuse, as the attempt to practice openness leads to a quest to radicalize theorizing of openness to make space for the closed.

As this growth takes place, perhaps even those opposed to relativism, and thus inclined so quickly to scent it in Gadamer, will see there are some versions of openness which do seek even amid commitment to history to learn from those who believe in what transcends history. Even if one disagrees with the exclusivist worries regarding collapse of communal boundaries unless Germantown is excluded, such concerns deserve attention. The attempt to define or maintain any communal values requires some forms of at least provisional closure; otherwise communities such as the Mennonites would cease to exist (and good riddance, some might say, but that is another story). Whatever one may think of the failure to converse the Franconia conversations exemplify, putting the matter in these terms does show why so many in the conversations thought so much was at stake.

Moving back to Gadamerian terms, an alternate way of putting the issue is this: without some closure the sensus communis ceases to exist. Mention of the sensus communis in this context then suggests that indeed it is not such an alien move to seek in Gadamer resources for closure. Surely a quest for communally-grounded ability to set limits is one reason Gadamer so often invokes the wisdom of the sensus communis (and by the same token one reason Gadamer's critics sense in Gadamer a conserving tendency). Thus a reading of

Gadamer which notes his simultaneous affirming of openness and of sensus communis can lead to paradoxical receptivity even to those who may challenge the foundation through which Gadamer believes genuine conversation proceeds.

Such a bringing together of openness and sensus communis may enable Gadamerian thought to become more fully congruent with itself and its commitment to a truth which evades relativism. It can reach such goals by opening itself not only to those perspectives most open to its call for openness but to all—including those who remind that to thrive and to be passed on the sensus communis can benefit from the quest for limits so central to the exclusivist and other limit-setting visions.[9]

CHAPTER SIX

WHO LEADS?
CHALLENGES OF APPLYING GADAMER RELATED TO ORGANIZATIONAL COMMUNICATION AND POWER

To this point I have primarily bracketed organizational or power dimensions of the Franconia conversations. My aim has been to generate as much insight as possible by applying Gadamerian categories to the conversation before considering such issues. Now I must address the costs and problems of such bracketing. My conclusion, as I will elaborate throughout this chapter, is that in relation to such agenda application of Gadamer raises a tangle of problematic if not entirely insoluble issues.

ORGANIZATIONAL COMMUNICATION

At one level of the Franconia conversations, discrete participants converse, and it is primarily at that level that I have aimed my analysis. This appears to be the level most appropriate to a Gadamerian analysis of conversation, because Gadamer's thought primarily emerges from and focuses on the model of conversation between individuals.Hopefully the preceding chapters provide evidence that focusing the Gadamerian lens on this level provides learnings.

MODERATOR ROLES

In addition to such learnings, there may be insights to be gleaned from analyzing moderator interactions through Gadamerian categories before focusing more sharply on the institutional implications of their roles. Such analysis suggests that all three moderators—Bradley, Robert, and Willis—make at least three noteworthy contributions.

First, all clarify the issues at hand and set goals for the conversations they are directing. Robert (C2) says that

> "The purpose of the cluster meetings this evening and all over the Conference is to speak to the proposal. It's not intended that we have a debate over homosexuality. That debate is underway, and if we spent two to three hours on it, my hunch is that positions wouldn't change. The issue here is, is this a proposal that seems in your judgment" to be an appropriate stand for now "in light of all the process" that has led to it, "or do you have council" regarding changes. "The committee is open to modifying the proposal on the basis of suggestions. If this is not acceptable, do you have suggestions to make it so?"

To summarize the issue, the question is, "How should we or can we relate to the Germantown congregation in light of all the information you have in hand?"

Through such moves moderators seek to foreground the subject matter and to allow it to take the initiative in guiding the conversations. Second, all three seek, through such means as repeatedly soliciting delegate opinions or taking straw votes, to highlight which prejudices are "yours" and "mine"; they encourage delegates to be clear about the shapes of the prejudices they hold and are placing in play. Willis tends to be least active in doing this himself and often turns to Ronald, another Conference leader, for help in discerning delegate prejudices. Ronald then offers that

> "I'd like to summarize the three positions I'm hearing. The first is the document doesn't go far enough toward discipline. Second is it's all right with a few changes. Third is it goes too far, not enough trust in Germantown. Could we have a straw vote, not binding, just to see how it comes out?"

Similarly Robert indicates that

> "Now I want to get a sense of the meeting—if the five suggestions were included, would you lean toward or against the proposal? Now we could take a secret ballot, but hopefully we don't need that, we've had open and honest conversation, that's how we do church. Are you willing to give an indication of your stand assuming the concerns you've expressed are incorporated?"

And Bradley likewise asks for a report from the secretary summarizing the positions presented but without requesting a straw vote.

Third, all three, but particularly Bradley and Robert, are strong advocates for placing and maintaining opposing prejudices in a mutually enlarging relationship. Repeatedly Robert, for example, makes statements such as this: "Can we simultaneously affirm the Franconia position and that Germantown is not in compliance, yet retain the relationship as spelled out here?"

Early in his leadership of cluster one, Bradley combines all three moves. He keeps the subject matter in focus, stresses that "The *relationship* is central," solicits "the opinions of *all*," and provides a summary of underlying principles, which include—

> "To keep in mind and to affirm the churchwide and FC position drawn up ten years ago.
>
> "The *relationship* is central, not what we believe. We need to find a way to maintain fellowship and relationships in the Conference.
>
> "The Holy Spirit guides us and we are trusting that guidance through this stage of discipleship.
>
> "Continue to pray as church and individuals are getting to know each other better.
>
> "We are on a journey of faithfulness—all are committed to God's grace faithfully as believers seeking a right relationship with God and one another.
>
> "The opinions of *all* are invited. We have the privilege here of being smaller than other clusters.
>
> "I encourage people to stay with the process—process is the important part—rather than get hung up on something. Not getting hung up is not always easy, of course."

After further comments summarizing the history and aims of the discernment process which has produced this meeting, Bradley emphasizes that

> "We can ask questions about anything here and just dialogue as brothers and sisters. This is the best effort by the joint committee to find a way to maintain the relationship and value wider discernment on this issue in the Conference."

Then he has the full third-way statement read and placed on the record before opening the conversation fully to participants.

Other learnings of applying Gadamerian categories to the moderators before emphasizing their institutional roles could include assessing the prejudices held by each. For example, though all seem to fall broadly in the category of a third-way prejudice, each seems to hold an identifiable variant. Bradley appears to be the strongest advocate for additional enlargement of the third way through further inclusion of Germantown. Robert seems most resolutely committed to the third way without shading his comments either toward inclusion or exclusion.

Willis appears ambivalent regarding whether his third-way advocacy in written Conference statements has gone too far toward inclusion. He reports his own involvement in generating the third-way statement but without strongly advocating for it and frequently noting that "We're open to change." When criticized for writings (Miller, 1997) in which he may have implied that homosexuality would someday become acceptable, he responds,

> "I wasn't predicting that homosexuality would someday come to be acceptable. I was just noting that we've seen division over the years—over issues like wedding rings, TV—that we now come to see as okay. So I just meant to say, let's be careful what we decide. I was talking about the process, wanting us to work at caution and patience. But you make a good point."

In addition, a significant question that might be asked in relation to the moderators is the extent to which they risk their own prejudices for the sake of enlargement. Take the case of Robert. He appears most staunchly committed from the outset to the third way. Yet he also repeatedly welcomes feedback that moves the third-way statement in the direction of further exclusion.

How is this to be interpreted? When Robert says, "I hear that the proposal [with which he has initially aligned himself] needs to state more strongly Franconia's stand on its position," is Robert allowing his initial prejudice to grow? Or is he simply operating as an ostensibly neutral institutional representative, whose responsibility it is to encourage expression of all prejudices regardless of how he personally views or is affected by them? How is the researcher to evaluate Willis' (C3) expectation, expressed after introducing the third way, that "We assumed there'd be changes, modifications, additions; they're welcome"? When the personal and institutional roles intersect, how are prejudices risked, and how is this risking identified by a student of such dynamics?

Organizational Dynamics

Now the organizational dynamics of the Franconia conversations become inescapable. Now the fact that the Franconia conversations are replete with organizational ingredients cannot be evaded.

Their very reason for existing is organizational: the need for the Franconia organization to generate a decision regarding a member congregation is what has triggered them. The structure in which the conversations unfold is organizational. Each cluster conversation is helped by a moderator selected and empowered by Franconia to help lead and structure the conversation. The participants are not simply conducting a conversation, though they do engage in it. They are also delegates asked to represent the congregations which have appointed them and to contribute to an organizational process of discernment.

An important implication of the fact that the conversation unfolds in this organizational framework is that—even as it can include the many characteristics of Gadamerian conversation I have identified—it also appears to preclude from the outset fully Gadamerian conversation. As affirmed by the moderators and generally accepted by the delegates, the goal of the conversation is ultimately to contribute to an institutional decision regarding the fate of a Franconia congregation. This need to make a decision hinders full expression of conversational play. The subject matter determines the conversation, but the participants also experience and participate in a preimposition of the subject matter. Moderators regularly steer the conversation back to it. Full freedom is lacking to let the "thing" itself—which seeks according to Gadamer to present itself to those who are fully open—make itself known.

Viewed from one angle, the foregoing, which might be viewed as Gadamerian criticism of the form the Franconia conversations took, suggests Gadamer may provide modest tools for assessing even institutional conversations. Viewed from another angle, however, the very existence of such institutional agenda points to the likelihood that, no matter how the research is defined and what its aims are, Gadamer does not provide a full range of tools for interpreting organizational communication and roles. It may be that conversational play can be envisioned in such a way that it does take into account institutional dynamics threading their way through a conversation, but it is unclear how to derive such a picture entirely from Gadamer.

This is the conclusion reached also by Stanley Deetz. He turns to Gadamer as provider of an inspired definition of "genuine conversation" (1992, 165-167). Next, however, Deetz moves to Habermas (168ff.), Foucault (ch. 7), and others for the tools Deetz believes are necessary to probe the "systematic distortions" as well as the "disciplinary power and discursive formations" he discerns in the organizational and institutional communication dynamics of the work world (165-167).

There may be ways to start with Gadamerian questions, then stitch into them mediating interpretive grids as modeled by Williams (1995) in relation to Gadamer and Garfinkel. Indeed research into organizational communication inspired by Gadamer seems likely to be fruitful, but the details of implementation are unlikely to be found in Gadamer. Here I see no way satisfactorily to undertake a thoroughly Gadamerian study. I conclude philosophical hermeneutics is modestly and indirectly applicable to research related to organizational communication.

The aftermath of the Franconia conversations falls outside the defined scope of this study and its focus on the conversations themselves. However, perhaps a number of pertinent observations (here as well as again in chapter 7) based on knowledge of the outcome of the conversations are in order. Several weeks after the conversations which form my database, the delegates of all the clusters met on April 26, 1997, to discuss and decide at a formal assembly what outcome should be implemented in relation to Germantown. Their deliberations were focused by a statement (Recommendation for Delegate Action, 1997) issued by Franconia leaders two days before the Assembly. This statement noted that

> In light of counsel received from the congregations and clusters of the Franconia Mennonite Conference in response to the statement from Germantown Mennonite Church that it cannot abide by the policy of the conference on homosexuality (as stated in 1984 and 1995), the delegates to the spring 1997 Assembly agree as follows:
>
> With much pain and regret, we recognize the Germantown Mennonite Church as not being in full fellowship with Franconia Conference. We confess our own indifference and limitation on understanding the meaning of Christ's love for all persons in our day. We commit ourselves to continue in love and pray for the membership of the Germantown congregation and its urban ministries which we appreciate. We desire to maintain a relationship with the members of the Germantown congregation and invite their attendance at Assemblies and other Conference activities as they desire. In view of current interim pastoral arrangements, the Leadership Commission will hold the credentials of pastors at Germantown through 1997. We ask the Executive Committee to appoint a group of conference persons to maintain ongoing conversation with the Germantown congregation as would be mutually beneficial, always

with the desire for the restoration of full fellowship in the body of Christ.

The statement, which in soft language but with a big stick deemed Germantown as "not being in full fellowship," placed on the table a motion to exclude Germantown rather than adopt the third way. Delegates were given half an hour to speak publicly in favor of or opposition to this recommendation. Of the eight who spoke, seven articulated third-way or inclusion prejudices and Raymond, quoted earlier, opted for exclusion. The overseer at Germantown, who took the second response turn, offered a passionate declaration that though he had experienced many dangers and pains during a lifetime of urban ministry, including muggings, break-ins, and bullets headed his way, he had never felt so much anguish as now, with the anticipated exclusion of Germantown just minutes away.

When the time for a straw vote on whether to cast a decision-making vote on the recommendation itself arrived, the vote failed. Thus the recommendation to exclude Germantown was not acted on. The Conference moderator announced that in the absence of a decision to decide, the Germantown status quo—an associate membership relatively similar to the third way—would remain in force. If or when future action might be taken was left unclear.

What is an analyst to make of this situation? It is possible, for instance, to argue that in effect the inability to decide forced a messy but shared decision to continue enlarging prejudices. But this is a stretch, particularly once the later decision (see below) to exclude Germantown is taken into account. Regardless of how the researcher proceeds, it is evident the analysis will not receive firm guidance from Gadamer. Little in Gadamer permits detailed application to a situation involving votes and an evaluation of what is taking place when a community seeking to clarify its polity rather than individuals seeking to understand are in focus.

POWER

The moment the problem of applying Gadamer to organizational communication is acknowledged, a related problem rears its head. As Deetz highlights by turning to Foucault's understanding of power as a tool for organizational analysis, organizational dynamics and power considerations intertwine. That is surely the case in the above example, in which not risking of prejudices—though this may be taking place—but the number of votes cast on either side of the issue at hand determines the outcome. The question of power is one of the knottier ones to be faced in assessing Gadamer's applicability. To explain my odd conclusions, which are that Gadamer is both inapplicable and applicable in relation to power agenda, and in addition that Gadamer shows why sometimes power is preferably bracketed, requires the particularly complex chain of reasoning to which I now turn.

There are several levels at which it is a challenge to apply Gadamer in relation to power. One level, that of organizations, has already been introduced. Another level has to do with power at the broader, macrocosmic level of sociocultural forces—and with how (as in Foucault, see below), such power may be implicated in producing even the individual's sense of being an individual.

GADAMER, ORGANIZATIONS, AND POWER

If Gadamer does not address the implications of his thought for organizational communication, then it stands to reason that power as a crucial aspect of that communication will be undertheorized. The lack of a framework in which to analyze power as a factor in the Franconia discussions is evident when they are examined with power in mind. What immediately leaps out is the ubiquity of power in the conversations and its likely perturbations of the conversational dynamics. Here I am operating with a relatively simple, basic understanding of power as the ability to be or to do.[1] Compliance. Control. Who has the power to change the rules and how. These are among the power issues relevant here and evident in the comments below of Deborah as well as Harvey, Heather, and Bradley.

Deborah (C1) is addressing the Franconia power to impose silence and resistance to it when she points out that "Some say we should be associate members too, to be in solidarity with Germantown." She explains that if all in the Conference took that stance, then none would have the right to persuade others of their view on homosexuality, because associate members would be silenced. Then everyone would have to be silent, and it is obvious what a ridiculous outcome that would be. The process would then have been appropriately subverted.

Harvey, Heather, and Bradley (C1) exchange comments riddled with power agenda:

> Harvey: "There are a lot of things that could be said, but the bottom line is how to relate to a congregation not following the principles of Conference. It has nothing to do with homosexuality. As for me, I bless GMC on this issue. But that's not the point. It's how we as a Conference continue to dialogue

with a congregation that has purposefully in some respects gone outside guidelines of the Conference. Now those guidelines I hope will change, then it will no longer be an issue. But presently they're still the issue."

Heather: "But how can Conference change? By not always following the rules?"

Harvey: "No. But what is the process? Is associate membership an intermediate stop? Is a better way to say the Conference continues to have a position on an issue and sort of ignore a congregation not in keeping with this? I could see the same sort of thing with the military issue. It's happened in Virginia on that issue. To me we're discussing noncompliance with Conference, not homosexuality."

Bradley: "And you represent someone deeply rooted in the Conference and even you react against it, control doesn't fit today."

Harvey: "But isn't that what this is about?"

Mitchell: "On one level, but it's a very selective issue. If the issue were noncompliance, we would add the military."

Leon, from Germantown, points to power when he says, "The Conference is free to add a word—we can't vote on it anyway!" Later in the same conversation there is a major interchange regarding the power over congregations Franconia exercises by determining who is qualified to receive the ministerial credentials endorsing a pastor's—and, by extension, a congregation's—legitimacy as a member of the Conference. And Heather initiates another power-focused interchange:

Heather: "If tested, would the majority throw us out?"

Leonard: "Delegates?"

Heather: "The majority of delegates, if there were not a third way, would they kick us out? I can see the negative comments from the congregations in the handbook; they make me sick."

Bradley: "I suspect it would be an Illinois Conference situation. There the vote failed, and they need to continue working."

Heather says she is trying to sense whether, in light of what is being said in the congregational responses, there are enough votes to "kick out."

Bradley: "That's what's being tested."

Harvey: "The majority say it's wrong, theologically, but that's not necessarily enough votes to kick out. That's my speculative observation."

Bradley: "I wonder whether even this compromise will fly?"

Andrew: "Two years ago I thought maybe we were back in 1642 or something. I think Germantown is out if no third way."

Leonard: "Pragmatically like we Anglos always talk, if we don't vote, withdrawals from the Conference are very likely."

Mitchell: "Then we really don't believe in family."

The Conference, Rachael responds, has troubles just "Like any family."

Bradley: "The Conference is like parent/child."

Rachel: "Who's the parent?" Rachel puts her arms around Lorena and Heather on either side, smiles, pats shoulders, and says, "My children!"

Who has power to do what to whom? What are implications for the conversations of delegates at the individual level when through analogy someone such as Rachel is associated with a conference labeled as "parent" and other delegates potentially experience themselves as powerless children?

And how do power, pragmatism, and Gadamer intersect? Pragmatism emerges several times as an issue, particularly in cluster one, where delegates tend toward the inclusivist prejudice and see the third way as the lesser of evils. "My pragmatism says take what you can get," notes Andrew. Harvey says that he's "a pragmatist—this is the only way we'll hold the brothers and sisters together. If this is what it takes, I support it, even if personally I disagree." Pragmatism is an issue in such instances because the delegates perceive that they lack the power to do other than accept the less preferred outcome. So the delegates pragmatically accept holding prejudices in relationship, but is this an instance of Gadamerian genuine conversation or primarily an effect of power?

Such questioning could continue indefinitely. Clusters two and three interchanges focused on power could be cited at similar length. Interesting observations could be made regarding the contrast between clusters one versus two and three power concerns. In cluster one, the focus is on the Franconia power to impose a discipline or exclusion most of the delegates oppose or at least question. In the other clusters, the more common worry is that Franconia will lack the nerve or power to impose the preferred discipline. This is exemplified by Morris (C3), who thinks that not excluding homosexuals is like being comfortable with having a doctor find a tumor but not treat it. "If we're comfortable with that," stresses Morris, "then FC polity is that the congregation has authority, not the Conference."

Unfortunately, there is insufficient reason to continue this line of analysis. No matter how much power is shown to intertwine with the Franconia conversations, only modest gains of insight can be achieved through Gadamerian analysis. The primary power-related contribution such analysis can make—and it is an important one, as discussed below—is to help establish preconditions for thoroughly Gadamerian conversation, which include ensuring that power is distributed with sufficient equity that participants in a conversation are not unjustly constrained by it.

Gadamerian analysis *can* probe whether conversational constraints are present and ask such simple but useful questions as whether some have more power, some less, some an equal amount. To the extent it can be established that power is shared, the Gadamerian analyst may be justified in bracketing issues of power as analysis proceeds according to those key Gadamerian terms from which power is mostly absent.

Employing such blunt tools for performing a power analysis of the Franconia conversations certainly suggests power is playing a role. Evident in just the few interchanges quoted are worries on the one hand about being dominated by persons or an organization with too much power or on the other hand lacking the power to dominate those one thinks should be dominated.

The quest to ascertain whether or not power is shared and the conversations unconstrained leads also to sensitivity regarding implicit effects of power. Deetz, for instance, notes that a potential "blockage" to Gadamer's genuine conversation is *disqualification*, which "applies to the determination of who has a right to have a say. Disqualification is the discursive process by which individuals are excluded" (1990, 236). There is the obvious disqualification of Germantown, whose members are explicitly asked in the third-way statement not to promote their view of homosexuality. The implied threat of disqualification also threads its way throughout the conversations. It would be hard to imagine any pastor in Franconia unaware that the Conference includes a Ministerial Committee empowered to evaluate whether pastors are accountable to official Conference polity—which explicitly rejects the inclusionist prejudice

In clusters two and three, delegates are under implicit threat of being excluded—literally, in the case of Germantown representatives—if they do not support at a minimum the third way or exclusion. The very fact that the meetings have been called to decide the level of sanction Germantown will face for inclusion makes clear the threat of disqualification for those who align themselves too closely with Germantown. And this potential disqualification has real teeth in relation to delegates who are pastors. They well know—it has been stressed in the third-way statement—that Franconia holds the power to disqualify by removal of credentials any pastor whose stance the Conference considers out of bounds. The most obvious danger, given that all can see the threat Germantown pastors are facing, is that those whose position is overly inclusivist will be formally disqualified through removal of credentials.

Meanwhile in cluster one, where all or nearly all participants hold a third-way or inclusivist prejudice, and no one speaks up on behalf of exclusion, to be part of this communal We is to be different than those Franconia "others" who favor exclusion. Here there is at least a lightly implied threat of disqualification of those who do not support the third way as minimal bottom line. The total absence of voices supporting anything but inclusion or the third way is likely to intimidate anyone inclined toward an alternate prejudice.

Though the argument, being from silence, is a speculative one, it is possible that in fact other voices are present but do not make themselves known precisely because they fear disqualification in the cluster—though clearly this is a mild and informal disqualification when compared to that which can be officially enforced by the Conference against any who stray too far toward inclusion.

Such analysis, which makes clear that the Franconia conversations unfold under significant power constraints, remains broadly Gadamerian and to some extent undergirds the applicability here of Gadamer. On the other hand, note that already, even in proceeding this modest distance, I have drawn on Deetz to provide a more refined tool of power analysis than seems to be available in Gadamer. This finally underlines why it would be poor stewardship of researcher resources to perform power analysis primarily through Gadamerian tools. The available equipment is simply not matched to the task.

This is underscored by turning once more to the aftermath of the conversations. Months after the decision not to decide what steps to take next, delegates received a packet of materials from Franconia Conference leaders. Included was a Rationale and Proposed Action (1997) explaining that

> Through extended discussion and discernment it has become clear that Franconia and Germantown Mennonite Church, while holding broad understandings of faith and practice in

common, experience a significant area of divergence over how to minister to gay and lesbian persons in our midst.

"In view of this divergence," the rationale continued, "the predominant perspective is that membership by the Germantown congregation in any form is no longer acceptable." The rationale went on to reaffirm with apparent good will, in terms similar to the third-way statement, the valued missions of both sides. It noted the continuing disagreement regarding how to view homosexuality and how to proceed. However, its conclusion (one rather similar to the assessment of the conversational failings I have offered in chapter 4), was that "Regardless of how long we remain in dialogue or discernment, there does not appear to be much change in the perspectives of our members on these issues, nor is there much openness to study the issue further."

While maintaining an ambivalent stance in relation to majority rule, the rationale nevertheless affirms it, with "reluctance and pain," explaining that

> The leaders of the Conference cannot keep trust with the delegates and members of the Conference if the majority voice is ignored and further processing is attempted. (As a Conference body we might well remember that the majority of the delegates may not in each situation express God's perspective or offer sound wisdom).

The relevance of Gadamer's normative understanding of conversation continues to be evident. The rationale itself includes notes of longing for something resembling the Gadamerian outcome that proved so elusive and grief that a more satisfactory destination was not reached. Through the warning that even a majority opinion does not guarantee truth, the leaders implicitly urge delegates in the majority to remain open to continued growth. The outcome is one many participants do not welcome. Among them appear to be the reluctant Franconia leaders, who schedule an "evening of confession" (V. Weaver, 1997a) for the next delegate assembly after the vote.

However, the misfit with Gadamer becomes ever more evident in tracing how inexorably power came to run affairs when further conversation was deemed futile. Not only did Franconia turn from further conversation, the decision was made that delegates would not even vote in person at a future assembly. Instead, ballots were included with the rationale and the delegates instructed to return their vote by mail. An October 14, 1997 letter (Clemens et al, 1997) to delegates reported the outcome:

The results of the vote were 218 ballots returned. Of those, 178 (81.5%) supported the proposal and 40 (18.5%) did not support it. Thus the proposal was passed and will become effective January 1, 1998.

Even here the Gadamerian longings persisted. "Our prayer is that God will continue to work among us and raise new life out of the ashes of this time. None of us holds all truth." Yet power would still rule: "However, the above action reflects the discernment of our community of faith on this matter for this time."

Again the importance of power arises and again it is unclear how to apply Gadamer when a community decides it will employ overt power to cut through the failures of its talk. To look at the world through Gadamer is not to make nuanced distinctions in relation to power but primarily to turn one's gaze in a different direction.

GADAMER, SOCIETY, AND POWER

This same tendency is evident when one examines the sociocultural dimensions of Gadamer's handling or nonhandling of power. Although analysis of the Franconia conversations does not unfold primarily at this macrocosmic level, it is one which nevertheless intersects with my research concerns.

If I were employing primarily a Foucauldian understanding of power, for example, I would not have been able in early chapters to focus on the role of an effective history which produces commonalities of understanding even between those who share divergent prejudices. I would have been drawn instead to emphasize the proliferation of fundamental differences produced by power, whose meaning particularly for the earlier Foucault seemed tied to division, to what Foucault called "Nietzsche's hypothesis" (1980a, 91): "should we not analyze it primarily in terms of *struggle, conflict,* and *war?*" (90).

If Foucault had been my guide to the Franconia analysis, I would very nearly have reversed my starting point. I would have viewed Franconia through the prism of power and difference, then perhaps pondered the implications of any commonalities. It is to explore the different direction set at the outset by choosing in relation to power to apply Gadamer, rather than such a thinker as Foucault, that I include this section as part of evaluating Gadamer's applicability to power.

The worry that Gadamer undertheorizes power is among common reasons for turning from the framework he provides. As mentioned above, this is the concern that causes Deetz to turn from

Gadamer to Foucault the moment he wants a nuanced treatment of power. It is in relation to power agenda that Gadamer suffers some of the sharpest blows from his critics. What is their case? Particularly a charge which might be framed as "pseudoinnocence" deserves attention.

The risk of Gadamerian pseudoinnocence

Drawing on Martin Buber and Rollo May among others, Ronald C. Arnett warns against the pseudoinnocent tendency to assume that the world is a loving place, that within its innocence I need only offer love and good will in trust that it will be returned. Then I minimize, ignore, or otherwise refuse to face whatever realities distort or block the innocent exchanges of goodness in which I see myself participating (1980, 44-49).

Something akin to pseudoinnocence is the danger many detect in Gadamer's thought. Despite appreciation for philosophical hermeneutics, Deetz contends that Gadamer does not "provide an adequate view of rhetoric or communication" because he assumes ideal conversation conditions rare in daily life. "There are more than matters of attitude at stake here," Deetz stresses. "There are real power relationships, manifested as institutional arrangements and structures of permissible discourse to preclude otherness and block conversation." Gadamer, he warns, does not address the dominances of those ideologies Deetz calls "protected prejudices." Gadamer, in short, lacks an "explicit politics" (1983, 437). Deetz's critique leads him to work at expanding the horizon of philosophical hermeneutics to include awareness of numerous potential blockages to conversation, such as the disqualification (determining who has the right to have a say, and disqualifying some) noted above (1990, 236).

Terry Eagleton is convinced Gadamer's hermeneutics cannot

> come to terms with the problem of ideology—with the fact that the unending "dialogue" of human history is as often as not a monologue by the powerful to the powerless, or that if it is indeed a "dialogue," then the partners—men and women, for example, hardly occupy equal positions. It refuses to recognize that discourse is always caught up with a power that is by no means benign; and the discourse in which it most signally fails to recognize this fact is its own. (1983, 73)

John D. Caputo claims Gadamer's "'tradition' is innocent of Nietzsche's suspicious eye, of Foucaultian genealogy. He does not face the question of the ruptures in the tradition, its vulnerability to difference, its capacity to oppress" (1987, 112). From a feminist perspective, Robin Schott argues that Gadamer "imports assumptions about universality which derive from an unacknowledged history of relations between subjects." Any viable hermeneutics must go beyond Gadamer to "incorporate analyses of power, of dominance and subordination, inclusion and exclusion" (1991, 208-209).

Kuang-Hsin Chen believes philosophical hermeneutics "should incorporate other contemporary discourses so as to account for the ideological nature of human understanding and the hidden politics of interpretive practices" (1987, 193). Chen names Foucauldian discourse among those to be incorporated, and thus joins Eagleton and others in posing a major challenge to Gadamerians who want to address at the fullest levels the implications of power.

Certainly whenever Foucauldian thought is invoked, the challenge to Gadamer is significant. This is because in Foucault power is ubiquitous, inescapable, "capillary," present not only in those societal structures normally associated with power but also in the very construction of the individual *as* individual. Power for Foucault is not primarily material, not economic, not that traditional domination exercised by institutions, premiers, sovereigns, not that which rules from a central point. Power does course through and sustain such sites but is not them. The head of the sovereign, of the old power (viewed as overt dominance), has in the modern regime, the regime of surveillance, discipline, and ensuing normalization, been lopped off (1980a,b; 1990a, 92-102). Now "power is everywhere; not because it embraces everything, but because it comes from everywhere" (1990a, 93). Now

> Power must be analyzed as something which circulates, or rather is something which only functions in the form of a chain. It is never localized here or there, never in anybody's hands, never appropriated as a commodity or piece of wealth. Power is employed and exercised through a net-like organization. (1980a, 98)

Power for Foucault is that in which humans live and move and have their being. It is what undergirds who we are, predetermines how we think, establishes what knowledges can be known, puts its own meanings into otherwise empty words, inaugurates the connection of this to that to create a unity which is actually "an unstable assemblage of faults, fissures, and heterogeneous layers" (1977, 146).

Then there is Jürgen Habermas' indictment, which sparked the years of interaction with Gadamer now remembered as the famous Habermas-Gadamer debates. Habermas accuses Gadamer of not facing power and its distortion of communication through structures of injustice that Gadamer's thought is powerless to address. Habermas' key contention is that Gadamer's hermeneutics lead to a pseudoinnocent conserving of tradition at the expense of a freedom to reflect beyond tradition to achieve emancipation. Habermas grants, with Gadamer, that rational reflection and knowledge are "rooted in actual tradition" and are "bound to contingent conditions." "But," stresses Habermas, meaning the *but* to be an enormous one—

> reflection does not wear itself out on the facticity of traditional norms without leaving a trace. It is condemned to operate after the fact; but, operating in retrospect, it unleashes retroactive power. We are not able to reflect back on internalized norms until we have first learned to follow them blindly through coercion imposed from without. But as reflection recalls that path of authority through which the grammars of language games were learned dogmatically as rules of worldview and action, authority can be stripped of that in it that was mere domination and dissolved into the less coercive force of insight and rational decision. (1988, 170)

Habermas' argument, as he elsewhere (1994) aims to illustrate through the example of psychoanalysis, is that there can be cases of dealing scientifically with language that do "not proceed by interpretation" (Nicholson, 1991, 159-160). Through retrospective reflection, reason can learn at least partly to free itself from what is hermeneutical and theorize what constitutes emancipated communication and what conditions are required for it to exist.

What responses to such criticisms are possible for any, including myself, who appreciate Gadamer's thought? One, which leads Graeme Nicholson to conclude that "Gadamer's replies to critical theory have carried the day decisively" (1991, 152) is that analyses of power and ideology need precisely the radical distance from what they analyze that hermeneutics problematizes. Nicholson's point is that it is never possible to rise sufficiently above hermeneutic challenges to arrive at a theory of power not ultimately shaped by the same tradition(s) whose power relations it claims ability to analyze.

A related response is that Gadamer's downplaying of power is appropriate in light of his central aim. His concern is not with power but the need to battle alienations inherent in scientific methodologies or aesthetic or historical consciousnesses which think they can distance themselves from their own humanity and conduct transcendent investigations into the nature of reality (1994a; 1976). As

Scheibler explains, though Gadamer can be interpreted to "support a naive and uncritical acceptance of the reality of existing conditions," his intent is to stress "the inescapable dimension of language" rather than to deny "the workings of ideology, forces of domination, or the existence of a non-linguistic, material domain" (2000, 85-86).

Although I see merit in such responses, as I will explore, they must not be offered too quickly, lest premature defensiveness leave unexposed the limits of any thought, including Gadamer's. Regardless of reasons, by focusing elsewhere Gadamer at the least marginalizes power agenda, as we have repeatedly seen in relation to Franconia. Thus one crucial response to his critics seems to me to be, "You're right; Gadamer's horizons do require enlarging." However, this seems no fatal admission. Hopefully Gadamer himself, champion of the partiality of thought, would grant that his own horizon is finite. Hopefully he would affirm that when power theorists seek to bring his emphases and theirs into conversation, they potentially enlarge his horizon as well as their own.

Chen, Eagleton, Schott, Caputo, Foucault, Habermas—any such critics or those who draw on them start from prejudices different than Gadamer's. According to Gadamer himself, they must understand him differently than he does to apply him to their own projects. As earlier noted, Gadamer is famous for stressing that, "Not just occasionally but always, the meaning of a text goes beyond its author. That is why understanding is not merely a reproductive but always a productive activity as well." So "we understand in a *different* way, *if we understand at all*" (1994a, 296-297). Even the meanings of philosophical hermeneutics go beyond the author of its texts.

Through engaging his blind spots, Gadamer's critics accept his invitation not only to reproduce but also to produce meaning. The meanings they produce in this case emerge as repeatedly they ask, "But what blockages and distortions produced by power, ideology, politics must be addressed before the hermeneutic process can freely unfold?"

The answer, Gadamer's many critics suggest, is that many potential blockages and distortions must be assessed. Whenever Gadamer is applied to Franconia or similar conversations, it must be recognized that in relation to such issues much potential insight remains concealed.

Gadamer's implicit theory of power

But that is not quite the entire story of Gadamer and power. As introduced earlier, once power is brought to the fore as an issue to be probed in Gadamer, it becomes evident that *Gadamer does incorporate an implicit theory of power.* This does not fully rescue him from pseudoinnocence nor fully address the challenge posed, for instance, by Foucault's radical understanding of power.[2] Yet it does suggest the risk may be somewhat less than a first glance might indicate.

The full complexities of what power is and how it is expressed are beyond this study's scope, precisely because the scope is set by Gadamer, for whom power is tangential though, as I am now exploring, not irrelevant. For my purposes here, let me simply note that one view of power compatible with Gadamer's ontological stance is, precisely, the ontological one. In Paul Tillich's striking words, "Being is the power of being!" (1954, 37). Tillich sees this power as more fundamental than "Sociological power," which he defines as "The chance to carry through one's will against social resistance. . . (36). Tillich does not sever the link between sociological power or "force" or "compulsion," which power "uses and abuses . . . to actualize itself" (47). But for him the heart of power is "the drive of everything living to realize itself with increasing intensity and extensity" (36). Thus for Tillich power is present whenever it is able to *be* over against the threat of not-being.

Drawing on Tillich and others, Arnett claims that "An ontological view of power equates the notion with being and cannot envision life without it. Power in the ontological sense is a social phenomenon between persons and events that is unavoidable and inevitable." To be, in short, is to have power (1986, 146-147).

If one defines power in that sense, then Gadamer is throughout his hermeneutics concerned that a right relationship of powers be maintained. For Gadamer, your power of being as expressed in the difference from me and my power as expressed through my being other than another must not overwhelm each other. Both must be maintained in any relationship that has integrity. For Gadamer my willingness to risk openness to you is balanced by knowledge that each of our differences is irreducible. To open ourselves to the other is never to relinquish our difference from each other. The indissolubility of my and your individuality is maintained.

Georgia Warnke (1993b) structures the argument less in connection with ontological views of power and more in relation to emphases on power as having potential to coerce which are indebted both to Habermas and to Nancy Fraser. However, Warnke also derives from Gadamerian emphases an implicit power theory which requires free and unconstrained access to a hermeneutic conversation for all participants and viewpoints. Though not explicitly referring to Gadamer at this point (she has earlier, 128-134), she describes a "hermeneutic conversation" in which all participants are educated by interpretations other than their own. To enable such education we "must both encourage the articulation of those alternative interpretations and make them as compelling as they can be" (157).

Then she connects these Gadamerian concerns with power: "And how can we do this except by assuring the fairness of the conversation and working to give all possible voices equal access?" The Gadamerian quest for openness to the claims of the other and for putting prejudices at risk in response to questions raised by the subject matter entail a conversation in which each participant contributes to a lowering of constraints so the other is heard (128-134).

Discerning implicit power theory in Gadamer does not simply let him off the hook here, of course. In the above paragraphs the implications have had to be teased out, argued for, which does underscore the explicit absence in Gadamer himself of such theorizing. And where Gadamer does speak more directly about power by addressing what he calls "authority" (1994a, 277-280), one can see why he makes Habermas and others nervous. Although he says that authority "has nothing to do with blind obedience to commands," he champions that positive authority of subject matter or person to which one should submit because it "is superior to oneself in judgment and insight. . ." (277).

This is not a surprising stance, congruent as it is with his persistent stress on risking prejudices in faith that the position of the other has something to offer. Neither, I think, is it automatically a mistaken stance; valuing the authority of the other is another way of stating the need to be open to the other, and the benefits of openness are hopefully by now clear. Yet it seems also clear why Gadamer and those who affirm him do need to be careful not to combine valuing authority with pseudoinnocent inability to grasp the risks of celebrating authority amid power differentials.

Why for Gadamer power is sometimes the wrong focus

There is yet another twist to the story of Gadamer and power. This twist has to do with the earlier-introduced (chapter 5) Gadamerian precept that the thing studied is always richer than any one perspective can reveal. In a conversation with Jacques Derrida noted by Lawrence K. Schmidt (1996, 269), Gadamer says "it is of decisive importance that 'Being' does not unfold totally in its self-manifestation, but rather withholds itself and withdraws with the same primordiality with which it manifests itself" (1989a, 25). Schmidt contends that through recognizing "This relationship of presenting and concealing in being," we see that "what comes to be is a perspective of the thing itself and so also implies the non-coming to be or concealing of other perspectives" (269).

Highlighted in such comments and in various ways throughout Gadamer's hermeneutics is the interplay between concealing and revealing. If my prejudices are a spotlight through which one set of insights emerge from the surrounding darkness, by their very act of lighting *this* they leave *that* concealed in the murk. Although my prejudices can grow, gradually widening what I see in the glow of my spotlight, they can never brighten the entire landscape.

This suggests the horizon of philosophical hermeneutics can and should be expanded in conversation with prejudices that spotlight power; that has been the goal of much of the foregoing. However, if the emphasis is placed too strongly on power, there will be loss of insight as well as gain; what I hope shines out below would be left shrouded.

Thus an important aspect of assessing Gadamer's applicability in relation to power is noting that Gadamer's inattention to power offers gain as well as loss. Here some of Gadamer's central themes deserve review as part of demonstrating that much of what is rich in Gadamer is enabled not despite his undertheorizing of power but by his very prejudice in favor of other agenda.

So what *is* gained by welcoming expansion of Gadamer through power criticism yet also allowing power agenda to recede into the background as the spotlight shines elsewhere? What then moves to the foreground is a relationality of commonality, which I see as accompanied by three key characteristics: not unmasking but being captivated by what we seek to understand, openness, and play.

Relationality of commonality

Emphasizing power frequently brings difference to the foreground and forces a *relationality of commonality* into the background. In speaking of a relationality of commonality, I mean simply to draw a contrast with forms of thought that affirm what might be termed a relationality of difference. In Foucault, for instance (as seen above and again below) relationships of power produce heterogeneities, antagonisms, differences. In Gadamer, relationships of commonality produce or are implicated in similarities, attractions, affirmations of the ties that bind together even the differences of difference. From here foreword, when I speak of relationality it is with this Gadamerian stress on commonality in mind.

To name just a few contemporary strands of thought which intertwine with a foregrounding of power, anyone observing settings touched by literary theory, postmodernism, poststructuralism, or by Derrida, Jean-Francois Lyotard, Foucault, knows how strongly difference is emphasized. Take Foucault's view of language. In at least the earlier Foucault's post-Saussurean, poststructuralist view, language is an empty system of signs in which a "statement" is "defined not by the treasure of intentions that it might contain . . . but by the difference that articulates it on . . . other real or possible statements. . ." (1994a, vii). This empty sign structure is then "filled" by discourse regimes imposed by this or that power. "We must conceive discourse," Foucault says, "as a violence we do to things, or, at all events, as a practice we impose on them; it is in this practice that the events of discourse find the principle of their regularity" (1972, 229). Here language and world lose their relational integrity.

Todd Gitlin arguably but passionately makes the case that Foucault has helped foment a cultural infatuation with difference indebted to

> Foucault's conviction that all knowledge and all social reality were reducible to power relations—that all being was local, all thinking self-interested, all understanding fatally circumscribed by history. The only common condition worth thinking about was the impossibility of commonality. (1995, 102)

Common in postcolonial literature and often also indebted to Foucault is power analysis. Much of it centers on theorizing an endless profusion of differences. Lisa Lowe (1991), for instance, wants to show how Foucault's overly binary conception of power can be made more heterogeneous. She fears Foucault's unrefined thought will contribute to viewing Occident-Orient as a stable binary. She wants to ensure that the "heterogeneities and ambivalences" which destabilize all binaries are kept in mind when the workings of power in Orientalism and any other terrain are analyzed.

My goal here is neither to address the full range of issues posed by such literature nor to oppose its many appropriate efforts to deconstruct false commonalities and unities. There is much to be affirmed in Foucault's thought as well as much complexity to probe, especially since it appears over the span of his career to emphasize varying aspects of power. Gitlin's view, for example, may be defensible in light of the "genealogical" Foucault evident in such readings as "Nietszche, Genealogy, History" (1977), who emphasizes the random play of meaning amid "fissures," "fragmentation," "heterogeneity"—but is less easily squared with the Foucault of "What Is Enlightenment?" who does look amid difference for "generality," "systematicity," "homogeneity." (1984, 47).

In addition, a Foucault read across the body of his work can be seen to make increasingly careful distinctions between the "most sophisticated structures of power" which are evident at the levels of society and government and are often "really demonic" (2000a, 311) versus the reality that power relations are so unstable that "many things can be changed, being as fragile as they are" (2000b, 458). Thus even individuals can resist the positions in which power places them. Foucault gives the example of his interviewer, younger than Foucault, being intimidated by the power of Foucault's age. But, stresses Foucault, the power conferred by age is unstable—therefore there may come a turn in the same interview when youth is power and, intimidating Foucault, turns the tables (1987, 12).

Amid such complexities and nuances, then, I simply want to note how prevalent power talk is and to worry about what can be lost in those settings in which a stress on power and difference dominates, even as I recognize that an appreciative reading of Foucault and others would make its own valuable contributions. When Gadamerian prejudices are brought to bear on the situation, it becomes evident, I think, that a potential key loss, and one philosophical hermeneutics can help remedy, *is* relationships of commonality.

To whatever extent those who highlight power do so to correct their own marginalization or exclusions they see others having suffered, their emphasis is crucial. The trust and openness to the other Gadamer foregrounds are blocked by conditions of abuse, marginalization, exclusion, oppression.

However, in light of my concerns it is troubling that many who foreground power and difference seem so little to mourn the loss of commonalities such emphases appear to encourage. Given that perspective, I am unsettled by the image of Derrida refusing, in a 1981 encounter with Gadamer in Paris (see Michelfelder and Palmer, 1989), Gadamer's invitation that together they overcome the polarizations of their own positions and explore the commonalities of Derrida's poststructuralism and Gadamer's hermeneutics.

Derrida has asked whether understanding, "far from being the continuity of *rapport* . . . is not rather the interruption of *rapport*, a certain *rapport* of interruption, the suspending of all mediation?" Derrida further charges that Gadamer's quest for a continuity of rapport is a return to metaphysics (1989, 53-54). As usual, Derrida's communicative style makes his meaning elusive, but this seems his intent: he means to enact precisely the interruption of rapport, of relationship, he describes. Josef Simon suggests that here "we have to do with a critique of good will from the standpoint of an other who feels misunderstood even in my best will" (1989, 169). Derrida appears to feel that Gadamer's terms for dialogue are not in fact ones that will enable Derrida's position to be heard. Thus he engages Gadamer only obliquely.

Gadamer responds that "surely" his quest for rapport is not metaphysical "but the presupposition that any partner in a dialogue must assume" (1989b, 56). He stresses that the very recognition of such limits to understanding as Derrida emphasizes would not be possible "if we had not traveled a long way together, perhaps even without acknowledging it to ourselves. All human solidarity, all social stability, presupposes this" (56-57).

Derrida (1989b) answers with commentary on Heidegger and Nietzsche and concludes that "In one blow Nietzsche thwarts all that governs the thought or even the anticipation of totality, namely, the relationship of genus and species" (71). Derrida says nothing at all regarding what Gadamer has just said. He never names Gadamer. He offers Gadamer only the presence of his absence, only his refusal to acknowledge that he and Gadamer have traveled a long way together. He thereby shows that Gadamer cannot assume they share a relationship of commonalities; in that sense and in that moment, Derrida proves Gadamer wrong. Derrida may have good reason for doing so; it may be that he cannot meet Gadamer on Gadamer's terms without losing his own terms, which value relationships of difference over relationships of commonality. He may be rejecting the potential imperialism of a Gadamerian commonality he concludes does not in the end respect but rather coopts the Derridean difference.

Thus Derrida shows it is possible to refuse relationship in Gadamerian terms and hereby points to an alternate path centered on a Derridean way some do find rewarding. Susan Biesecker-Mast (1999), for example, provides a positive reading of Derrida as a potential inspiration for a risk-taking encounter with the other in which an initial or communication-enabling commonality is deemphasized. By turning from the Gadamerian path and toward their own, Derrida and followers implicitly warn once more of the dangers that may lurk in the Gadamarian quest for commonality.

Meanwhile Gadamer's own persistent offer of relationship points to the gift Gadamer means through his hermeneutics of commonality to present to those who opt for it. Gadamer too stresses the ubiquity of difference, but with his own crucial difference. Differences do not proliferate in endless regression, making it difficult to discern where grounds for communion remain. Rather, Gadamer emphasizes ways *differences remain in relationships of commonality with each other.*

For Gadamer, such relationality is embedded at the most basic level, language itself. Rather than a violence we do to the world, language is that in which we are inescapably at home, because the only world we can know is the one language offers us. Our linguistically-shaped cognition and what we cognize through language are inevitably joined; "the object of knowledge and statements is always already enclosed in the world horizon of language" (1994a, 450).

Against Saussurean language models, John Stewart has drawn on Gadamer, among others, to develop his view of "language as articulate contact." We become who we are in the webbings of our linguistic exchanges with each other and the world. We cannot then rise above language to treat it as a "*system* that is instrumentally employed by *already*-constituted humans to represent aspects of their worlds and accomplish other goals" (1995, 113). We are inherently in relationships of commonality with—rather than alienated from—language.

Recall Gadamer's commentary (chapter one) on Plato's *Lysis* and the household in which we join as friends and his regular insistence that crucial to life in the oikos as well as to the hermeneutic journey is relationality. The point is not that this Gadamerian vision is the only one through which to interpret the world or such conversations as Franconia's. Rather, the point is that different perspectives on the data will be offered by this vision than by others. This vision justifies affirmation, for example, that in developing its third-way statement Franconia Conference did achieve something more or other than a mere manipulation of powers. Yes, power was integrally present and deserves attention, but more can also be seen and Gadamer encourages the seeing.

Not unmasking but being captivated. Backgrounding of power and foregrounding of relationships of commonality is accompanied by *not unmasking but being captivated by what we seek to understand.* Arnett (1986, 51) speaks of tendencies in "critical or deconstitutive hermeneutics" which have a bearing as well on the power theories I have mentioned. The critic suspects that one way or another what seems "normal" reality to most members of a community is actually a mask behind which can be discerned forces of domination or disintegration the ordinary person does not grasp.

When he calls for recovering a hermeneutics of trust in biblical studies in addition to one of suspicion, Richard B. Hays (1997) aims suspicion at the very ubiquity of suspicion and institutions and ideologies fomenting it. To underscore the point, Hays points to Frank Lentricchia, author of *Criticism and Social Change* (1983), who, as Hays quotes him, once urged treating literature "as the most devious of rhetorical discourses (writing with political designs on us all), either in opposition to or complicity with the power in place" (222).

But now, reports Hays, Lentricchia "repents publicly," as is evident in his telling us he has grown tired of students who, following his earlier injunctions, care only about the critical theory through which they unmask—and not about the literature itself, which they treat only as suspect. He is weary of criticism which

> stems from the sense that one is morally superior to the writers one is supposedly describing. This posture is assumed when those writers represent the major islands of Western literary tradition, the central cultural engine—so it goes—of racism, poverty, sexism, homophobia, and imperialism: a cesspool that literary critics would expose for mankind's benefit. . . . It is impossible, this much is clear, to exaggerate the heroic self-inflation of academic literary criticism. . . ." (Hays citing Lentricchia, 222-223)

Lentricchia's stand (and Hays') is complex; in reproving those who constantly unmask, he himself unmasks them and their "heroic self-inflation" and becomes a meta-unmasker. Perhaps I then continue the cycle, unmasking Lentricchia. So handling the unmasking hot potato is no simple task. But maybe the sense of unfair labeling likely experienced by those Lentricchia criticizes underscores the danger of the unmasking move, which so easily—and this is Gadamer's point—distorts the lived reality of those it targets.

As mentioned in chapter 1, Gadamer addresses critical, suspicious, and unmasking tendencies when he opposes the "methodical alienation" characteristic of any sciences, critical theories, or methods which abstract their analyses from life as actually experienced (1994b, 289-291). Apart from alienating consequences, however, Gadamer argues—and here he makes his key reply to Habermas and others who want their critical reason and power analyses to transcend hermeneutics—that there simply is no stance outside history, and thus hermeneutics, from which to understand anything.

However, the inability to stand outside history need never obviate concerns with power. Thinking no doubt still of Habermas, even as recently as 1997, Gadamer says,

And who would deny that there are real factors conditioning human life, such as hunger, love, labor, and domination, which are not themselves language or speaking, but which for their part furnish the space in which our speaking to each other and listening to each other take place. (1997a, 28)

But if Gadamer remains open to consideration of power, he remains convinced as well that someone such as Habermas, concerned to set up ideal speech situations which ameliorate distortions of power, can never move in this direction outside limits identified by hermeneutics. Habermas' very prejudices regarding what is undistorted speech are themselves artifacts of an effective history indebted to the Enlightenment and Western culture (1994a, 551-579). Rather stingingly, Gadamer charges that

> the attitude of the "critique of ideology" [*Ideologiekritik*] can itself be criticized as ideological, in that it represents antibourgeois interests, or whatever interests they may be, while at the same time masking its own tendentiousness as critique. (1989a, 39)[3]

In contrast to those alienating stances which mistakenly "privilege . . . distorted intelligibility" (40), Gadamer believes his hermeneutics can integrate critical moves "in the whole of human life" (1994a, 552). As introduced in my related chapter 1 comments on method as well as elaborated below (under "Play"), Gadamer does not rule out and even affirms critical and methodological moves—but only to the extent that they recognize their embeddedness in what they survey and remain open to its claims. Gadamer opposes any such claiming of transcendent ability to unmask the "true" nature of what is being probed as Lentricchia fears he recognizes in his students.

Analysis of the Franconia conversations focused entirely on power would exemplify, as I understand Gadamer, obsession with unmasking distortion or other power-related dynamics.[4] Various levels of power and distortion are present, I have concluded. But also there are the claims, particularly evident in the third-way statement, of what "captivates us just as the beautiful captivates us" (1994a, 490). They too deserve to be sought out and enabled to shine forth.

Openness. Implicit in the foregoing is *openness*, another characteristic of relationality and of course one already much-addressed in this study. Arnett helps clarify the contrast here between what Gadamer offers and what power focus provides. With such theorists as Habermas or Warnke, Arnett agrees a first step in taming our "communicative crisis" may be to encourage "a symmetrical communicative exchange between power equals," but he adds that this by itself "is often not sufficient to open up the channels of healthy communication in community" (1986, 19).

Arnett contends that in any number of situations, resolving issues of power does not resolve communicative breakdown. Following Bateson, Arnett notes that in the case of *schismogenesis*. This is a type of "runaway" conflict, such as took place during the Cold War between the United States and the Soviet Union, in which achieving power parity does not bring resolution and may in fact become a goal which feeds the conflict. Thus even if schismogenetic opponents achieve equal power, they remain locked in combat, gaining nothing from each other but ongoing competition and antagonism (19-23). Gadamer would want schismogenetic combatants to shift their focus from the *combat*, including frequently its power agenda, to the *resources* they can offer each other.

How did openness versus schismogenesis unfold in the Franconia conversations? That is the type of question made possible by following Gadamer rather than power critics. In fact there is considerable evidence that the power agenda inherent in this runaway conflict was of crucial concern. However, the very production of the third-way document would have been precluded if those involved in creating it had proved totally unable to transcend the schismogenetic cycle and the intertwining power agenda. This is an example of what Gadamer's non-power-focus opens the researcher to see.

Play. A final characteristic of relationality is play. Hermeneutics, as I have noted, is a form of play. The task is to understand. But the task sets in motion a dance larger than conversational participants which possesses or opens us to what we seek to understand before we, as subject grasping object, can understand it.

This helps turn a floodlight on Gadamer's passion to foreground play and move power to the background. If power is foregrounded, such moves as methodical alienation and unmasking may halt play. Can anyone truly bring to play the purposive, joyful abandonment to the play's task which makes play play—and at the same time stand outside the play as critic, analyst, unmasker of power dynamics thought possibly to be more fundamental than the play itself? Perhaps so, if the analyst learns how simultaneously to analyze and yield to play. Perhaps to the extent this study is successful, it aims at precisely such a version of the dance. But as I am amid experiencing, this is a delicate dance indeed.

Gadamer does not refuse all distancing moves; there can be misleading prejudices, players who do use the play to advance power interests, dancers who step on the other's toes. Gadamer insists he means not "to deny the necessity of methodical work in the human sciences (Geisteswissenschaften)" (1994a, xxix). Through various forms of partial distance, including temporal, from prejudices, we "distinguish the true prejudices, by which we *understand*, from the *false* ones, by which we *misunderstand* (1994a, 298-299).

As friendly critic Paul Ricoeur notes, Gadamer's openness to all traditions potentially allows him to incorporate even the critical tools of the Enlightenment, which, Ricoeur observes, "is also a tradition" (1991, 306) What this entails, says Warnke, is preserving "the Enlightenment ideal while rendering it compatible with the cultural and linguistic embeddedness of our understanding" (1987, 168).

But if Gadamer is open in theory to critical thought, rarely is this what he elaborates or champions. Always he returns to his deeper concern, which is "not what we do or what we ought to do, but what happens to us over and above our wanting and doing" (1994a, xxviii). Always he reminds us that even when we refuse to play, the play is playing us. When we aim critically to stand outside the play we risk not so much leaving the play as depriving ourselves of experiencing the buoyancy and energy of a playing which continues to possess us even as we seek to block its workings on us.

This view of play has affected my conduct of my research, inspiring me to use methods through which I seek partial distance from the Franconia conversations but never a full withdrawal from the play of a conversation in which I participated as observer, Franconia member, and 1980s pastor of Germantown Mennonite Church. Though I made almost no overt contributions to the conversations, I was in the ways mentioned a player in them and have sought in my reporting of them to remain in their play even when distantly so.

In relation to his sociohistorical analysis of his own branch of the Mennonites, sociologist Calvin Redekop (1998, 13-14) notes the difficulty of finding the right balance between distance from and involvement with his topic. He concludes that "only an ambiguous or a love-hate relationship" with a tradition being studied ensures that the analyst will care enough about the tradition both to study it and to remain distant enough from it to do more than repeat its traditional truisms.

He speaks for me. Without some distance, provided by deliberately using Gadamer as source of analytic tools from outside my religious tradition, I would have risked merely recirculating its clichés.

Without some immersion in the tradition, I would likely neither have undertaken this study nor understood the conversations sufficiently from within to grasp, for instance, how the trajectories of effective history could be discerned in the conversations under analysis.

This is consistent with Deetz' injunctions for critical interpretive research, which include the emphasis that "the interpreter should strive for the greatest degree of familiarity with the data to be interpreted" (1982, 144) and that "results of interpretive research should be applicable to the organization under study"—meaning that, as Deetz clarifies, "Accounts should be plausible to the organizational actors" (145). Unmasking of power dynamics need not necessarily violate such canons, but research conducted through Gadamer will always seek to avoid looking down—in that former (and present?) Lentricchia-like way—on poor subjects who misunderstand their own roles and will instead aim to conduct its analysis in a play of meanings accessible to the players.

ADDRESSING RHETORIC VERSUS HERMENEUTICS

The foregoing discussion of power may also point toward exploration of a matter which has been important from the start, as introduced in chapter 1, but has needed to await sufficient groundwork to enable further discussion. I am referring to the need to clarify the respective roles in conversation of listeners and speakers, and this will lead shortly to comment on rhetoric versus hermeneutics.

In the previous chapter I noted that assessing intention, difficult though this may be, may be one way to investigate whether risking of prejudices is being talked about or actually performed. But this points also to another challenge of applying Gadamer, which is *whether he provides a space for a speaker ever to intend to persuade* rather than ever and again to be open to being persuaded.

This is not so large a matter in the case of texts; there the author has already made her or his effort to persuade. There Gadamer's stress on openness to claims of the artifact the author has left behind as a written record now possessing its own autonomy makes sense. In the case of texts, Gadamer's approach does provide a means to allow the written word to speak again, to stimulate the question and answer of conversation, even in the absence of the author.

But matters are different in actual conversations. If the only genuine Gadamerian move in a conversation were openness to the other, the conversation would cease. Outside of the text-interpreter interchange, in which text already exists to be attended to, there can be no living conversation if participants seek only to listen. There must be someone to listen to, or the conversation does stop. So what is the role of the speaker in the Gadamerian conversation? *Does* Gadamer provide a role for her or him, or is Gadamer so attuned to the role of listener that he never defines the speaker's position?

So far I have handled this question by becoming myself primarily the Gadamerian listener analyzing the speaking of those Franconia participants whose spoken "texts" I seek to understand. But this has glossed over the complexity of what is unfolding in the Franconia interchanges as well as in the rhetoric of this study, whereby I seek to persuade the reader. Every conversational turn marks a transaction in which not only many are listening but someone is talking. What does a Gadamerian analysis make of this talker? The answer is complex and involves, I believe, at least two parts.

First, it seems clear that because Gadamer's application of his own thought is to texts—despite his high regard for conversation—he foregrounds the listener's role. The automatic bias of the Gadamerian lens when focused on conversation is to assume the existence of a text, written or uttered, which must be understood. How this understanding is to take place then remains Gadamer's persistent concern. This listening to written or spoken text and how it is accomplished *is* hermeneutics as Gadamer defines it.

Second, if listening is hermeneutics, then what is speaking? The answer is more implicit than explicit in Gadamer, but this seems to be not so much because Gadamer lacks an answer as because he assumes it to be so obvious it requires little clarification or justification. And the answer is that speaking is rhetoric.

Such definitions of listening and speaking are consistent with Richard E. Palmer's view that rhetoric and hermeneutics "Conceptually . . . appear distinct: rhetoric has to do with speaking well and hermeneutics with understanding and interpreting a text." As is so often the case in the struggle to maintain distinctions between the two rhetoric and hermeneutics, Palmer also points to overlap, noting that "The Greek verb *hermeneuein* seems to refer to oral interpretation: i.e. rhetoric" (1997, 113).

Here is one way Gadamer words the distinction:

> The rhetorical and the hermeneutical aspects of human linguisticality interpenetrate each other at every point. There would be no speaker and no such thing as rhetoric if understanding and agreement were not the lifeblood of human relationships. There would be no hermeneutical task if there were no loss of agreement between the parties to a "conversation" and no need to seek understanding. (1994a, 280)

Elsewhere Gadamer contends that "Hermeneutics may be precisely defined as the art of bringing what is said or written to speech again." He immediately proceeds to suggest that "What kind of an art this is, then, we can learn from rhetoric." Then what is rhetoric and the art it teaches? Gadamer stresses that

> Clearly the ability to speak has the same breadth and universality as the ability to understand and interpret. One can talk about everything, and everything one says has to be able to be understood. Here rhetoric and hermeneutics have a very close relationship. The skilled mastery of such abilities in speaking and understanding is demonstrated to the utmost in written usage in the writing of speeches and in the understanding of what is written. (1986, 119)

Gadamer's near-conflation of rhetoric and hermeneutics is so consistent it is a challenge to disentangle one from the other in his thought. Gadamer can be faulted for assuming too much with too little clarification.[5] Still, some detective work at least yields tentative outlines of the distinctions. If hermeneutics is the art of understanding, rhetoric is "the ability to speak" and its close relationship with hermeneutics appears to revolve around the assumption that good speaking is speaking which can be understood—even as good hermeneutics is that which allows good speaking to shine forth.

But there is more. Gadamer explicitly draws on the notion of shining forth when he connects rhetoric to the concept of the beautiful. "We have said," he recalls, "that, like everything meaningful, the beautiful is *einleuchtend* ('clearly evident,' 'shining in')." He then links this evidentness of the beautiful

> to the tradition of rhetoric. The eikos, the verisimilar, the "probable" (*wahrscheinliche*: "true shining"), the "evident," belong in a series of things that defend their rightness against the truth and certainty of what is proved and known. Let us recall that we assigned special importance to the sensus communis.

Remember the chapter 5 discussion of truth, which for Gadamer is that aspect of the thing which captivates us rather than we it. Gadamer is placing rhetoric in the context of such thought. He is saying that rhetoric, going back to ancient Greece, is the model for forms of thought—including philosophical hermeneutics—which do not seek the true or good in some realm of objective verifiability. Rather, they experience truth and goodness through opening themselves to what is evident in the currents of history and their shaping of the sensus communis.

This sensus communis, a concept important to Gadamer, as he himself stresses, is "that sense that is acquired through living in the community and is determined by its structures and aims" (1994a, 23). The sensus communis has to do with that "sense of the community" whereby it "mediates its own positive knowledge" (23), its own practice-tested learnings, and still pursues truth amid history as an outgrowth of that "structure of living, organic being in which the whole is in each individual. . ." (29).

The sensus communis, the beautiful, and rhetoric are linked for Gadamer. This is because the sensus communis generates the initial contextual frames in which the beautiful emerges as self-evident. Rhetoric is then persuasive to the extent it is able to mobilize among those to whom it speaks a sense that is grounded in and speaking amid at least minimal agreement regarding what is valid and true. Gadamer believes that rhetoric depends for its persuasive power on its alignment with, openness to, and communication of what those in a communicative community experience as being evident, as truly shining, as supported by what Gadamer terms the "Socratic legacy of 'human wisdom'. . ." (1997a, 31).

Thus the space Gadamer creates for the speaker in a conversation is that of rhetoric. The speaker is a rhetor, and as rhetor, she or he seeks to enhance the ability of the subject matter—and that which is "beautiful" or self-justifying in it—to make its claim on all conversational participants. If the rhetor's task is to be such a servant of the subject matter, then Gadamer would oppose coercive or manipulative rhetorics, those Wayne Brockriede labels rape and seduction (1972). As W. S. K. Cameron notes (though in language probably more transcendental than Gadamer would affirm), Gadamer joins Habermas in assuming "something like a transcendental or regulative ideal of communicative action. If 'agreement' is the result of manipulation, it is not agreement" (1996, 163). To put it another way, if agreement is imposed rather than emerging from mutual openness to the claims of the thing around which all in a conversation are gathered, then it is not agreement. The subject matter must be free to speak!

When the stress on rhetoric as cooperation with the subject matter is linked to Gadamer's concept of prejudices as the "biases of our openness to the world," more insight emerges. My prejudices are treasures, the biases of my openness to the world. I owe you the most persuasive articulation I can offer of why I find compelling the horizon my prejudices allow me to gaze on. Such a perspective allows Gadamer to support a rhetoric conceived in relatively traditional terms as intending to persuade, provided that openness to the subject is ever maintained. Through such a view of rhetoric's relationship with hermeneutics speakers are given space to claim their own perspective—*and power*.[6]

But of course the rhetorical move is only one of two moves. Also crucial is the hermeneutic move whereby I open myself to the potential correctness and persuasiveness of what I learn about the subject matter in play between us through the alien claim of your prejudices. Thus I have never truly entered the dance or play of communication unless I participate in the back-and-forth rhythms of rhetoric and hermeneutics. We must each be true to our own prejudices if they are to be available as our perspective on the subject matter with power to enlarge the other; that is our rhetorical move. But we must also each risk our prejudices in openness to the other if our horizons are to be enlarged by their perspective on the subject matter; that is the hermeneutic move.

This dovetails with all the categories of successful conversation identified in the Franconia conversations, but perhaps particularly with goodwill highlighting of prejudices as yours and mine and prejudices in relationship. It helps show how the prejudices can with goodwill be highlighted, then set in motion as a play of or dance between rhetors and hermeneuts who in relationship are gracefully matching each other's Gadamerian steps so a genuine conversation has opportunity to unfold. Future research can benefit from this clarification regarding who dances how to the Gadamerian music.

CONCLUSION:
THE VALUE OF FOREGROUNDING THE DANCE

Here again the value of allowing issues of power to recede becomes, as Gadamer might put it, evident. A rough parity of power is necessary for the true interpenetration of rhetoric and hermeneutics to take place. The speaker must have enabling power to speak and the listener must have space to listen and risk without coercion. Any number of power analyses along the way may be required to help establish the enabling context. As the ubiquity of power perturbations in the Franconia conversations makes clear, Gadamerian prejudices need the enlargement provided by such moves and their theoretical underpinnings. Then, however, ballroom floor ready, it is time to assess whether the players are also able to play, to dance their dance, to relinquish themselves to the joy of the conversation which according to Gadamer holds the potential to possess them there in the household of those who as friends see difference as dear.

Sadly, the tendency toward absence of playing or dancing in the Franconia conversations is striking. Mostly the delegates seem to enter the discussions grimly committed to their initial prejudices and to leave little changed. For all, regardless of which prejudice they hold dear, the stakes are too high, the risks too great, for trust that through open conversation the subject matter can provide for the delegates the enlarged range of options they cannot provide for themselves and in the end fail to find.

What Gadamer helps foreground here is not the dance which has taken place but that it did not take place. This absence is itself meaningful, providing a way of probing the gap between a potentially genuine conversation and the less-than-genuine conversations which mostly unfolded. To evaluate through Gadamer's gaze less toward power and more toward dance what could have happened but did not seems to me more fruitful than to never notice the absence because one never expected anything else to be present in the first place. And it provides cause for celebration in those too-brief but shining moments in the conversations and even more in the third-way statement when the dance steps found their rhythm and for an instant turned lovely.

SEVEN
CHAPTER

CONCLUDING DANCE:
A "WE" BRIGHTENED,
SHADOWED, AND DAPPLED

So what has been learned through observing, with Gadamerian lenses, that fractured dance which was the Franconia conversations? What has become of that "We" able to dance with differences I set out to seek on the path of this study, walking a trail blazed by Gadamer? Is the We more or less present? Are its outlines sharper or muddier?

This We, I conclude, now both shines more brightly and has been cast deeper into shadow. I trace first the shape of what the Gadamerian spotlight has brought into view, then ponder what turns out to be harder in the end to see, amid the shadows cast by life's complexities and the limits of Gadamer's applicability.

Now I have stressed from the start that, given Gadamerian precepts, my data and research methods are neither fully generalizable nor should be. The conclusions below, based on work with Gadamer and Franconia, are tentative. Different findings might have emerged from applying Gadamer to data derived, for instance, from a more heterogeneous sample than Mennonites, whose self-understanding includes high valuing of community.

Thus I offer not generalizations I expect to provide guidance wherever applied—but trajectories or arrows pointing one direction or another. Without claiming to see precisely where the arrows will fall, let me at least describe the direction in which they appear first to take flight.

SHINING WE

Never from my study does an unambiguously shining We emerge. There is no "smoking gun," no waving wand, no panacea to be found in my research which produces the outlines of commonality and difference in perfect balance, ideal integration, utopian synthesis, flawless dance. In practice, this We has proved elusive.

A NORMATIVE VISION

However, the very insights gained from counterposing Gadamer's vision of the We with the We actually discerned point to the value of Gadamer's normative understanding of what constitutes "genuine" conversation. His view of the characteristics of conversation, translated in my efforts into categories of success and failure, has provided a language for evaluating what worked and what did not in the Franconia conversations. Gadamer has provided a language pertinent not only to the researcher but also the participants themselves, many of whom likewise experienced the conversations as failed and wished for something better.

This is evident in one more look at the aftermath. As even the *Philadelphia Inquirer* (O'Reilly, 1997) and other news outlets[1] reported when the news broke that Franconia had removed the oldest Mennonite church in North America, the Franconia leaders who shared the outcome with Germantown took no joy in it. In a dramatic moment that crystallized the failure and its consequences for many, Ken White, a gay Germantown member, asked leader Donella Clemens "to escort him to the door of the historic 1770 meetinghouse to 'cast me out of The [sic] Mennonite Church and body of Christ'. . ." (R-1). Clemens was reluctant, "saying she had no personal wish to see any church member expelled" and did not interpret the vote as calling into question Germantown membership in the body of Christ. However, under pressure from Germantown insistence that she and other leaders

> accept the implications of their actions, Clemens accompanied White to the door, saying she did so "as a representative of the 81 percent of delegates" who had voted for expulsion. (R-1)

Not only White but many others at Germantown mourned the decision.

> "It's like you know that someone is going to die—you think you are prepared for it, but it still has a finality about it," said Germantown pastor Richard Lichty the day after the church was informed of the decision. "Yet it's not like a death in that

the church we love is still there; we're just not allowed to be a part of it." (V. Weaver, 1997a)

At the first delegate assembly held after the expulsion, the gathering at which conversation would have continued had it not been terminated by mail-in vote, there was a time of "confession," in which "delegates acknowledged . . . areas of brokenness and separation as occasions for grieving. These included the recent separation of the Germantown congregation. . ." (Delegates gather to pray, 1997). During a public "prayer of confession," delegates read in unison: "We confess a deep sense of loss, and mourn the broken fellowship with Germantown. . ." (A prayer of confession, 1997). Earlier that evening, and outside the church hosting the assembly, an "unofficial group" held an outdoor prayer vigil accompanied by a sign saying, "Grieving the brokenness in Franconia Mennonite Conference and the pain of Germantown Mennonite Church" (Germantown loses membership, 1997).

Meanwhile, in the primary editorial comment to appear in *Gospel Herald*, Valerie Weaver (1997b) poignantly articulates the high price of the Franconia decision. She begins by quoting Marge Piercy: "We lose and we go on losing as long as we live, a little winter no spring can melt." Then she outlines four things the church is losing: history, trust, innocence, and relationships. The church needs "models of discernment and not divorce, of relationship and not rejection," she says. "No matter what one thinks about the decision, this loss must not slip by without acknowledgment," she urges. "Considering our losses may help us handle our disagreements with clarity, compassion, and reflection. It may help us decide what more we're willing to lose." Building on the Piercy imagery, she mourns over the many in the church who

> will count their losses and ponder their grief, either at being cut off themselves or at losing conference ties with their friends or relatives and sisters and brothers. Through the frosts that come and go, these will live in the winter loss—a winter that, depending on the church's decisions, may not thaw.

Here the "fit" between normative Gadamerian analysis and the conversational data seems confirmed. Franconia (as well as those in the larger church for whom Weaver speaks) wanted something more, something better than what the conversations found, not permanent winter but winter pregnant with hope of spring. Though they failed to achieve it, at least some participants were aiming toward some such norm as Gadamer aims to theorize.[2]

As always in applying Gadamer, however, misfits also move into view. For one, not all in the conversation yearned toward Gadamerian norms (a point connected to the chapter 5 discussion of truth). Appearing to perpetuate the failure (by Gadamerian norms) of the conversations themselves, some in Franconia and the larger church welcomed the outcome. Not atypical among the flood of letters to the *Gospel Herald* was José Solano's (1998) comment that "There should be no doubt about how the church should respond to blatant unrepented immorality of all sorts." Solano adds, "Thank you, Franconia Conference, for your courage to act on the truth." Meanwhile George R. Brunk II (1998) scores "The cries for tolerance and dialogue" accompanying the "courageous disciplinary action" of Franconia.

Weaver's editorial also triggered many critical letters, such as these: "The perspective of the *Gospel Herald* editorial is confusing," says Steven E. Landis (1997) "Should not the official magazine of the Mennonite Church affirm the biblical beliefs of our denomination and respect the decisions of area conferences?" Likewise Bishop Shant. S. Kunjam (1997), writing from Rajnandgaon, India, comments that it seems Mennonites in "North America are troubled by issues of human sexuality." He then contends that Weaver has been swayed by sentiment rather than submitting to Jesus' call for humans to cease sinning. Rather than expressing an opinion incompatible with the views of Jesus and the official stand of her church, an editor such as Weaver should "honour [sic] and voice official positions of the church. . . ."[3]

The combination of such fits and misfits sets the stage for discussion of the remainder of my conclusions, in which for every mention of strengths glimpsed in Gadamer, comment on application challenges must quickly follow. Turning first to strengths inherent in Gadamer's normative vision, additional aspects of a We which respects difference do shine forth.

THE COMMONALITIES OF EFFECTIVE HISTORY

Effective history, my study suggests, is crucial in making the We shine. Gadamer's great contribution to those who hope to discern commonality amid difference is summarized in this oft-quoted statement, which provides one of the most pointed and reliable summaries of a key Gadamerian emphasis: "Is it not, in fact, the case," he asks, "that every misunderstanding presupposes a 'deep common accord'?" (1976, 7). And this deep common accord is generated by effective history. If human perception is fundamentally shaped by a history mediated through language, and if the broad forces of a common history have shaped the languages which provide people with access to the world, then there will inevitably be commonalities of understanding. These commonalities precede that on which we agree or disagree, Gadamer insists. We also cannot misunderstand each other—at least we cannot misunderstand and in any meaningful way recognize that we have done so—if there is not some understanding from which the misunderstanding is a deviation.

As we have seen, Gadamer has of course been taken to task for relying on a view of effective history as a homogeneous unity. The critics, such as Eagleton, then contend that if effective history, or the tradition which is roughly a synonym for it, is actually more riddled with disjunctures and heterogeneities than he perceives, deep common accord cannot after all be affirmed. Bernstein, in general an appreciative reader of Gadamer, similarly worries that Gadamer presupposes a version of community which does not exist in today's situation of societal breakdown. Bernstein wonders "what is to be done when we realize how much of humanity has been systematically excluded and prevented from participating in . . . dialogical communities?" (1983, 226).

These concerns deserve the serious attention they have hopefully earlier received, yet they can be at least partly answered. One important response is that no matter how fragmented a tradition or a community may be, so long as the very notion of its fragmentation persists, this provides powerful evidence of the point Gadamer wants to make. The commonality of effective history is not found in understanding something the same way; this can hardly be the case for a thinker whose motto is that understanding understands differently if it understands at all. Rather, the commonality is seen whenever anything remains legible, significant, meaningful, no matter how much disagreement, protest, criticism it may elicit.

As P. Christopher Smith points out, suppose I say to you, "That's mean." If it signifies something to you for me to identify something as mean, if so to speak, the fact that something is mean "computes" for each of us, then we both remain shaped by a heritage which has produced in us assumptions about what it means to treat people meanly. A tremendous web of buried yet still living ethical norms either held in common or at a minimum discernible or legible to the two of us begins to come into view (1991, 280-281). Together we may ponder, discuss, and possibly move in directions we both agree are not mean as we probe what commonalities underlie our mutual ability to understand something as mean.

Or suppose I insist a community has been dismembered or a tradition can be seen to be riddled with heterogeneity. The very meaningfulness of dismemberment or of heterogeneity requires the legibility as well of community or homogeneity. As Margolis (1995, 170) so nicely summarizes it, "The detection of conceptual incommensurability is a mark of cognitive and communicative competence, not evidence of its local defeat or failure." It is at the levels that make incommensurability detectable that Gadamer insists deep common accord operates. And it is at such levels that a fragile yet significant We may perhaps be sought.

This seems at least partly evident in the Franconia conversations. A fully satisfactory We is never found by the participants. Differences remain in tension—an often angry, hostile tension. In the aftermath of the Franconia decision, the long-term status of Germantown remains unknown, and it is unsafe to predict what further evolution there may be in the Franconia and churchwide stands on homosexuality. For now it appears that the Franconia decision has brought no closure to controversy but has rather triggered continuing churchwide debate regarding the validity of the decision.

Yet also discernible throughout the conversations and their aftermath are those great webbings of commonality produced by a Mennonite effective history. This is perhaps the commonality that enabled the structures of the new Mennonite Church USA to be ratified in 2001 despite tensions over homosexuality. This history has made meaningful to all, regardless of their prejudices, a discussion powerfully shaped by affirmation of the cruciality of the Bible, of the body of Christ, and of a church with which all, even those now formally excluded from it, remain in some form of relationship.[4]

Obviously the We revealed in the Franconia conversations is no comfortable, seamless waltz of homogeneities. For all the talk of family, at least in relation to homosexuality no happy family is to be found. One reason for this is likely that, as we have seen, multiple strands of difference and prejudice are woven into the very fabric of effective history. Thus multiple and sometimes contradictory emphases emerge from biblical effective history, which is so thoroughly intertwined with each of the three primary Franconia prejudices that adherents of each can claim their stance as biblical. Likewise tensions inherent in the effective history producing the body of Christ can lead some in this body to emphasize being *rightly* joined to the body and others to emphasize maintaining *relationships* in the body.

Nevertheless, amid the differences, antagonisms, and conflicts, some form of We undeniably exists; without it, the conversations would not even take place. To be in the conversations at all and then to follow what unfolds in them is to participate in a We even in the act of fighting over what We, if any, can satisfy all involved. The Franconia story is filled with missteps, and major ones, as Weaver mourns—yet amid and through their anger, sorrow, and more, even the Germantown members remain in a fractured dance with not only their supporters but also those who have evicted them.

CHARACTERISTICS OF THE SHINING WE

Characteristics of the We enabled by effective history have been earlier addressed at length and so require being only lightly touched on here. But to review, my study indicates, first, that a *goodwill highlighting of prejudices as yours and mine* is one significant feature. The We evident through Gadamer does not suppress but rather highlights differences in faith that through seeing what is best in what is other enlargement comes. It is as the framers of the third-way statement lay out charitably *and* unflinchingly their different prejudices that the journey toward growth is set in motion.

Second, *awareness of finitude* is required to enable the journey to begin. Only if there is still some lack in my position, some falling short of completion or perfection, do I see a need to grapple with myself to what is other. In Franconia, awareness of finitude allows a few—and only a few!—to seek to move beyond their initial stances.

Third, awareness of finitude can promote my *openness* to allowing the spotlight cast by your prejudices to join mine and thus brighten a larger horizon than either of us can alone. The Franconia conversations are a living attempt to break an impasse of opposing prejudices by seeking means to join the prejudices of all in a We able to view a larger horizon without eradicating the original visions. There is an implicit and even occasionally explicit acceptance among some participants that openness to viewing the thing from a variety of angles offers more access to it than reifying one perspective as *the* transcendent one able to grasp unerringly the thing itself.

Finally, the power of merely maintaining *prejudices in relationship* is evident. Regardless of what Franconia participants do or do not say to each other, Gadamer helps identify how potent is the mere presence with each other they enact to the extent they continue relating. So long as they remain present in relationship, much of what Gadamer values in genuine conversation will be promoted. The simple realization that you are not the same as me prods me to remain aware of the questionability of my prejudice—and thus to become aware of my finitude and in so doing potentially open myself to you.

SHADOWED WE

As noted, the Franconia conversations, which aimed specifically if perhaps somewhat unknowingly for a kind of Gadamerian interchange, show cause for glimmers of hope that a We able to respect difference can be sustained. However, they indicate at least as strongly just how many shadows darken the chances of such a conversation to succeed. Two primary sources of sobering conclusions regarding the extent to which the We is shadowed rather than shining appear to emerge from my study. One is that human frailties and realities frequently subvert the Gadamerian vision, however valuable its normativity may be. The other, to be noted under suggestions for further research, is that—partly because of this normativity and its potential to remain above such a tussle as Franconia proved to be—Gadamer may not at points be useful for adequate theorizing of the data.

FAILURES OF CONVERSATION TO BE GADAMERIAN

Among failures of conversation to be Gadamerian, five stand out. First, *antagonistic highlighting of prejudices as mine and yours* subverts the process.

As some Franconia participants ridicule and distort opposing prejudices, seeking the worst in them, they promote a second failure, which is *closure*. This failure involves intolerance of ambiguity or the possibility that initial positions will be invited to change.

Antagonism toward other prejudices and an attitude of closure in relation to one's own is enabled by a third failure, *certitude*, which is the assurance that one can securely know what is right and what is wrong, based on such foundations as an inerrant Bible or objective standards thought to be fully knowable.

As these other failures unfold, the progression to a fourth, *severing relationships*, seems natural. Given that one's own position is correct and requires no further enlargement and the other's is wrong, it makes sense to aim for severed relationships as a way to minimize the risk of having one's own prejudice made questionable by the continuing presence of the other's prejudice. Or, to respect how those holding exclusivist prejudices might see it, it makes sense as a way to maintain the *right* fellowship.

And if the conversation is taking place in a context in which one set of prejudices can potentially gain the power to impose itself on others, then understandably a fifth failure, *coercion*, may emerge.

As such failures unfold, it also becomes evident how *ambiguous the commonalities of effective history can be.* Despite the We or deep common accord which with Gadamer I contend can be discerned as products of effective history even amid fragmentations of tradition and community, some Franconia participants do not see these commonalities as sufficient to sustain their preferred versions of the We. Thus for instance they may define a We in relation to shared commitment to a given prejudice regarding the level of inclusion or exclusion they believe Germantown should experience.

I conclude it is possible for a We to be discerned as the background of even a failed conversation—yet such a We cannot necessarily prevent the failures. And it may be experienced by the participants as a We more thin and tenuous than the We by which they want to be defined—such as the We comprised of those who want the church either to change or to maintain its traditional exclusion of homosexuals. Even as the Franconia participants operate in the common We established by Bible, body of Christ, and other characteristics of their effective history, many more see their differences as outweighing their commonalities. This is why eighty percent are prepared formally to declare some of their members no longer a part of the We as they define it. Effective history serves as resource for transcending differences when other characteristics of Gadamerian conversation are present—but can be at the same time trumped when participants turn away from what it offers.

CLOSED OPENNESS: A GADAMERIAN FAILURE

However, if failures of Gadamerian conversation are understandably most evident in those conversational moves which are themselves non-Gadamerian, the paradoxical potential for closure in the Gadamerian moves themselves must always be remembered. The Franconia evidence suggests that the drive for openness at all costs as the only measure of and means for the shining forth of truth can founder in self-refuting paradox. If Gadamerian openness can find no way to open itself to those prejudices whose integrity requires forms of closure, then perhaps it has not yet found full openness.

In my chapter 5 comments on this issue. I found no obvious path through such paradox, nor do I offer one here. I simply stress that in Franconia a crucial reason for the frequent failures of genuine conversation appears to include the requirement on the Gadamerian side that all parties first enter *its* prejudices before the conversation can unfold. This, it seems to me, underlines a potential weakness of the Gadamerian vision. If finally a Gadamerian prejudice must trump all other prejudices, must assume the superiority of its own stance rather than continue to anticipate the completeness of even those stances so at odds with this one, then here perhaps philosophical hermeneutics risks ceasing to be itself. A way through this self-refuting tangle seems a worthy goal of Gadamerian enlargement.

POSSIBILITIES FOR FURTHER RESEARCH

In light of successes and failures I identify in working with Gadamer in search of commonalities that dance respectfully with difference, where to from here? The many failures of genuine conversation I have identified may discourage other researchers from looking for successes elsewhere. But I hope I have detected enough tantalizing hints of success to tempt others to try again, to continue probing what it is that makes the occasional conversational move succeed, even amid what may typically be overwhelming odds in favor of failure.

For those who may be so tempted, it must first be stressed again that my research has been highly exploratory. To the best of my knowledge (and bolstered by Williams' similar conclusion, 1995, 6-7, as reported earlier), no previous research quite like mine has been undertaken. Thus I have hoped mainly to chart a few lines on uncharted territory, to suggest that this one may go somewhere, that one not. The categories of Gadamerian and non-Gadamerian talk fit under this exploratory heading. I sensed even as I worked with them—and this is the only way it could have been, says Gadamer—that I could have sliced the data differently, pushing this category one way, that another, de-emphasizing this, reconceptualizing that.

My hope is less that other researchers will duplicate the same categories in relation to other data and more that they will benefit from my initial thinking as they produce their refinements. There may be ways, for instance, for someone more microanalytically oriented to find in Gadamer a finer gridwork of roads than I have been able to by first setting out on the few large interstates I have hoped to construct. But needed is not primarily replication of my research, which by Gadamerian precepts can after all never be duplicated. Called for rather are related efforts of others who share my interests and perhaps even experience some fusion of horizons with mine— but who then take the research in their own unique directions as their prejudices guide their applications to their chosen data.

AREAS OF INAPPLICABILITY

In addition, other researchers can hopefully benefit from my recording of the dead-ends or false trails which seem to be risks of

Gadamerian research. If my assessments are correct, two key potential dead-ends relate to organizations and power. One will rarely want to turn to Gadamer for microanalytic analysis of institutional or organizational processes of understanding and communication. And except to make modest judgments about whether conversation is unconstrained, one may not want to start with Gadamer in settings where power is a crucial issue. However, at a more general level one may want to start with Gadamer as a way of spotlighting those dances, not spied through power analysis, in which the beautiful claims the dancers.

FINDING THE RIGHT LEVEL OF ABSTRACTION

Also deserving mention is the challenge of operationalizing Gadamer at the appropriate level of abstraction. Gadamerian application of Gadamer appears most congruent with Gadamer the farther above the "world" it remains. When employed as source of relatively abstract theory and vision, he stimulates rich heuristic exploring. Whether or not such probing has been fully successful in this study, it is here exemplified; without Gadamer, to state the obvious, this work would cease to be. Second, Gadamer himself is unsuited to microanalytic research conducted in terms drawn from Gadamer; Gadamer's thought proceeds at a level of abstraction above that necessary for generating microanalytic tools. Third, if tied to mediating or complementary theories (as in Williams, 1992; Deetz, 1992), he can potentially provide fruitful inspiration for microanalytic work guided by tools drawn from other theorists.

SOME SPECIFICS OF POTENTIAL FURTHER RESEARCH

Amid such constraints, researchers interested in furthering the application of Gadamer to conversation which I have tried to pioneer may glean results from focusing on conversational dyads or small groups whose conversations unfold over several testing stages. After working intensively with Gadamer, I suspect it is primarily in relation to such settings or even the lone reader seeking to understand texts that he developed his hermeneutics. Thus for all the effort I have made at points to follow the trajectories of his thought beyond his own implementation of it, at the application level the most natural fit of his theories may be with few rather than many persons, and with settings in which systems and regularities are less important than discernible events.

As noted earlier (chapter 5) fruitful sources of data may include those which provide access to intentional or introspective states as well as longitudinal cues. Sources to be considered include retro-spective self-reports, diaries, interviews, or other means to assess initial prejudices and growth in them. But if chosen, potential prob-lems of using such tools must also be assessed. The potential unreli-ability of tools dependent on self-reporting must be considered.

In addition, if longitudinal tools seem to fit Gadamer's empha-sis on prejudices which change, Gadamer's focus is not on precisely when they change, how they change, how they may be held fixed long enough to be studied. Gadamer's stress on the prejudice which welcomes the *new* implies that a changed or changing prejudice will continue to change, which for a researcher poses the challenge of as-sessing a moving target. Whatever the challenges of qualitative re-search, certainly Gadamerian research is unlikely to benefit from sta-tistical or experimental methodologies but will rather seek access to lived experience congruent with the sensus communis.

Although the density of some of his thinking suggests he could have held himself even more accountable to practice, Gadamer stresses that from the start his hermeneutics arose from his "effort to be theoretically accountable for the style of my studies and teach-ing." He explains that "Practice came first. For as long ago as I can remember, I have been concerned not to say too much and not to lose myself in theoretical constructions which were not fully made good by experience" (1997a, 16). Here is a motto for Gadamerian research.

Such research may want to consider the possibility that aspects of philosophical hermeneutics make little sense if the internal, intro-spective experience of the psyche pursuing the act of understanding is not pertinent. If, despite problems more raised than resolved in this study, self-reporting holds potential to make a valid contribu-tion to Gadamerian research, then a researcher's own self-reporting holds potential to provide pertinent data. Depending on how the re-search is structured, the introspection of the researcher herself or himself may yield insights into how the Gadamerian vision in real-ity unfolds. Indeed it may be that Gadamer himself, who in an intel-lectual autobiography refers to the "effective history" which shaped him (1997a, 27), turned to introspection as a source of data for his theorizing.

Here too, as so often in applying Gadamer, there are tensions and challenges. If introspection is useful, then how are the conversa-tional, interactive dimensions kept in view? The chapter 5 study of Gadamer's view of the interaction between texts and conversations is aimed at this concern—and that discussion underscores the com-plexities. If a case can be made that Gadamer means in theory to give priority to conversation, it is also evident that in practice his application is primarily to written texts. And if the focus is a written text, then conceptualizing the act of understanding in relation to the solitary reader seeking to comprehend the text is a natural move. This leads to ambiguities and tensions in Gadamerian thought regarding the relationship between living conversations and conversations teased out of texts. Any application of Gadamer will collide, as my study has, with these tensions and the need for a path through them.

Turning specifically to the issue of homosexuality, one other fruitful avenue for further research might be for scholars to conduct a Gadamerian assessment of the style of conversations on homosexuality in other denominations or in other deliberative settings. Among interesting questions to consider, to name just a few, would be these: first, to what extent are the tendencies toward successful or failed conversation seen in the Franconia conversations observable in other denominational or conversational contexts? Second, is there any discernible difference in the style of the conversations that might or might not be attributable to the absence in other settings of a peace church tradition as well as such traditional Mennonite traits as gelassenheit and humility?

ALLOWING THE OBJECT TO OBJECT

As elaborated in Appendix A, Stanley Deetz contends that methods of research should be chosen that fit what is being analyzed: "The appeal for the appropriateness of method needs to be made to the object of analysis, not the existing standards of the research community. Only in this way can research be objective—to allow the object to object." (1982a, 143) Hopefully I have earlier made a reasonably convincing case for the value of using Gadamer to explore the meaning of the Franconia conversations. However, particularly in light of the many tendencies toward failure I have identified by using Gadamerian evaluative norms, I owe it to give the "object" at least least some opportunity to object.

To achieve this I have shared summaries of my research with persons involved in the conversations and have found particularly helpful the the reaction of James M. Lapp, FMC Conference Pastor (meaning pastor of the conference) and leader in the FC process, who in personal interaction non-defensively noted that a different theory would have generated a different view of the process. If viewed through the lens of Gadamerian theory the process largely failed, what, Lapp wondered, would have been glimpsed through an alternate theoretical perspective, such as systems theory?

This is a fruitful question. What if, for example, the thought of Edwin H. Friedman had guided the study? Friedman's *Generation to Generation: Family Process in Church and Synagogue* (1985) has emerged as a classic in its field and has been cited often in recent years in FMC leadership settings. Discerning to what extent that theory actually guided the FMC decisions falls outside the scope of my project, yet it is possible at least to note that some actions may be viewed differently if understood as emerging from a systems framework.

Friedman's theory highlights, for instance, how important it is for leaders in systems to be "self-differentiated," meaning that they "take nonreactive, clearly conceived, and clearly defined positions" (229). He suggests that leaders who function according to this and other systems-informed principles will not "simply be leading people to a goal or to feeling good about their togetherness." Rather, the effectiveness of such leaders "must also be judged by criteria such as the growth of the followers and the long-term survival of the family [or other system] itself" (249). Self-differentiated leaders effect change less by imposing a given vision and more by assuming that their non-anxious taking of clear stands will contribute to healthy transformation of the system, whether or not the outcome precisely matches a leader's personal preferences.

It might be possible, then, using Friedman's approach, to theorize at least some constructive outcomes from the actions of FC leaders. The decision to implement a mail-in ballot whose results, by a large margin, dictated excommunication of Germantown was a clear stand that cut through years of ambiguity, preserved the FC "family" (there was at least a possibility of dramatic FC disunity if leaders had ratified the Germantown position), and set in motion a range of lively dynamics whose outcome is still being written and thus cannot yet be fully evaluated. What potentially healthy results might a longer-term systems assessment of the process turn out to discern?

My point is not that Friedman's theory is then the best for assessing the FC conversations or that it could not itself be used to detect failure in addition to success. Surely a thorough evaluation of Friedman would show that this theory too has its limits, its need for enlargement, and surely it might also be applied to call into question the FC process. In addition, if Friedmann offers one alternative theory, any number of additional ones might be envisioned, including an interpreting grid some might prefer, which is whether the conversations were or were not biblical. Each approach then would include its own potential for generating or clouding insight.

My hope, then, is simply to make two points: First, Lapp is indeed correct to note, on behalf of the "object," that other theories could have been used and would have generated different analyses. Second, the very fact that this is so points again to the need for all prejudices, including Gadamerian, to continue to seek transformation through conversation with contrasting stands—and even competing theories.

DAPPLED WE

As so often with Gadamer, I find that binary categorization is not quite enough. Yes, there are points at which Gadamer and application of philosophical hermeneutics can be argued to succeed, and places where they fail. A strength here, a weakness there can be pointed to. But also repeatedly in Gadamer, something is not quite either/or. Perhaps it is that third possibility which Gadamer says "brings us very near Platonic or, better said, human secrets." Gadamer is speaking here of the "neither/nor" which is linked to and participates in the "two alternatives in a conceptual opposition" but is neither precisely the one nor exactly the other (1980, 13). This is the neither/nor in Gadamer of that which links us in commonality—but not fully, or all would be same and movement would cease; that which is alien—yet not entirely, or the strangeness would prevent even our discerning of it and would cease to be for us.

Perhaps it is this neither/nor that makes Gadamer himself such a paradoxical figure. On the one hand, he is widely acknowledged to be one of the intellectual giants of his century, in whose years he has aged in lockstep since his birth timed in 1900 to the emergence of the century itself. On the other hand, the largeness and the imprecision of his concepts can make him frustratingly and sometimes irritatingly difficult to apply. Is Gadamer genius or failed researcher? Perhaps he himself might see this either/or as a false choice and choose some fresh neither/nor both linked to yet different than such categories.

And perhaps the challenge of assessment is itself well-exemplified by the question of how to evaluate what might be labeled Gadamer's mysticism. Much has been said already about Gadamer's vision of an openness to the claim of what is beyond the self, of a readiness to yield to the play of life and the words in which it dances into our experience and cognition. Perhaps what yet remains to be said is that Gadamer himself admits or celebrates (depending on the critic's prejudice), that his exultation (is that finally too strong a word?) in the beautiful which captures us before we even know it

has arrived "may be an echo of the mystical, pietistic-sounding illu-
minatio, illumination. . ." (1994a, 485).

What sense can anyone not already inclined toward the mystical finally make of a Gadamer who makes an admission like that?
This is why, I suspect, such a scholar as Margolis (see chapter 3) takes
pains to disassociate himself from that Gadamerian agenda connected to the beautiful and rooted in Plato. Gadamer may have contributions to make, such a critic may agree, but aspects of his thought
are better left aside.

On the other hand, what sense is one like myself, member of
that tradition which in the Franconia conversations speaks so often
of God, Jesus, the Holy Spirit—openness aimed not only at one another but beyond—to make of things if left only with categories that
make no mention of, or space for, the mystical? In Gadamer, the two
perspectives are oddly, unsettlingly, and often controversially joined.
But may it be here, where the joints seem to creak, where the clarity
and mysticism seem to run inseparably together, that what Gadamer
is trying to tell us comes most fully into view? Here we can see what
it looks like for like and unlike to come together yet maintain their
difference, to dance with each other yet remain neither/nor.

This vision leads me to speak, then, not only of the shining we
and the shadowed we but also of the dappled we. If I can say little
else with certainty after much wrestling with Gadamer and my data,
I think I can at least confirm that Gadamer points to a longing of
many to be in relationship with each other—to avoid that "brokenness" of relationships so many in Franconia and Germantown are
grieving—and likewise a longing of many to have what makes them
different respected and affirmed. The crosscurrents these longings
set in motion eddy and clash and swirl with and against and around
each other with more complexity than any theory or research method
can penetrate. Every move toward relationship risks setting in motion rapids of coercion which overwhelm precisely the difference
that makes relationship relationship, because sameness cannot relate to sameness but becomes indiscernible from itself. Every move
toward difference risks ripping that difference from the fabric of
sameness in which it defines itself and from which it draws strength.

Gadamer is trying, in his murky, maddening, creative way, to
do justice to it all even as he tells us as many times as he tells us anything else that no perspective on anything does anything justice. This
is because the thing is not just either this or that, the thing is neither
this nor that, though it is all of that and more, and how is such a thing
ever fully to be known? It is not to be, that is Gadamer's point. And

that is why any researcher inspired by Gadamer can know much, but only so much. It is why we humans can begin the journey of knowing and communicating and dancing with each other on the way, but we can never know in advance precisely where we will end up. It is why Gadamer, quoting nearly word-for-word a saying of Jesus, is certain amid all his uncertainty of one thing: "One must lose oneself to find oneself" (1989, 57).

EPILOGUE:
ONE MODEST APPLICATION

My analysis of the Franconia conversations constitutes my primary application of Gadamer. Yet necessarily the scholarly purposes of that application have kept it at some distance from the lived daily experience of the Mennonite Church or other denominations facing comparable agenda.

Thus I want to include here one modest attempt to apply Gadamer more directly and intimately to church issues. "Becoming Dear Friends," below, is a brief and simple discussion of how Gadamer might be useful even in church settings where few have heard of him or would be interested in exploring his more esoteric assumptions. In varying stages of development, I preached this material as a sermon in three Mennonite congregations, including one in Franconia Conference, and the current version was eventually published in the Mennonite press (King, 1998).[1] Though surely there are other ways Gadamer can be drawn on as a resource for church efforts to promote quests for Gadamerian understanding, this at least offers one example—without significant focus on homosexuality—of how Gadamerian abstractions might be applied in congregational or denominational contexts.

BECOMING DEAR FRIENDS:
HONORING YOUR STANCE AND MINE
IN THE BODY OF CHRIST

"You're too authoritarian, conservative, legalistic," charges one group. "You value rules over God."

"And you're too liberal, worldly, even heretical," worries the other. "You forget to say, `Go and sin no more.' "

They split.

For 500 years Anabaptist-Mennonites have stressed faithful living *and* community. We have believed we must practice what we preach in relationship with each other. Sadly, we have often been true to our ethical stances while violating our vision of mutual accountability.

Repeatedly we have disagreed regarding how to be faithful. Frequently we have resolved the clash by affirming our own stand at the expense of continuing fellowship. We see this in the history of splits in denominations, conferences, congregations, and even families which continue to this day.

Is there another path? Is there a peacemaking way forward which allows us, members of a historic peace church, not to hate but to love the enemies we make of each other? Is there a way *to be true to our deepest commitments without splitting from those whose passions don't match ours?*

Seeking ways to live together without losing our own hearings of the gospel has been one of my scholarly goals. I want to share pointers glimpsed in the work of Hans-Georg Gadamer. This German Christian philosopher has studied how we can at the same time honor our original perspectives *and* be blessed by other viewpoints.

SEEING PREJUDICES AS TREASURES

One of Gadamer's key points involves *prejudice*. We often see prejudice as a bad thing we must replace with an objective view of whatever's really in front of us. But for Gadamer prejudices are simply initial prejudgments—unavoidable "biases of our openness to the world." He means we never see exactly what is before us. Rather, we see through the lenses of our histories, backgrounds, peeves, loves.

This is as it must be, thinks Gadamer. We see only through the lens of who we are. Our biases spring from our beings and are the lenses through which we see whatever we see. These lenses are life's and God's gift. We cannot take them off any more than our personhood. People aren't microscopes, instruments which relay impersonal data. People are people. And people see through drawing on the rich mix of relationships and thoughts and feelings and memories we all are.

But Gadamer isn't done. Yes, as initial lenses through which we see, prejudices are treasures. But to stop there would be tragic. Then we'd be locked into observing only what we first see. Then there would be no way for our understandings of each other, the church, the Bible, God to grow.

BECOMING DEAR FRIENDS

How do we grow? *By becoming friends.* A friend isn't just like me. If you and I are entirely alike, we're boring blobs of sameness. "Opposites attract," we say. So is the best friend the enemy most unlike me? No! Friends are enough alike to feel connected. "Birds of a feather flock together." True friendship is a blend: friends have enough in common to want to journey together. But as your friend I'm also drawn to what is unlike me in you which I sense can help me become the better person I yearn to be. Gadamer calls "dear" that part of you which can enlarge me, complete me, bring me home to the richer person I'm called to become.

If we saw each other as friends, then prejudices we treated as reasons for splitting we might instead see as dear to us. Imagine if not every clash of prejudices were cause for suspicion. Imagine if instead we asked, "Is your prejudice something that could be dear to me, complete me, cause me to grow into the larger person God is calling me to be?" Gadamer is telling us there *is* a way to be true at the same time to ourselves and each other. That way invites us first to cherish our own prejudices. It then requires us to treasure the other's prejudices. It's as simple and as complicated as that. If all sides of a potential split truly make these two moves, they begin to step back from the fissure.

This remains a big *if*, however. *Both* sides must honor *both* sets of prejudices. Often only one condition is met: we value *our* prejudices. This in itself is right; I must be faithful to *my* truth for it to complete *you.* The problem is my not meeting the second condition of delighting in and risking being enlarged by *your* prejudices. Then again we exchange those "too-too-too" epithets. Positions harden.

BECOMING DEAR IN CHRIST'S BODY

What might soften them? It's time to ask Paul, who in 1 Corinthians 12-13 anticipated Gadamer. We may not squabble over exactly the spiritual gifts Paul focuses on, yet our theological and moral stances can be seen as gifts Paul also helps us manage. For Paul Christians are alike as members of Christ's body. Yet God gives us different gifts. We're as unlike as hands, noses, feet. Paul joins our common affirmations and different gifts by emphasizing that no gift can survive alone any more than can a foot. As parts of the same body, we're all dear to each other.

Paul stresses that now "we know only in part," we see only "in a mirror, dimly. . . ." All the parts, all the dim half-knowledges of this life, will pass. No gift, no stance, no matter how sure we are we're

God's prophets, will endure. Only one thing never ends. Only that which allows us to cherish what is dear in each other never ends: "Love never ends."

Love which never ends because it lives and moves and has its being in God is what may soften us. If love does spread among us, maybe we *will* treasure the *other's* prejudices as well as our own. Maybe we'll see splitting as a detour around the work of being completed by the other.

Such work may not prevent all splits. Some differences may truly be irreconcilable. My proposals open cans of worms I don't have space to address, am not aware of, or which at this time in our church life are wriggling too hard to hold. But though I need others to help me enlarge it, my prejudice is that the effort to remain in relationship is worth making.

NAMING EACH OTHER DEAR HOMEMAKERS AND EXPLORERS

One way to begin might be to give each other not labels arising from enmity but names springing from friendship. Two names seem to me to highlight what in each other's prejudices we might see as the hand, arm, or leg which could become dear to us.

One is *homemaker*. Many amid today's chaos ache for home. This is why Frederick Buechner has called a recent book *The Longing for Home* and why he reflects on our love for earthly homes and that great Home toward which we're traveling. Their opponents label some people conservative, legalistic, rigid. What if as friends we named them homemakers?

What if we saw that we all—without those prejudices through which homemakers make church home—would be homeless? My prejudice has been to focus on line-drawing dangers. But homemakers are teaching me much. What if I and we saw drawing lines, clarifying boundaries, conserving tradition as homemaker callings? What if we saw we can no more have church homes without such things than physical homes without walls and roofs?

Oh, but what if our longing for home grew obsessive? What if we only hunkered down? Then someday, food gone, lights out, the roof itself would cave in, the walls tumble. There at home we'd die. We need a second group. What if we named them *explorers*? Their antagonists call them liberal, worldly, heretics—and indeed the labels hint at explorer tendencies to scrimp on home maintenance. But what if as friends we saw them instead as scouts, sent out to explore the territory, to ponder how in changing times food and light can still stream into church homes?

What if we applied such renaming, for instance, to divorce and remarriage? Homemakers stress the holiness of marriage bonds, consequences of breaking them, and the danger that easy remarriage will cheapen all marriage. But they risk making the divorced the church's homeless. Explorers want to update old church homes with the track lighting of God's forgiveness. But they risk weakening the walls which sustain marriage.

Homemakers and explorers can complete each other, however. This is the consensus emerging in some congregations. Homemakers are bolstering church walls with "divorce-is-tragic" policies requiring members to process divorce and remarriage in congregational accountability structures. But explorer emphases are present in the move from eviction to faith that amazing grace shines even amid this sin.

Homemakers. Explorers. The names oversimplify; all of us are more complex than any one name can capture. But seeing one another through these or similar names may help us at least begin to grasp how dear we are to each other. Together we can maintain home and bring in food and light, if only we learn amid our dim half-seeing to perceive this one thing fully: love—that true love from God which endures all things—never ends.

APPENDIX A:
THE STUDY AND ITS METHODS

THE STUDY

PURPOSES

Although the pursuit of a We that respects difference was the original impetus for my study, it remained too broad to stand alone as a viable research question. Narrowing it to manageable scope yielded the following as my formal research question(s): *to what extent is it possible to (a) apply the philosophical hermeneutics of Hans-Georg Gadamer so as to (b) recognize in the Franconia conversations instances of successful Gadamerian conversation and (c) recognize as well failures of such conversation?*[1]

GADAMERIAN FRAMEWORK

To apply Gadamer with integrity requires conceptualizing the study in a Gadamerian framework. Here is a challenge indeed. This is a scholarly study, and its structure must follow the forms expected of it. However, I also intended as much as possible not only detachedly to *analyze* Gadamer but also to *enact* his thought. Thus I must find a way simultaneously to meet scholarly requirements *and* perform the precepts of a theorist hostile to those methodological aspects of research he considers alienating.

Speaking of *phronesis* (see note 1, below), or that practical wisdom inseparable from the life of the community, Gadamer (1983, 263) says he "cannot really make sense of a *phronesis* that is supposed to be scientifically disciplined, although I can imagine a scientific approach that is disciplined by *phronesis*." Evident here is the challenge of applying in some disciplined way a thinker who has put the larger part of his energy into showing that phronesis cannot be disciplined rather than exploring how a scientific approach might be disciplined by phronesis.

The primary path I discerned for proceeding which held the possibility of being not only in theory but in performance truly Gadamerian is the one

I adopted. Interestingly, the fact that such a path is now feasible in academia is a tribute to the effect Gadamer—and those who from varying perspectives at least share his emphasis on "lived" reality[2]—has had on scholarship. In the space such thought has constructed, the form I offer is akin to narrative. I have aimed not simply to present in orderly fashion the results of my research but to see the *plot* of the research, the stages it has undergone in arriving at the outcomes—or climactic moments of the tale—as being nearly as pertinent as the conclusions themselves. Let me elaborate.

It is abundantly clear, and sometimes incites such criticisms of Gadamer as Habermas (1988, 1994; see chapter 6 for more) famously leveled, that Gadamer is passionately opposed to the reduction (as he would see it) to method of the quest for knowledge. Gadamer wants nothing to do with scientific methodologies or aesthetic or historical consciousnesses which think they can distance themselves from their own humanity and conduct transcendent investigations into reality. Gadamer scores the "methodical alienation" characteristic of many modern sciences and any critical theory which abstracts its analysis from life as actually lived. One role of hermeneutics is to show the terrible price of such alienation: "how much screening and abstraction it demands, and how, in the process, it leaves natural consciousness perplexed behind it. . ." (1994b, 289-291). Gadamer's contention is that alienating methods yield results which appear scientific but in the process lose access to the very humanness they purport to clarify.

In contrast to the alienating stance taken by critical rationality and science, Gadamer believes his hermeneutics can resituate the critical drive "in the whole of human life" from which it springs and which carries it forward (1994a, 552). The key distinction here is between an alienated rationality which criticizes from outside and an at-home rationality which accepts the indissolubility of its relationship with what it criticizes. Such rationality can continue to criticize but never is closed to whatever "is meaningful" in what we seek to understand—whether text, art, or horizons of another—which "captivates us just as the beautiful captivates us" (1994a, 490).[3] Not the critic standing over the other but the humble reasoner open to and experiencing the claim of the other is what Gadamer envisions.

METHOD

For some years, as I made my intellectual journey ever deeper into Gadamerian terrain, I wrestled with how to reconcile such Gadamerian precepts with the demands of an at least quasi-social-scientific book on applying Gadamer to conversation. I grappled with how to place in conversation with Gadamer the fruits of content analytic or ethnomethodological methods and learned, I hope, much from them.

Partly under helpful guidance from my dissertation committee, I aimed as much as is possible for one trained more in Gadamer than such methods to benefit from criteria for analysis provided by Earl Babbie (1995), Barbara Montgomery and Steve Duck (1991a), Robert M. Emerson, Rachel I. Fretz, and Linda L. Shaw (1995), J. P. Spradley (1980), Robert Philip Weber (n.d), Klaus Krippendorf (1980), and more. Such resources were informative as I struggled with what categories to generate for applying Gadamer to my data. I valued and learned from them in the Gadamerian spirit articulated implicitly by Montgomery and Duck (1991c). They are weary of research program polarizations which lead to "entrenched advocacies," that imply the existence of this or that one true method; they call instead for "a risky openness that could be the basis for true dialogue" (324).

Nevertheless, I have discovered that some moves toward method, at least as more systematically conceived, seemed to throw me off rather than place me on the trail my nose has seemed to scent. This stands to reason in the case of research inspired by Gadamer's understanding that

> every dialogue we have with the thinking of a thinker we are seek-
> ing to understand remains an endless conversation. It is a real con-
> versation, a conversation in which we seek to find "our" language—
> to grasp what we have in common. Consciously taking up a histori-
> cal distance from one's partner and placing the partner in an histori-
> cally surveyable course of events must remain subordinate move-
> ments of our effort to achieve understanding. As a matter of fact,
> they represent a self-assurance by which one actually closes oneself
> off from one's partner. (1997a, 36)

As Dieter Misgeld notes, Gadamer "does not so much analyze the rule-guided conventional-dependent character of speech" as he does "speaking as a discursive activity" in which can be discerned "intentions to make sense of something at work in it." Gadamer's focus is not primarily on cod-able regularities evident in speech. His concern rather is with the "meaning" or sense participants in conversations experience. In Gadamer's emphasis, conventions of communication recede to the background as "a precondition for the competence to think, in and with language, and formulate what is worth saying. . ." (Misgeld, 1985, 157).

And so, as I have aimed to conduct a Gadamerian conversation both with Gadamer and the Franconia data, the form of this study has become as much its contribution as its content. The form represents my effort to resolve the problem of research based on a type of thought which opposes method and to balance requirements for disciplined research with openness to the conversation which plays me in addition to my playing it. Bochner et al (1991) stress their view of "decisions about methodology as contingent on the purposes of inquiry" and note that according to this approach the research question shifts from "How do you know?" to "Why do you talk that way?" (30-31).

CONSIDERATIONS OF TALKING THAT WAY

I "talk that way" for the Gadamerian reasons noted. But if that points to the why of how I talk, what are in fact some of the ways I do talk, or what considerations does such talk entail? Eight deserve mention.

My initial prejudices

First, I have seen my own prejudices as productive and as providing the initial perspectives through which to organize and set in motion my research. I am a product of the Mennonite effective history whose outlines I explore in chapter 2. This history has produced in me prejudices in favor of the very We which respects difference which I am here seeking. I am the product of a people who, as has been elaborated, have struggled regularly for 500 years with how to handle differences of opinion regarding truth and doctrine while maintaining a community identified as the "Body of Christ," a body in which differences are to be managed in relationship— uneasy though the truce between differences and relationship has often been. So I set out on the journey impelled in directions already predetermined by my heritage.

Joining my initial prejudices with Gadamer's

Second, I sought for some years before undertaking this study to broaden my initial Mennonite prejudices through interaction with Gadamer. My belief and hope is that this has enlarged my perspectives and provided me a set of prejudices indelibly colored by my own initial ones yet aligned with Gadamer's to the extent I may perhaps now label them Gadamerian. Thus I bring not only my initial but also Gadamerian prejudices to bear on the data.[4]

In addition, the very act of applying Gadamer has, as Gadamer might see it, stimulated continued growth in my understanding of Gadamer, impelling me into a spiral of thinking in which I began with a more rudimentary understanding of Gadamer, deepened it as I applied it to the data, then used this deepened insight to yield similarly deepened insight into the data. This is a never-ending spiral, Gadamer makes clear, so in a sense the decision to call a halt to the study, to write the last line, is arbitrary. Yet I at least aim to show a slice of the journey, to provide evidence of movement through several of the spirals.

Asking the data to speak back

Third, not only does my enlarging of Gadamerian prejudices shape my view of the data; I ask the data to speak back. I asked the data, according to Gadamerian terms I later explored, to show me how they need to claim me rather than I them. I sought to be open to the resistances they offer my and Gadamer's initial prejudices and thus to show me how not only my own but Gadamer's prejudices require enlargement.

In relation to this agenda as well as the broader question of appropriate methodology, Stanley Deetz makes an important plea congruent with my own concerns and approach:

> Many existing quantitative and qualitative methods may and need to be used in interpretive research. The issue is not the research methods but the use to which they are put and their relation to the phenomena under study. The appeal for the appropriateness of method

needs to be made to the object of analysis, not the existing standards of the research community. Only in this way can research be objective—to allow the object to object. (1982a, 143)

Projecting a finite whole and parts

Fourth, I hoped through such means to project finally a whole in which the parts made sense while recognizing from beginning through end that I could have made different decisions regarding where to cast the spotlight which would have yielded a different whole and parts. I did so believing that the many different possible outcomes are not merely self-canceling or contradictory but rather that varied perspectives on the "thing" allow it to become present as ever more spotlights unite in brightening its qualities.

Making data available for engagement by other prejudices

Fifth, throughout my study I sought to provide access to the material on which I base my analysis so other readers may evaluate for themselves and through the grid of their own biases my handling of the data.

Conducting deductive-inductive data analysis

Sixth, I performed a mixed deductive-inductive analysis of my data. There would be no point in seeing my research as Gadamerian if I did not approach the data through categories drawn from Gadamer. Generating and applying these categories was the deductive move. However, a study would equally be non-Gadamerian if only the imposition of initial prejudices took place and the data had no chance to talk back. Thus I saw my initial categories as precisely that—initial, tentative, flexible, needing to change as the research proceeded and the data and prejudices continued to converse with each other. This was the inductive move.[5]

Performing exploratory research

Seventh, as I hope has become abundantly clear, the nature of my research was heuristic and exploratory. I sought more to ask fruitful questions in an exploratory mode than to achieve definitive answers.

Asking Gadamerian questions

Eighth, I set for myself a series of questions to ask as part of assessing to what extent Gadamer was applicable. The questions are engaged throughout the study as appropriate and provisional answers are summarized in my concluding chapter.

1. Is it possible to identify a "deep common accord" (Gadamer, 1976, 7) or "horizon" (Gadamer, 1994a, 306-307, 374-375) which makes contrasting prejudices intelligible to each other? This search for common accord was a quest for what shared framework, paradigm, or premises are required for holders of different prejudices even to make sense of the other's prejudice.

2. Are there prejudices or horizons so divergent they make "deep common accord" questionable?

3. What happens when an attempt such as this one is made to apply Gadamer? Does it work or not? Categories establishing and implementing criteria for success and failure are applied in chapters 3 and 4.

4. When failures to operate in a Gadamerian view of understanding occur, are they failures of praxis or Gadamerian theory? Especially chapters 5 and 6 explore this question.

THE CATEGORIES

Appendix B details the stages and theoretical background that led to establishing the categories whose implementation to conversation is comprehensively described in chapters 3 and 4. Treating Gadamerian thought as source of normative descriptions of genuine conversation, and aware of challenges which would eventually require comment, I established categories of success and failure.

Categories of conversational success

The categories of conversational success are (1) effective history producing commonality, (2) goodwill highlighting of prejudices as yours and mine, (3) awareness of finitude, (4) openness, (5) risking prejudices in relationship.

Categories of conversational failure

The failure categories are (1) effective history producing commonality; (2) antagonistic highlighting of prejudices as yours and mine; (3) certitude; (4) closure; (5) severing prejudices; (6) coercion.

Process and unit of analysis

My analytic process was guided by such resources as Emerson et al, who describe movement from "open coding," in which all categories of potential significance are noted (1995, 150-155); through selecting "core themes," in which themes of central importance to the research and potentially linked to each other are isolated (157-160), to more "focused coding," in which additional subcategories are pursued (160-162).

Early attempts were to analyze the conversations using sentences as the "recording units," the "basic unit of text to be classified (Weber, n.d, 21). This approach proved too microanalytic for my categories. Conversational turns likewise proved to be slices of data too narrow to be meaningfully categorized. The appropriate method for the categories proved to be discerning thematic units. The final wording of the categories presented above was achieved in this way, as I aimed to allow the data to define for me what it was actually thematically presenting to me. I then accepted the loss of precision entailed in de-emphasizing material in conversational turns that seemed to fit no meaningful thematic categories.

An alternate approach would have been to develop finer-grained analytic categories, but the Gadamer who himself says that "to make me into a sociologist is something no one will succeed in doing"[6] (1993, 265) simply does not provide tools adequate to such microanalysis. This study attempts to discover how far one can go in applying Gadamer. Then when difficulties arise, they are resolved not by attempting to make Gadamer more microanalytic than he is, but by discussing, particularly and in detail in chapter 5, the key challenges of applying Gadamer that become apparent in the sometimes-failed attempts to do so.

APPENDIX B:
THE PROGRESSION OF CATEGORIES

As part of enacting Gadamer and recording that performance, I offer here an account of the three stages through which I moved in establishing initial categories for applying Gadamer. I include this record because it is called for by the goal of not only summarizing my research results but also revealing how it unfolded. To do so is to show the messiness of the process, to include the backstage handling of sets and not only to show the polished play. Such a record illustrates key principles Gadamer insists describe the unfolding of human knowledge. As the narrative shows, my own work has moved forward in contingent steps, each step the result of finite and imperfect decisions made when at the many forks in the road the researcher chooses this path and not that, even while knowing that an argument for the other path could also have been made.

STAGE ONE
During the first stage I asked this early question: what tendencies are evident in the handling of prejudices seen in the data? My initial projection was that at least five tendencies might be identifiable (and indebted to Brockriede, 1972; Barnlund, 1979, as cited in Czubaroff; and Czubaroff, n.d.[1]), falling in three possible foci identified by Stewart and Thomas (1986): In comments on "dialogic listening" influenced by Gadamer (among others), Stewart and Thomas contend that listeners can focus on *my*, *your*, or *ours*. The *my* stance foregrounds my perspectives, viewpoints, prejudices and thus does not truly attend to the other. (Here they move closer to pathologizing "my" than does Gadamer, so committed to the productive aspects of prejudice). Stewart and Thomas argue that before deliberate efforts to move to other stances, the my stance is most common (181).

Then to transcend the my stance, some aim to nurture the *your* stance. Through this stance of empathic listening[2], one makes an effort to walk in another's shoes, to "get inside" another (181-183). However, though they value the "your" stance's fostering of openness to the other, Stewart and

252

Thomas believe this position is problematic. It is finally impossible to lay myself aside; thus a focus purely on the other is partly a fiction in which, even as I imagine myself into another, I remain grounded in my "own attitudes, expectations, past experiences, and world view" (182). This is congruent with Gadamer, who (see chapter 1) calls us to put *ourselves* in the other's position.

The ideal position is the *our* stance. Here neither "mine" nor "yours" is dissolved at the expense of the other. Rather, as mine and yours contribute to a common conversational project, ours emerges. Two features of the our stance particularly deserve mention. First, and again congruent with Gadamer's highlighting of play, it is open-ended and playful; its focus is not closure and certainty but the ongoing, buoyant creativity of participants who are mutually sculpting something new (184-187). Second, the our stance emerges "in front of." Although they are not irrelevant, the emphasis is not on the internal states "behind" the conversation from which conversation partners may draw contributions. Rather, insights emerging "between" conversational participants as they mutually address the subject matter before them are foregrounded (187-188).

The first two tendencies below, coercion and seduction, fall under the my stance. Either more actively and overtly or more seductively and covertly, each tendency highlights mine at the expense of yours. The third tendency, submission, falls under the your stance. Here the risk is loss of mine in an ultimately illusory adoption of yours. The final two tendencies work at ours. Principled love remains rooted in mine but actively seeks to respect and honor yours in the process. Dialogic love is an effort to move more fully toward co-creation of what is ours from what was initially mine and yours.

As will be seen, important in assessing each of the five tendencies is their handling of power and also finitude. What I mean by the latter is this: Gadamer stresses that the hermeneutic process requires awareness of the interpreter's finitude. Czubaroff and Whelan (1995) highlight this precept in their own effort to apply Gadamer to pedagogy. They suggest that such awareness is nurtured and marked by ability to see "the particularity of our perspectives and experiences and grasp that there are other possibilities of belief and experience." Awareness of finitude is accompanied by openness, curiosity, questioning, humility, and awareness of diversities in which my particularity is one of many options (8).

Here are the five tendencies placed under the my, your, or our stances.

"My" Stances

1. *Coercion.* Some, exemplifying Gadamer's "shadow" hermeneutics, may defend their own prejudices, actively attack prejudices of others, aim to censor or silence others, attempt coercively (Barnlund, 1972) to impose their own views. Coercers may operate through "Threats, intimidation, ridicule, sanctions" (Czubaroff, n.d., 9).

The coercer, contends Brockriede (1972, 3), intends to establish power over the other.

Awareness of finitude is lacking in the coercive stance, which is likely to emphasize the supposed universality of the coercer's perspective and to include "musts" and "oughts."

2. *Seduction.* Some may exploitatively (Barnlund, 1982, 204), seductively, selectively, and potentially deceptively enhance the appeal of their own prejudices and minimize the appeal of other prejudices. Seducers may offer "Subtle promises of reward, enticements, charm, deception. . . ." They may also withhold information—whether negative; about alternatives; or regarding self, intentions, methods (Czubaroff, n.d., 9). Brockriede includes deliberate use of such fallacies as "ignoring the question, begging the question, appeals to ignorance or to prejudice" (with prejudice here being used with common pejorative connotations rather than conveying Gadamer's ironic and positive twist) as well as "quoting out of context, misquoting an authority or witness, misrepresenting a factual situation, drawing unwarranted conclusions from evidence. . ." (1972, 4).

The seducer seeks power over the other but lulls him or her "through the argumentative equivalent of soft lights" (Brockriede, 1972, 4).

Missing again is evidence of awareness of finitude. However, the "musts" and oughts" of coercion are likely replaced by exclusions of alternatives which make the correctness of the presented view appear self-evident rather than imposed.

"YOUR" STANCE

3. *Submission.* As introduced above, the first sets of tendencies involve minimizing the tension between one's own and others' prejudices by affirming one's own against the other's. Submission tendencies reduce the tension by replacing one's own prejudices with another's. Such strategies may be rare but are conceivable and in Mennonite circles have sometimes even been encouraged as evidence that the individual accepts the norms of a group or its authorities. Mennonite historian C. J. Dyck (1993, 144) notes, for example, that for the Anabaptist from whom Mennonites descended "A key word in true community was *Gelassenheit*—meaning yieldedness, self-denial, trust." In addition, the Mennonite trait of humility, as elaborated on in relation to Schlabach, Liechty, and Brenneman in chapter 2, has strong affinities with the idea of submission.

Evidence might include a historically verifiable shift by the writer from one position to another, the writer's self-report that a position once held has been exchanged for another (of the genre, "How My Mind Has Changed"), or moves to adopt from another without awareness of or commitment to what is one's own. Submission does not indicate hermeneutic competence. Gadamer proposes that understanding requires a complex, dynamic fusion of or meaningful contact between horizons, not a simple foregrounding of another's stand at the expense of one's own.

The submitter willingly relinquishes power to the other. Rather than carrying certainty to an extreme, the submitter may carry awareness of finitude to an extreme. "I'm not sure," "I don't know," "You know better," may not be balanced by "I think," or "It seems to me," however tentative.

"OUR" STANCES

4. *Principled love.* The final two tendencies begin the hard work of maintaining two sets of prejudices in tension. Principled lovers are committed to handling their own prejudices and those of others sensitively and accurately. However, their primary aim is to persuade others of the value of their own prejudices. Missing is full implementation of dialogue. Principled lovers incorporate "honest, full report of relevant information and biases; 'heart' appeals consistent with the facts" and are "open to critical response" even as they show respect "for other points of view" (Czubaroff, n.d., 9). They may aim accurately to paraphrase positions which contrast with their own.

Although the principled lover's respect for the other softens the power-over aspects of the coercive and seductive stances, they remain present in the unilaterality of this tendency (Czubaroff, n.d., 7, 9).

Principled lovers have made significant strides toward awareness of finitude. They position their stance as one among many respectable options. However, they remain provisionally committed to the preferability of their position. They may say, "I know my prejudice is one among many, but I still see it as better than—"

5. *Dialogical love.* Those who manifest "openness to the other point of view, effort to understand, and seeking of critical response" (Czubaroff, n.d., 9) are dialogical lovers. They place mine and yours in conversation to create a new "between" which is ours. They show evidence of intuitive or explicit grasp of the Gadamerian call to risk initial prejudices through ability to incorporate a.) such traits of principled love as handling opposing prejudices accurately, respectfully, appreciatively; and b.) such added traits of dialogical love as efforts to improve, enhance, or enlarge one's initial prejudices through incorporating into them elements drawn from another's prejudices. Here "One listens with the desire to bring out the strength rather than the weakness of what is said—to find that which is different yet applicable to one's position" (Deetz, 1982b, 6-7, cited in Simons, n.d.).

Stewart and Thomas (1986) identify "Say more" and paraphrasing as among dialogic traits. "Say more" marks my encouraging you to continue speaking, clarifying, elaborating (190). Paraphrasing in dialogic situations goes beyond restating your position in my words. The addition is provided by attempting to answer, "Now what?" If we are together creating what is ours, then I not only aim to check whether I have heard you accurately, but probe what this hearing may contribute to our ongoing project (191-192).

Here power parity leading to "free assent to propositions" and establishing of truths "in an open environment" (Brockriede, 1972, 5-6) is present. Evident is a facilitative environment in which "Words are used to inform, to enlarge perspective, to deepen sensitivity, to remove external threat, to encourage independence of meaning" (Barnlund, 1972, 204).

Dialogical love is strongly aware of finitude. Openness, curiosity, questioning, humility, and awareness of diversity are evident. "I'm not sure's" and "don't know's" are accompanied by, "Let's together do the exciting work of probing this mystery or seeing what creative insights we can co-discover or create."

STAGE TWO

As I began to move closer to actual data analysis, I found the above categories problematic in two ways. First, implications of power were too quickly and easily assumed. I had partly to address power as a category but also partly to separate it out as a troublesome area of applying Gadamer (as detailed in chapter 6).

Second, I found many of the categories too fuzzy to be fully usable. Though drawing significantly on them and theory that undergirded them, I proposed to sharpen them into two sets of categories, one for probing successes of Gadamerian conversation, the other for identifying failures.

STAGE TWO CATEGORIES OF CONVERSATIONAL SUCCESS

Those categories characterizing successful Gadamerian conversation were these: awareness of finitude, initial focus on difference, prejudice, or "my"; subject matter sets agenda; openness to other; willingness to risk; readiness to dialogue; movement from "my" to what is "ours" and "between"; turning my and your prejudices into mutual resources for co-construction; focus on what is "in-front-of"; (implied) freedom from conversational constraints.

STAGE TWO CATEGORIES OF CONVERSATIONAL FAILURE

This was my own initial list of potential failure categories culled from asking what shadow hermeneutics, counter-hermeneutics, Gadamerian theory turned inside-out might look like: certitude; initial focus on difference, prejudice or "my" combined with final focus on difference, prejudice, or "my"; agenda imposed on subject matter; closure; rejection of risk; nondialogic; focus on what is "behind"; sharpening prejudice by contrasting one's own stance with opponent's; (implied) constraints on free conversation; possibly submission to "your."

STAGE THREE

By the time I began to interact with actual data from the Franconia conversation, I had already sharpened the stage one categories into those of stage two. The stage two categories were those I first applied to actual conversations. I attempted through the grid they provided to identify instances of them in the data. I found that the data both cooperated and resisted.

Categories of Conversational Success

On the cooperation side and in relation to the categories of successful Gadamerian conversation, much of the concern with prejudices, finitude, openness, and relationship seemed congruent with what I was seeing.

On the resistance side, I found that particularly those categories which were efforts to isolate the subject-matter orientation of the conversations bore little fruit. They or versions of them might well be important categories for studying other conversations, but they proved not particularly useful in the Franconia conversations because these interchanges were already, by definition, determined by a given subject matter. I found few instances where it seemed fruitful to determine that here the subject matter was guiding the play of conversation, here not. What was important was not so much whether the subject matter was in control—it generally was—but whether participants were opening or closing themselves to its claims. Such determination seemed better achieved through other categories.

Although the decision to handle the subject matter in this way seems justified in relation to this particular data, it may also point to challenges in applying Gadamer. If it was difficult in this context to find instances meaningfully categorizable as control by the subject matter, to what can this be attributed? Is the difficulty in applying this central Gadamerian precept due in this case only to the fact that if the subject matter by definition controlled the conversation, it proved a superfluous category? Or may it be that in any conversation, whether ostensibly controlled by the subject matter or not, discerning this control is a very tricky matter? Such questions are addressed in chapter 5 along with assessment of other challenges of applying Gadamer.

Amid awareness of challenges which would eventually require comment, in the end I revised the stage two success categories to the following, detailed in subsequent chapters: (1) effective history producing commonality, (2) goodwill highlighting of prejudices as yours and mine, (3) awareness of finitude, (4) openness, (5) risking prejudices in relationship.

Added to the original list is effective history. Other categories remain recognizable but with revisions. Initial focus on difference, prejudice, or "my" becomes goodwill highlighting of prejudices as yours and mine. The aim here was to find a way to signal, in some contrast to Stewart and Thomas's devaluing of the "my" stance, that the *initial* focus on differences or prejudices is potentially positive, congruent with Gadamer's positive view of prejudice. This is the function of "highlighting" prejudices and distinguishing between your and my initial vantage points. For this positive assessment to carry, however, the highlighting must be done with "good will"; otherwise there is no distinction from a failed highlighting of prejudices, described below as "antagonistic." As my study shows, these are complex matters and tricky distinctions to apply, given that the line between positive and negative highlighting of prejudices is potentially such a fine one.

Those categories which originally particularly sought insight regarding the handling of the subject matter—and had to do with "between," co-construction, and "in-front-of"—have been combined into prejudices-in-relationship. Freedom from constraints is addressed in chapter 6 in relation to issues of power.

STAGE THREE CATEGORIES OF CONVERSATIONAL FAILURE

Once I applied the stage two failure categories to a first assessment of the Franconia conversations, I concluded that the resistance of the data to being viewed in precisely these terms suggested the need for these revised failure categories: (1) effective history producing commonality; (2) antagonistic highlighting of prejudices as yours and mine; (3) certitude; (4) closure; (5) severing prejudices; (6) coercion.

As before, and for the same reasons, I dropped or modified the categories most related to the role played by the subject matter. I also eliminated entirely the stage one "your" stance and stage two "submission to your" category. Stewart and Thomas's belief that some conversational moves can be so characterized remains persuasive to me, particularly given the importance of submission in Mennonite tradition. However, I detected no instances of submission in the Franconia conversations and thus chose to let this resistance of the data to such categories carry the day. The first category, effective history producing commonality, emerged late in the process, when dissertation committee readers pointed out that if a major thrust of my study was to show that even amid failure to converse there is "deep common accord," then paradoxically this category of success must accompany even categories of failure.

APPENDIX C:
DRAFT PROPOSAL FOR A GERMANTOWN MENNONITE CHURCH RELATIONSHIP WITH FRANCONIA MENNONITE CONFERENCE

INTRODUCTION

In April 1995, concern over the presence of gay and lesbian members at Germantown Mennonite Church (GMC) led Franconia Conference (FMC) delegates to give GMC the status of associate member for two years. This initiated a two-year discernment process. Through it, Christ has revealed to us that GMC and other FMC congregations have substantial unity of faith and purpose. Christ has also given us a clearer understanding that serious areas of disagreement remain unresolved.

GMC and its supporters in FMC focus on the unity and prefer that GMC be restored to full membership. Those who see GMC's position as a threat to unity prefer that FMC's relationship with GMC be completely terminated. Many others find themselves seeking a "third way."

Full inclusion or complete exclusion need little explanation. But we offer a "third way" for consideration by the delegates. This third way seeks to embody Christ's call to maintain both unity and purity of faith. It suggests a GMC-FMC relationship that recognizes both the integrity of GMC's faith journey and the faithful concerns of a majority of FMC congregations that believe GMC errs in one important aspect of faith.

CONFESSION AND AFFIRMATION

In a spirit of brokenness, we pray for God's mercy and for the Holy Spirit to enable us to pursue healing and holiness in our relationship. Our recent history reflects that GMC has felt betrayed by the Conference in its selective attention regarding the congregation's faithfulness to Conference actions. On the other hand, the Conference has felt betrayed by GMC for moving in a direction that did not have the Conference's full sanction. Out of this brokenness of our communication, trust, and social isolation, we seek to find unity of purpose and spirit.

Both Conference and GMC affirm the importance of our relationship. GMC values the nurture, resources, and mutual accountability that can come from a body bound together with a common purpose of growing in faithfulness to Christ and the gospel. FMC recognizes the continued enrichment of the urban challenge that GMC offers and acknowledges that many aspects of GMC's vision may serve the larger body as we enter the twenty-first century. We have many rich gifts to benefit one another. In this light, the differences between GMC and FMC may seem small.

Yet these differences are not inconsequential. GMC, affirming the earlier FMC call to be "a people of invitation," welcomes persons of faith and commitment to Jesus Christ including some who are living with a partner of the same gender. GMC believes it would be unfaithful and destructive to revoke the membership of persons who actively contribute to its spiritual life. On the other hand, the majority of FMC congregations believe it would be unfaithful to continue to sanction membership for people who are gay and lesbian.

Persons from both sides of the issue wish to respect the conviction of those who, out of conscience, hold a different position. Both share a concern for faithfulness, authority of the Scriptures, holiness, and holy living. In this apparent impasse, GMC takes inspiration from Paul's counsel to an equally divided Roman church to welcome those who are "weak in faith" but "not to doubtful disputations" (Rom. 14:1). Though, as sinners in common, we may not agree who is the "weaker" party, we can seek a relationship that does not center on disputation.

PROPOSED FORM OF RELATIONSHIP

1. GMC will continue its non-voting association with FMC. This associate membership frees from close relationship with GMC those congregations who feel their own ministry and integrity are compromised by close ties to GMC. It allows a caring liaison between GMC and FMC congregations who feel nurtured by ongoing ties.

Although it allows GMC to discern and pursue ministry in its context, it acknowledges FMC's firm and continuing opposition to including gay and lesbian people in congregational membership.

2. GMC and the other congregations of FMC will continue to be a resource to each other by:

a. remaining open to dialogue with those who desire it and respecting those whose faith leads them to discontinue such dialogue.

b. continuing to search the Scriptures, welcome counsel, and maintain a teachable spirit on issues of sexuality.

c. continuing to support the ministries of FMC in prayer, gifts, and communication to others about the Conference.

APPENDIX C / 261

3. GMC will honor this associate membership in the following ways:

a. GMC delegates will not vote at FMC Assembly.

b. GMC will clearly acknowledge that its inclusion of gay and lesbian members is not consistent with the FMC position.

c. GMC will not ask FMC or other FMC congregations to adopt its viewpoints on homosexuality. In FMC-sponsored meetings and Assemblies and in FMC congregations, GMC will address its views on homosexuality only by invitation.

4. FMC will honor this association in the following ways:

a. FMC will provide an overseer for GMC and include GMC in Philadelphia area cluster activities.

b. FMC will invite GMC to participate in Conference events (e.g., seminars, retreats, etc.) on a non-voting basis, and provide access to its Resource Center.

c. FMC's Leadership Commission may, at its discretion, continue to hold the credentials of GMC's ordained pastors and participate in the credentialing of future GMC pastors but will not be compelled to do so.

We recognize that this association does not fully satisfy the deepest concerns of GMC or other FMC congregations. Yet we desire that FMC and GMC will together experience more fully God's intention for the church of Jesus Christ through this relationship. In it, we recognize opportunities for some mutual accountability and growth, while not ignoring the important difference that exists concerning homosexuality. May the Spirit of God guide us to welcome one another respectfully while putting behind us distracting disputations.

Overseer Advisory Committee:
Willis Miller, Chair
Hubert Schwartentruber, Ovsr.
Libby Caes
Joe Haines
John Ruth
Carl Yusavitz

Germantown Cong. Reps.:
James L. Derstine, Pastor
Richard Lichty, Intm. As. Past.
Anita Bender
George Hatzfeld
John Linscheid
RaMona Stahl
Tina Swartz Burkholder

NOTES

AUTHOR'S PREFACE

1. See for example my description of such interaction in King (1997).

2. As Stanley Hauerwas delights in stressing in such sources as 1994a and 1994b, where he opposes "the hegemony of liberal discourses" in academic settings such as his at Duke and mine at Temple.

CHAPTER 1

1. See note 4 below for explanation of why *Gospel Herald*, still the denominational publication of the Mennonite Church at the time the first phases of this study were being conducted, ceased publication.

2. Due to maintenance of focus on Gadamerian analysis, only occasional explicit links with the literatures of rhetoric and speech communication are made, but the implicit links are numerous. Williams (1995) surveys over 100 speech communication sources, many of them background reading for this study, which interact with Gadamer. Gadamer himself (1997a, 30) connects his understanding of hermeneutics with the field of rhetoric and notes, for example, the important affinities with his thought present in Perelman and Olbrechts-Tyteca (1969).

Implications of his hermeneutics intersect with the rhetorical or rhetoric-related thought of Arnett (1986b), Bineham (1990, 1994, 1995), Brockriede (1972), Brummett (1976, 1982, 1990a, 1990b), Burke (1969a,b), Fish (1989), Gearheart (1979), Hollinger (1985a,b), Kontopolos (1995), Margolis (1995a,b), McKerrow (1989), Orr (1978, 1990), Perelman and Olbrechts-Tyteca (1969), Rorty (1979, 1989), Scott (1967, 1973, 1976), Simons (1985, 1989, 1990), Stewart (1978), Stewart and Thomas (1986), Toulmin (1964), Warnke (1987, 1993), White (1984, 1987)—to name just a few.

Certainly these scholars are not of a single mind nor are all rhetoricians; the details of their concerns vary dramatically and at a good many points place them at odds with each other. However, each contributes to a view of understanding, communication, rhetoric, or philosophy in which differences are respected yet woven into larger horizons through modes of thought having affinities with Gadamer's emphases. Perhaps it can at least safely be said that in their varying ways they unite in affirming this: first, transcendent foundations of knowledge either do not exist or cannot be fully known. Rather, knowledge is historically situated.

Second, in the absence of transcendent or invariant foundations of knowledge there are nevertheless broad fields of thought and reasoning, or areas of the probable and tacitly assumed, which enable communication to unfold with some coherence and success. Practical reason and wisdom—*phronesis*—strongly shaped by the history and context in which it finds itself, inhabit this region of that which is probable, assumed, or agreed-on, but not provable. Rhetoric is one of the principle languages this practical wisdom speaks. Gadamer himself connects phronesis and rhetoric to his hermeneutic project, noting that "Rhetoric from oldest tradition has been the only advocate of a claim to truth that defends the probable . . . and that which is convincing to ordinary reason. . ." (1976, 24).

3. The Franconia conversations on which this study is based took place April 1997 in three eastern Pennsylvania locations where three cluster meetings—geographically-organized sub-units of that total delegate body empowered to make decisions (as detailed under note 4, below)—were hosted. Cluster one was hosted in an aging church building in a relatively rundown urban neighborhood. This cluster includes Germantown Mennonite Church and delegates from other urban or semi-urban congregations. Eighteen participants, including six Germantown observers, were present. Except for two African-Americans, all were white.

Cluster two was hosted in one of the largest and most prominent congregations in Franconia Conference, located roughly at the Conference's geographic center. Present were thirty-six participants from the largest congregations in the Conference. Except for one Latino, all were white. Cluster three was held in a large and historic congregation located just east of the Conference's geographic center. Present were thirty-two participants, all white.

Three sets of transcripts totalling about eighty typed, double-spaced pages were captured through my attending the meetings with a co-recorder trained in taking field notes. Tape recording was forbidden due to the perception of Franconia leaders that the conversations were so sensitive recording might lead to unwanted distortions. In addition, attendance at the clusters considered most polarized was not possible. Leaders selected for my attendance the three clusters they considered best able to manage the presence of observers without undue impact. Though I have no reason to believe these clusters yielded dramatically skewed data, the fact that they were considered among the least polarized suggests that any tendencies toward conversational failure observed here were likely even stronger in other clusters.

In the absence of taping, my goal was to take notes as much as possible non-interpretively, aiming to record word-for-word all conversational turns. In practice, as is true for any transcription of this nature, recording of every word proved impossible. However, in general all the words I considered key were recorded precisely as spoken and typically in such a way that syntax was maintained. Primarily omitted were the small linking words—the and's, the's, and so forth—which can be inferred from context when not present in a transcript.

Immediately following each meeting, I spent up to fifteen hours reconstructing the conversations from my notes, from context, from cross-checking with my co-recorder's notes, and in a few cases from memory. Despite such care, inevitably many decisions, particularly in relation to punctuation, were interpretive, even if hopefully minimally so. And the impossibility of recording every word, especially those which seemed redundant, led to production of transcripts which are surely slightly more polished than the more ragged actual conversations.

On the other hand, I intended to observe such criteria for sound fieldnote production and ethnographic recording as described by Emerson et al (1995, especially chs. 2, 3, 4) as well as by Spradley (1989) and by Lofland and Lofland (1984). Aiming to preserve actual wording, syntax, and style of speech led to transcripts which are as accurate as possible in the absence of tapes. It is doubtful, in light of my Gadamerian approach, that tape-based transcripts would have provided significantly better data.

As a general rule, names of participants in the conversations have been changed. In a few instances, it has been nearly impossible fully to mask identities, such as when a participant in a conversation interacts with his own on-the-record written statements (as in Miller, 1997). In addition, the analysis of certain conversational turns would make little sense without identifying that the speaker is from Germantown Mennonite Church. Here also names have been changed to conceal the exact identity of the speaker, but the Germantown relationship has been revealed.

Generally material taken from the conversations is in quotation marks, indicating that within the limits described above, a Franconia participant is being directly quoted. Occasionally a block quote, for instance, may include a few phrases not enclosed in quotation marks. Here I felt confident enough of what was said to describe it but not to treat it as direct quotation.

4. For more on the conference/congregational polity of the Mennonite Church, the Mennonite denomination on which this study focuses, see Stutzman (1993). As he notes, "Twenty-one district conferences comprise the Mennonite Church in the U.S. and Canada. The conferences are primarily made up of congregations in the same geographical regions" (368).

The structures Stutzman describes remained in place during much of this writing but were changing as a merger of two separated denominations, the Mennonite Church and General Conference Mennonite Church, was being completed, with many new structures being formally ratified by 2001. Early evidence of the merger is found in the discontinued publication of the *Gospel Herald*, cited often in these pages, as of January 1998. In anticipation of full merger, the denominational periodicals of the Mennonite and General Conference Mennonite churches were integrated just as data gathering for this study was being completed. *The Mennonite*, the resulting integrated periodical, was first published in February 1998.

In Franconia Conference, congregations have considerable autonomy to direct their own affairs. However, each congregation sends delegates to bi-annual decision-making assemblies. There decisions can be made—as in the Germantown case—regarding the terms congregations must honor to maintain Conference affiliation. When an egregious violation of statements or doctrines considered important by the conference takes place, the conference has the authority, ultimately through appropriate majorities of delegate votes, to take action against the offenders, with excommunication being perhaps the most severe penalty.

5. Based on a computer search of such databases as *Communication Index*, *Sociological Abstracts, Inc.*, *Philosophers's Index*, several years of immersion in the primary and secondary literature of philosophical hermeneutics, and the corroborating statement by Williams that she is aware of no "empirical research which specifically labels itself as 'Gadamerian'" (1995, 6-7).

6. Gadamer himself has worked at application (as in 1992 and 1996). However, even Gadamer's applications remain relatively abstract, certainly more abstract than the study I am attempting here.

7. These and other splits and details of Mennonite history are examined in the four-volume Mennonite Experience in America series: MacMaster, 1985; Schlabach, 1988; Juhnke, 1990; Toews, 1996.

8. Although he also often notes contrasts between his and Heidegger's thought, here as at many points Gadamer is deeply indebted to Heidegger, as he frequently notes (see for instance Gadamer, 1976; 198-229; 1994; 1994a, 265-271; 1997, 7-8). In addition, Bruns (1992), Caputo (1987), Weinsheimer (1985), Warnke (1987), and many of the essayists in Wright (1990) and Wachterhauser (1994) are among the innumerable commentators on Gadamer who could be cited in this regard.

9. Though his comments pertain more to Dilthey, a hermeneut Gadamer both drew on and attempted to move beyond, E. T. Gendlin helps clarify how the process of fusion and understanding can be perceived to work:

> Dilthey held that we never really have the same understanding as the author had. If we understand a work at all, we understand it *better* than its author did. We must create the author's process out of our own, thereby augmenting both. In our terms we can say that they *cross*: some of each becomes *implicit* in the other. The author's statements do not change, but *implicitly* they now contain our own experience as well. So they constitute a "better" understanding than the author's. . . . (1997, 14)

Gendlin, who notes that "Dilthey's point is largely lost today," appears to prefer Dilthey's formulation to Gadamer's. He contends that "People follow Gadamer who says we always understand another person *differently*, as if understanding had to be the same or different." Gendlin adds that "Gadamer does not mean that we can only misunderstand, but to say what he wants requres the kind of terms we are developing" (14).

Though Gendlin explains well one way of conceptualizing a fusion of horizons, it is not quite clear why he thinks Dilthey more helpful. As I understand Gadamer, he means to say roughly what Gendlin wants him to say but thinks he does not say, which is indeed that understanding is not duplication of an author's original meanings but a productive crossing of the horizons of both original speaker and interpreter.

10. See Caputo (1987, 112); Chen (1987); Gadamer (1994a, 566-571, 1994b); Habermas (1987, 1994); Misgeld (1991); Nicholson (1991); Schott (1991), as well as other sources noted in chapter 6.

11. See Appendix A for details of how these Gadamerian precepts then shaped my study and its methods.

CHAPTER 2

1. As it is put by John Ruth in *Maintaining the Right Fellowship* (1984). The title of this history of Franconia Conference derives from Ruth's perception that the concern to maintain a rich, satisfying community *and* the "right" one pose a tension present at the very core of the Conference and throughout its history—beginning, ironically enough, with the founding of the conference by the establishment of Germantown Mennonite Church in 1683.

2. From this point forward clusters are identified as cluster one, C1; cluster two, C2; cluster three, C3; also, Franconia Conference is often referred to as FC. I concluded that a formal comparison and contrast of the three clusters would constitute over-analysis of the data, particularly because clusters two and three were too similar for comparisons to yield significant results. Yet it seems worth noting that Germantown Mennonite, the congregation whose actions triggered the discussions, belongs to C1 and is represented by delegates in attendance there. Throughout my reporting on the conversations, I *do* nonsystematically note contrasts between this cluster, the only one lacking strong prejudices toward exclusion, and the other two.

3. See Snyder (1995, 374).

4. See MacMaster (1985, 46-49).

5. See Dyck (1993); Snyder (1995).

CHAPTER 3

1. A fuller record of avenues of inquiry not finally pursued can be found in Appendix B, where I record the progression in my development of the Gadamerian categories whose application I describe in chapter 3.

2. In clarifying his use of the term *horizonal*, through which he summarizes his understanding of the philosophical implications of the historicization of human life and thought, Margolis both joins and distances himself from Gadamer:

> I use the term more or less in Gadamer's sense, without commitment to his own themes of authenticity, the universal poet's voice, the "classical," the scaled-down adherence to Heidegger's conceptual orientation, or anything of the kind. (1995, 337)

3. As confirmed on copyright page, this text and all Bible quotations in this study are taken from the *New Revised Standard Version of the Bible* (NRSV).

4. See Swartley for a Mennonite affirmation of this multivocality, which leads him to note that one reason Christians disagree on many issues is that

"the Bible itself gives mixed signals, especially on the surface of the text." Although Swartley appears concerned not to implicate God in this diversity, he does unhesitatingly acknowledge the role of history in creating it. He argues that the diversity is "due not to the nature of God but to the fact that divine revelation comes into and through history and culture" (1983, 203). He notes as well the diversity of models for interpreting this diverse book (ch. 5).

5. Turns discussed in such resources as Bernstein (1983), Bertens (1995), Best and Kellner (1991), Dickens and Fontana (1994), Rosenau (1992), Simons (1989, 1990 and of course in countless resources in that countless set of tributaries which in their varying ways feed the great river known as postmodernism. Also pertinent are such Anabaptist treatments of postmodernism as found in the following sources, which are part of a growing body of literature making Anabaptist prejudices an integral part of conversations about postmodernism and how to live faithfully with it: Biesecker-Mast and Biesecker-Mast (2000), King (1990, 1997, 2000), and Weaver (2000). Clearly Gadamer's thought began to move in what some might label at least a postmodern direction long before postmodernism(s) recognizably emerged, so Gadamer's lifelong concerns have not so much been shaped by contemporary postmodernism as have fed some of its tributaries.

6. The discussion here being analyzed has other interesting features. Noteworthy, for instance, is the interchange regarding whether the church better fits the analogy of parent, family, or brotherhood. Here and elsewhere metaphors and images are sprinkled throughout the conversations and help structure them. However, even as I point this out as a conversational feature of interest from other theoretical perspectives (such as the analysis of metaphor which is a specialty of Lakoff and Johnson, 1980; and Lakoff, 1996), I suggest that Gadamer does not provide tools for "thick" analyses at this level of discourse.

CHAPTER 4

1. Such reasoning also reflects challenges of applying Gadamer to be elaborated in chapter 5, including questions of how goodwill is discerned and evaluated and how ambiguous statements are to be assessed.

2. Whether this "slippery slope" stance is an accurate reading of consequences is not the point here, but it does foreshadow an issue to be addressed in chapter 5: can Gadamerian openness be structured in such a way as to recognize merit in the concern to maintain boundaries, or forms of closure?

CHAPTER 5

1. This is just a sampling of recent Mennonite peace resources. The *Herald Press Catalog* (2000-2001), which lists resources available from the official Mennonite publisher, includes under "Peace Concerns" 34 books in print and scatters throughout the catalogue scores of other books that include comments on peace.

2. The depth of the concern is attested to in Peachey, 1996b; J. D. Weaver; 1996, V. Weaver, 1996.

3. Of course here and throughout this study the possibility that limitations discussed are not Gadamer's but mine must be kept in mind. While reading, in the interchanges included in Hahn (1997), Gadamer's many responses to critical assessments of his work, I have been struck by the sheer scope and power of Gadamer's thought and by his ability to offer responses it would not have occurred to me to give. Surely at times Gadamer himself could capably defend ground I have ceded to his critics. Thus I assume my own thought is by definition in regular need of the growth Gadamer calls for and demonstrates at levels of mastery exceeding my own.

4. As mentioned in chapter one, another example of a rhetorical approach which places priority on "highlighting instabilities of discourses on controversial public issues" (1997, 30) rather than, in hermeneutic fashion, seeking the commonalities that unite more stable interpretive communities is provided by Smith and Windes (1997; 2000).

5. This is not only an issue for Franconia exclusivists. Any who champion standpoints on truth independent of tradition are likely to find themselves in tension with Gadamer here. Warnke sees Okin for instance, as seeking a tradition-independent standpoint when she assumes ability to find a stance somehow outside tradition from which to criticize theories (such as Gadamer's), which through relying on "'shared understandings' . . . reveal their tendencies to reinforce patriarchy. . ." (Okin, 1989). With Gadamer, Warnke contends that even the stance from which Okin criticizes a tradition has somehow been yielded up by the tradition (1993a, 1994).

I share this perspective—but also believe the challenge for the Gadamerian faced with claims to standpoint-independent truth is how to remain open to them. The Gadamerian temptation is to aim overly quickly to trump such positions through the argument that all standpoint-independent claims are after all tradition-bound. Gadamerians openness risks closure to the possible validity of *any* closures.

6. Among those who charge relativism are Donald Rothberg (1986), who sees truth for Gadamer as "located in the consensus between interpreter and object, in the acceptance of the validity claims of the object by the interpreter" (357). He contends that this pointing toward truth is not adequately theorized, for several reasons. First, Gadamer makes inadequate provision for distinguishing false from true prejudices (357-358).

Second, through his concept of the "anticipation of completeness," Gadamer gives "privileged status to the object" to that other we are seeking to understand and before which we place our prejudices at risk. Rothberg wonders, however, if this privileging of the object can be taken to be operative in all moves toward understanding—such as conversation "between two persons." But if the object is not privileged, then from where may anything called "truth" be derived (358-359)? Finally, why should it be assumed that, whatever fusion of horizons results when prejudices clash and attempts are made to enlarge them, this process "moves toward truth"? (359). Rothberg concludes that though such problems may be answerable through further "extension of certain aspects of Gadamer's work," they are serious and do plague Gadamer's thought (360).

Another critic is Karl-Otto Apel. As Apel himself notes, Apel's lifework has involved a running conversation with Gadamer regarding Apel's preference for "transcendental" hermeneutics over Gadamer's version (1997, 67ff). Apel is convinced that despite its many valuable contributions to his own work, Gadamer's thought wrongly locates "the question of the *validity* of understanding in a *temporal ontology* of understanding as a *truth-happening*"; rather, validity must be sought through "*regulative ideas* for a *normative* orientation of understanding." (70-71).

Apel believes Gadamer's approach wrongly collapses the distinction between that form of truth (the *aletheia* version Gadamer derives from Heidegger) which is disclosed only through what is historical, and "the *always already* recognizable norms" which comprise the "fore-structure" or foreknowledge in which Gadamer's (or Heidegger's or Wittgenstein's) discussion of foreknowledge as an effect of history itself unfolds. Apel argues that through philosophical analysis of the very conditions that make such discourse possible can be discerned "universally valid" regulative norms without which discourse could not proceed (85-90).

Apel is not simplistically charging Gadamer with relativism but is restating from another angle Rothberg's concern that Gadamer's handling of validity and truth is problematic. Apel's similar worry is thàt Gadamer's radical historicism in the end risks leaving him trapped in whatever tradition he initially begins to converse and the truths it makes available. Apel, in contrast, thinks he can provide "universal norms of critically understanding and judging traditions independently of these very traditions" (85).

In response, Gadamer doubts any such vision of universal norms as Apel dreams of can be implemented. "It would be just as likely," he memorably comments, "that a stabilization of the world's climate could occur by means of a type of global air conditioning." Whatever universal norms may in theory be abstractable from historicized existence cannot, Gadamer contends, sustain such existence. The philosopher's rarefied understanding of such norms is not comparable to whatever truths must be sustained by "the lived solidarity that is alive or should be alive in every culture" (1997b, 97).

In addition, Gadamer stresses that there can be no universal perspective, because "One perspective darkens another. A universal perspective comprising everything is a contradiction in itself which at most the metaphysical concept of God could assume." A perspective is an angle of vision, an angle shaped by history which can be called a prejudice. Except possibly for God, there can be no prejudice which combines all prejudices and thus ceases to be one (95-96).

7. See similar arguments in Madison, 1992; Rothberg, 1986; Steuber, 1994; Wachterhauser, 1994; Warnke, 1986, 1990.

8. Bullock notes that not only Gadamer but also Jacques Derrida (as in 1972) uses play "to denote a collapsing of the subject-object dichotomies that characterize the modern world" (Bullock, 1996, 157-159). But Bullock observes that for Gadamer "play manifests a way of being" and thus "con-

veys 'truth,' " but Derrida, as Bullock cites him, sees "no closure beyond the ceaseless play of dissemination" (Derrida, 266, cited in Bullock, 159).

9. Here again the types of issues raised in the Warnke-Okin debate (see above, note 5) deserve attention. The quest is for an understanding of Gadamer that sees spaces in his thought for seeking to affirm, for instance, feminist values or a variety of concerns for social justice requiring the closure entailed in drawing certain lines here and not there.

CHAPTER 6

1. In a classic study of power, Steve Lukes (1974) offers a variety of definitions. At least two dimensions of power, among the many Lukes addresses, deserve mention: first, at one basic level power is power over or against, power in some way to impose on or obstruct the freedom to act or to be of another; second, power has institutional and societal manifestations, including the power to set or eliminate agenda, the power to set procedures, the power of ideology to form and constrain thought.

2. This is partly because there is no simple way to reconcile Gadamer and Foucault, particularly for application. I do believe they can mutually enlarge each other's thought and have taken a few steps in that direction in this chapter. In addition, a strong effort by Kögler to work at a critical (Foucault) hermeneutics (Gadamer) deserves mention. Kögler does a masterful job of probing some of the vulnerabilities in Gadamer I have been addressing in this chapter, then similarly criticizes Foucault before finally moving toward integrating their strengths in what he views as a "situated, yet not power-blind form of reflexivity" (1999:275).

However, even as I conclude that work to integrate Foucault and Gadamer is likely to bear continuing fruit, their "first principles" are dramatically different (a contrast evident in Foucault's rejection of hermeneutics as starting point, as explored in Dreyfus and Rabinow, 1983). In light of this, I conclude that the most productive way to apply them to a given database, at least given the current state of both Gadamerian and Foucaultian studies, is to give one or the other primacy—then explore, as in this chapter, what is thus gained and lost. That is why I have aimed briefly to point toward potential gains of starting with Foucault even as I now move toward examining the gains of working largely with Gadamer.

3. See also related comments in Gadamer (1984).

4. The issue of unmasking also helps explain my decision to make Gadamer rather than, say, Foucault, the primary resource for my Franconia analysis. Gadamer's hermeneutics seems closer to addressing life as the Franconia participants experience it than would have been the case had Foucault's anti-hermeneutic thought been foregrounded.

If Franconia participants read this study, at least some are likely to perceive distance between their experience and even my Gadamerian treatment, despite my concern to honor Deetz' call (elaborated in Appendix A) for a method that allows "the object to object" (1982a, 143). But they would likely experience considerably more alienation from an approach that treated their entire conversations as produced by the effects of a power so radical it has constructed even their perception of themselves as subjects. This is not to say such an analysis would lack merit; indeed it would likely generate fascinating and productive insights. It is simply to point to the likely loss, in addition to any gain, that would result from proceeding so far in an unmasking direction.

5. Rather than risk over-emphasizing tangential matters, I have aimed in commenting on distinctions between and interpenetrations of rhetoric and hermeneutics to maintain focus on those aspects of the discussion particularly pertinent in relation to Gadamer and my project. However, if my aim were to examine more comprehensively the relationship between rhetoric and hermeneutics, there would be other significant matters to consider.

Among them is the question of whether Gadamer's views here gloss over large issues. This is a question posed by the dissatisfaction of some analysts with any picture of rhetoric and hermeneutics that permits fuzzy overlaps. Calvin O. Schrag, for one, wants sharper distinctions than Gadamer draws. "Surely there is a close connection between hermeneutics and rhetoric," he contends, "Yet the one cannot be simply analyzed into the other. They overlap, they interconnect, they supplement each other; but one cannot be reduced to the other" (1997, 136).

Paul Ricouer likewise presses for clear demarcations. He sees rhetoric as "the art of arguing with a view to persuading an audience that one opinion is preferable to its rival" (1997, 71). Meanwhile he prefers that hermeneutics be viewed as interpreting texts in the absence of the original author to discover "new dimensions of reality." Ricoeur does not rule out a "hermeneutics of conversation" in which the goal is mutual understanding but thinks this "would only be a pre-hermeneutics" because oral exchange eludes the complexities that arise in texts when the speaker is no longer present and thus is severed from her or his intentions (67).

Schrag cites approvingly Ricouer's (1997, 71) definitions of rhetoric and hermeneutics. He wants to retain the distinctions to highlight the superior ability of rhetoric to foreground and manage "the role of the other and the play of differences," in contrast to the preferability of hermeneutics when the concern is to show, as we have so often seen Gadamer aiming to do, that "Even in the throes of disagreement, partisans of dialogue and partisans of agonistics continue to face each other as they announce to the world, "We cannot agree!" (1997, 137).

Altieri too draws sharp lines. He explicitly aims to "put pressure on the ease with which Gadamer tries to link the domains of rhetoric and hermeneutics, admitting as different only the demand for immediate effects basic to the rhetor's actions." He stresses that "hermeneutic theory dwells on how we can hear what the other is saying. . . ." In contrast, "most rhetorical theory occupies itself with how an author can move or position those auditors so that they will be disposed to perform certain actions" (1997, 95).

Such perspectives do help delimit what is sometimes fuzzy in Gadamer. They also cast in bolder relief than Gadamer does the danger that Gadamer's hermeneutic bias permits him not to notice the options for managing difference perhaps more available in a rhetoric less allied with hermeneutics.

6. Here another question posed by the rhetoric-hermeneutics interplay comes into view: does Gadamer's handling of the relationship participate in that larger undertheorizing of power to which I have devoted so much attention in this chapter? This is a frequent theme in a special issue of the journal *Studies in the Literary Imagination* (1995) devoted to the relationship between rhetoric and hermeneutics. For example, Thomas Crusius sees insight in Gadamer's faith in the common accord that underlies every disagreement but believes that through his vision of the ineradicable difference of—yet relationship between—identification and division, Kenneth Burke more adequately accounts for the tensions between a hermeneutics of trust (such as implied in Gadamer's stance on common accord), and of suspicion (ever alert to the machinations and insinuations of power). Crusius concludes that

> The tension is permanently beyond resolution. There is no way out of the conflict of interpretations, no master critical theory that can draw the lines securely, no metahermeneutical synthesis that can make the voices sing in harmony. In certain contexts we may in fact wish to distinguish hermeneutics from rhetoric. Yet interpretation *is* rhetoric, and vice-versa. The process of interpretive conflict is rhetorical, and resolution, insofar as there is any, is also rhetorical. What counts is who best persuades. (89)

Note the insistence that hermeneutics and rhetoric in the end are inseparable if distinguishable in theory. Note also the links with the chapter 5 valuing of Burke's nimbleness as rhetorical analyst.

Stephen Mailloux, without explicitly taking on Gadamer, at a minimum aims in a different and more power-oriented direction when he calls for a "rhetorical hermeneutics" centered on power (1989) in which the focus is "less on the interaction between reader and text than on the relations among historical interpreters arguing about and otherwise using texts in specific cultural conversations at particular historical moments" (1995, 55).

Krista Radcliffe wants materialist-feminist redefinitions of rhetoric and hermeneutics which

> offer marginalized groups the possibility of redefining their commonly perceived margins as viable centers. Likewise, this authority would challenge dominant groups to expose or reveal their own assumptions about where the center is located and to critique how this location constructs possibilities and limitations, both personal and cultural. Such gendered listening-in-the-world can help each of us to articulate and negotiate our own cultural positions with others, to recognize the kinds of truths that must be challenged, and to remember that such processes are ongoing. (73)

Note again the combination of both articulation (rhetoric) and listening (hermeneutics) in the context of power.

As can be seen in some of the above quotes, if there is on the one hand a greater inclination than in Gadamer to underline power, on the other hand the tendency to theorize rhetoric and hermeneutics as so closely intertwined as to be nearly inseparable remains strong—and perhaps in need of the correctives suggested by the commentators summarized in note 5. Nevertheless, repeatedly rhetoric does emerge as the speaking side and hermeneutics the listening side of a continuing dance. The criticisms of Gadamer continue to deserve attention but the congruence with Gadamer is also noteworthy.

CHAPTER 7

1. As reported in *Franconia Conference News* (Germantown loses membership, 1997), "The final vote generated a flurry of secular news coverage."

2. In their own analysis of cultural conversation on issues of sexuality, Smith and Windes contend that "Nowhere in either the gay or antigay interpretive packages does one find the notion that the opposition consists of another set of agents with justified grievances against society." They conclude that "Refusal to acknowledge any similarity with the opposition arises from a sense that such an acknowledgment would legitimize the adversary" (1997, 39).

I suspect their analysis is correct and offers clues to the comparable lack of seeking similarity with the other observed in the Franconia conversations. Here Smith and Windes again show the ability of rhetorical analysis to probe what is occurring among speakers who show little evidence of aiming to understand each other. However, the grief expressed by many in Franconia and the larger church over the breakdown of understanding also again underscores Gadamer's ability to provide a language for analyzing what has broken down and how those who *do* want to understand each other and find commonalities amid difference may set out on that path.

3. And with such misfitting twists of the data, once more it becomes evident why rhetorically-biased analyses can complement hermeneutically-prejudiced assessments. Rhetoric can continue to probe what is unfolding even after the hermeneutic quest for commonality is derailed.

4. Even Smith and Windes, who are seeking not hermeneutic commonalities but rhetorical tracking of differences, highlight the extent to which conversational opponents define themselves in "relationships" with each other—"oppositional" and antagonistic though this relating may be (1997, 30-31, 38-39; see also 2000, 197-198 for more on the quest for commonality).

EPILOGUE

1. This material was originally published under the title "What if 'Bias' Isn't a Bad Word After All?" (King, 1998).

APPENDIX A

1. These research goals delineate the scope of my scholarship. To elaborate on comments under the heading of "Literature and Cultural/Mennonite Contexts," potentially my project intersects with massive bodies of literature and research related to homosexuality, queer theory, feminist theory, analytic and continental philosophy, Mennonite and other-denominational history and theology, speech communication, rhetoric, the various streams of hermeneutics in addition to Gadamer's, sociology, ethnomethodology,

literary theory, poststructuralism, postmodernism, conflict resolution, and much more. As appropriate, I link my comments with such literatures, but I aim to keep the core of my analysis focused sharply and persistently on Gadamer. Whatever claims I make based on my scholarship here are pertinent primarily to Gadamer and to the issues involved in the application of philosophical hermeneutics—and only secondarily to those other literatures and disciplines with which my concerns intersect.

2. Such as Bourdieu (1977, 1990, 1991); Bourdieu and Wacquant (1992); Geertz (1973, 1980); the many rhetoricians of the human sciences in Nelson et. al (1987); or the rhetorical theorists who comment on related matters in Simons (1990).

3. Gadamer stresses that he does "grant the social sciences full recognition in their field" but wants to ensure that they remain connected to the lived reality of the sensus communis, or the common wisdom of the human community. This is because he is "concerned with the fact that the displacement of human reality never goes so far that no forms of solidarity exist any longer" (1983, 264). Then, in a lighter vein, after noting his willingness to continue to "get something new into this old head," he concludes that "Admittedly, to make me into a sociologist is something no one will succeed in doing, not even myself" (265).

4. My preparation for this analysis includes years of researching and reading the secondary Gadamerian literature. This material has played a crucial role in providing me access to and clarification of the thought of Gadamer, which is at points highly complex and at first encounter so dense as to be nearly impenetrable. However, grateful though I am to many secondary sources, a debt I have tried to repay by giving due credit throughout, I have found it more helpful to turn first to Gadamer at many points, rather than to simply reiterate or summarize the secondary commentary. One reason for this is the hope that at some junctures I am doing work which breaks ground not yet well-plowed in secondary sources.

5. While there are significant divergences in our aims and methods, I am indebted to Marcia Witten (1993) for providing a research path that sent me in a helpful direction even as I have taken freedom to travel other byways when my project called for it. Witten's methods were an important inspiration for mine; the parallels between hers and mine as I have sketched them will hopefully be obvious. In relation to her research on sermons, Witten describes her approach as a search for "a combination of methods that does justice to the richness and fullness of the texts' expression."

To accomplish her goals, Witten precluded "attempting a priori to reduce the examination in analytical categories, or to simplify the task by sampling parts of sermons. . . ." Instead, she "undertook a close textual analysis of all parts of all sermons. The analysis was guided to some extent by theory and to a larger extent by inductive readings of the texts" (25). Most likely my decision to approach the data with a loose but nevertheless pre-determined set of initial categories posed the sharpest distinction between my approach and what Witten describes here. Nevertheless, the difference appears to be primarily a matter of degree. If theory likely predetermined my project to a greater degree than it did Witten's, with Witten I aimed to allow inductive readings of texts to test and if necessary modify theory, as indeed at a number of important points in this study (especially in chapters 5 and 6) I report that it has.

She notes the more general bodies of literature through which she established a context for her analysis, then emphasizes that though such resources provided background, she "allowed the topics of substantive concern . . . to emerge from the texts themselves. In other words," she explains,

> I decided to deal with particular topics based less on a pre-existing scheme of what "ought" to appear in such an analysis than on the presence, degree of elaboration, and appearance of importance or problematization of these issues in the texts themselves. (25)

Then Witten describes how she proceeded with the actual analysis and in so doing sketches a scheme remarkably similar to the one I found myself following as I attempted to develop those Gadamerian categories for analysis of conversational success and failure I describe later in this chapter. She says,

> Once the general themes of the analysis were identified from the sermons, I proceeded simultaneously in two ways, consonant with techniques of analytical induction (Katz, 1983). First, I looked for the appearance of rhetorical formulations that marked similarities and differences in the ways in which speakers treated each general topic (for example, the key terms and clusters of imageries that constituted patterns of speaking about the characteristics or behavior of God). As these patterns appeared to emerge in the analysis of the sermons ("initial coding," Charmaz, 1983, 113), I undertook an interactive process of refining them through checking their fit with the rest of the data. As tentative patterns emerged, I looked for their disconfirmation from cases that didn't seem to fit, to refine the categories ("focused coding," Charmaz, 1983, 116). After several rounds, I was satisfied that the categories that had been identified were both appropriate and sufficient for capturing the general patterns of discourse about each substantive topic. (26)

6. For more context, see note 3.

APPENDIX B

1. Brockriede originated a three-fold model for viewing communication in terms of rape, seduction, love. Drawing in addition on Barnlund and others (including Gadamer and Plato), Czubaroff has expanded and sharpened the model to include principled love and dialogical love. I have relabeled rape as coercion, added the category of submission to Czubaroff's model, and drawn on her definitions while appropriating them in a more explicitly Gadamerian framework and the intersecting work of Stewart and Thomas. As noted, this initial effort to bridge the gap between Gadamerian abstraction and my application of philosophical hermeneutics continued to sharpen as work on the project continued and data collection and analysis proceeded.

2. Here I am summarizing one stage in the process Stewart and Thomas describe but are not themselves necessarily affirming, given their own move to "what is in front of us"—one way of stating Gadamer's prioritizing of the subject matter. I am not making an unproblematized statement of their or my own eventual position. As is indicated at a number of points throughout my study, including in the chapter 5 discussion of Gadamer in relation to issues of psychology and human relationships, Gadamer sees the process of understanding as unfolding primarily when the subject matter, not human relationships, are foregrounded. Thus it is unlikely he would want to give empathy a key role.

BIBLIOGRAPHY

A prayer of confession (1997, November). *Franconia Conference News*, 1.

Abelove, Henry, Michèle Aina Barale, and David M. Halperin (Eds.) (1993). *The lesbian and gay studies reader*. New York: Routledge.

Ahlgrim, Ryan (1995, February 7). [Letter to the editor]. *Gospel Herald*, 5.

Ahlhgrim, Ryan and Stanley Bohn, Marjorie Reimer Ediger, Eldon E. Esau, Calvin Flickinger, Matthew C. Friesen, James Gingerich, Steven Goering, Susan Ortman Goering, Gary Harder, Elfrieda Hiebert, Rhonda Horsch, Dorothea Janzen, LeRoy Kennel, Pauline Kennel, Kathy Landis, Weldon Nisly, Bonnie Neufeld, Chuck Neufeld, Brenda Sawatzky Paetkau, Miles Reimer, Steven G. Schmidt, Myron Schrag, Earl Sears, Ann Showalter, Joyce M. Shutt, Marlene Smucker, Stan Smucker, Muriel T. Stackley, Rod Stafford, Donald R. Steelberg, David Swartz, Jerry Toews, Leann Toews, Dorothy Wiebe Johnson, Steve Wiebe Johnson, John Waltner, David M. Whitermore, Bruce Yoder (1995, June 20). An open letter to the Mennonite Church and the General Conference Mennonite Church. *Gospel Herald*, 4.

Albrecht, Darl D. (1995, May 16). [Letter to the editor]. Gospel Herald, 5.

Altieri, Charles (1997). Toward a hermeneutics responsive to rhetorical theory. In Walter Jost and Michael J. Hyde (Eds.), *Rhetoric and hermeneutics in our time* (90-107).

Anderson, Richard C. (1996). *Peace was in their hearts*. Scottdale, Pa.: Herald Press.

Apel, Kart-Otto (1997). Regulative ideas or truth happening?: An attempt to answer the question of the conditions of the possibility of valid understanding. In Lewis Edwin Hahn (Ed.), *The philosophy of Hans-Georg Gadamer* (67-94).

Armour, Ellen T. (1999). *Deconstruction, feminist theology, and the problem of difference: Subverting the race/gender divide*. Chicago: University of Chicago Press.

Arnett, Ronald C. (1980). *Dwell in peace: Applying nonviolence to everyday relationships*. Elgin, Ill.: Brethren Press.

────── (1986a). *Communication and community: Implications of Martin Buber's dialogue*. Carbondale, Ill.: Southern Illinois University Press.

────── (1986b). The inevitable conflict and confronting in dialogue. In Stewart, John (Ed.), *Bridges not walls: A book about interpersonal communication* (272-279).

Babbie, Earl (1995). *The practic of social research*, 7th. ed. Wadsworth Publishing Company.

Bachman, Charles and Isaac Beiler, Howard H. Hanna III, Isaac Lapp, Jonathan Lapp, Melvin G. Lapp, Walter Martin, Earl E. Mast, Kenneth Mast, John Smoker, Mel Smoker, Clair Umble, David M. Weaver, Samuel Yoder (1995, August 29). [Letter to the editor]. *Gospel Herald*, 6.

Balch, David L. (Ed.) (2000). *Homosexuality, science, and the "plain sense" of Scripture*. Grand Rapids, Mich.: Wm. B. Eerdmans.

Bakelaar, Philip (1997). The issue culture of the gay and lesbian religious controversy in the age of AIDS: Moral argumentation in American mainline religious communities as a symbolic contest between competing interpretations. (Doctoral dissertation, Temple University, 1997).

Barnlund, D. C. (1979). Toward a meaning-centered philosophy of communication. *Journal of Communication*, 197-211.

Beachy, Alvin J. (1977). *The concept of grace in the Radical Reformation*. Nieuwkoop, Holland: B. De Graaf. Original work published 1960.

Bender, Harold S. (1956). *Mennonite encyclopdia*, vol. 2 (277-278). Scottdale, Pa.: Mennonite Publishing House.

Bernstein, Richard (1983). *Beyond objectivism and relativism: Science, hermeneutics, and praxis*. Philadelphia: University of Pennsylvania Press.

────── (1987). One step forward, two steps backward. *Political Theory, 15*, 538-563.

Bertens, Hans (1995). *The idea of the postmodern: A history*. London and New York: Routledge.

Best, Steven and Douglas Kellner (1991). *Postmodern theory: Critical interrogations*. New York: The Guilford Press.

Biesecker-Mast, Gerald and Susan Biesecker-Mast (2000). *Anabaptists and postmodernity*. Telford, Pa.: Pandora Press U.S.

Biesecker-Mast, Gerald J. (1998, April). Mennonite public discourse and the conflicts over homosexuality. *Mennonite Quarterly Review 72(2)*, 275-300.

Biesecker-Mast, Susan. The aporetic witness. In David W. Shenk and Linford Stutzman, *Practicing truth: Confident witness in our pluralistic world* (130-147). Scottdale, Pa.: Herald Press.

Bineham, Jeffery L. (1990). The Cartesian anxiety in epistemic rhetoric: An assessment of the literature. *Philosophy and Rhetoric, 23*, 43-64.

—— (1994). Displacing Descartes: Philosophical hermeneutics and rhetorical studies. *Philosophy and Rhetoric 27*, 300-12.

—— (1995). The hermeneutic medium. *Philosophy and Rhetoric 28*, 1-15.

Bochner, Arthur P., Kenneth N. Cissna, and Michael G. Garko (1991). Optional metaphors for studying interaction. In Montgomery, Barbara M. and Steve Duck (Eds.), *Studying interspersonal interaction* (16-34).

Borntrager, Naomi, and Merritt Gardner, Ruth Ann Gardner, Suella Gerber, Nancy S. Lapp, Steven L. Mullet, Dorothy Yoder Nyce, John Nyce, Arden Shank, Meribeth Shank (1995, August 1). [Letter to the editor]. *Gospel Herald*, 4.

Boswell, John (1981). *Christianity, social tolerance, and homosexuality: Gay people in Western Europe from the beginning of the Christian era to the fourth century.* Chicago: University of Chicago Press.

Bourdieu, Pierre (1977). *Outline of a theory of practice.* (Richard Nice, Trans.). Cambridge, England: Cambridge University Press.

—— (1984). *Distinction: A social critique of the judgment of taste.* (Richard Nice, Trans.). Cambridge, Mass.: Harvard University Press.

—— (1990). *The Logic of practice* (Richard Nice, Trans.). Stanford, Calif.: Stanford University Press.

—— (1991). John B. Thompson (Ed.). *Language and symbolic power.* (Gino Raymond and Matthew Adamson, Trans.). Cambridge, Mass.: Harvard University Press.

Bourdieu, P. and L. J. D. Wacquant (1992). *An invitation to reflexive sociology.* Chicago: University of Chicago Press.

Brawley, Robert L. (Ed.) (1996). *Biblical ethics and homosexuality: Listening to Scripture.* Louisville: Westminster John Knox, 1996.

Brenneman, John M. (1863). *Christianity and war: A sermon setting forth the sufferings of Christians.* Chicago: John F. Funk.

——. (1886). Pride and humility: A discourse setting forth the characteristics of the proud and the humble. Elkhart, Ind.: John F. Funk.

Brethren/Mennonite Parents of Lesbian/Gay Children (1993, May 25). [Letter to the editor]. *Gospel Herald*, 4-5.

Brockriede, W. (1972). Arguers as lovers. *Philosophy and Rhetoric 5*, 11.

Brooten, Bernadette (1996). *Love between women: Early Christian responses to female homoeroticism.* Chicago: University of Chicago Press.

Brummett, B. (1976). Some implications of "process" or "intersubjectivity": Postmodern rhetoric. *Philosophy and Rhetoric 9*, 21-51.

—— (1982). On to rhetorical relativism. *Quarterly Journal of Speech 68*, 425-430.

—— (1990a). A eulogy for epistemic rhetoric. *Quarterly Journal of Speech 76*, 69-72.

—— (1990b). Relativism and rhetoric. In Cherwitz, Richard A. (Ed.), *Rhetoric and Philosophy* (79-104). Hillsdale, N.J.: Lawrence Erlbaum Associates.

Brunk, George II (1998, January 6). [Letter to the editor]. *Gospel Herald*, 5.

Bruns, Gerald L. (1992). *Hermeneutics ancient and modern*. New Haven and London: Yale University Press.

Bullock, Jeffrey Frances (1996). Preaching with a cupped ear: Hans-Georg Gadamer's philosophical hermeneutics as postmodern wor(l)d. (Doctoral dissertation, University of Washington, 1996).

Burke, Kenneth (1945, 1969a). Appendix D: Four master tropes. *The grammar of motives* (503-517). Berkeley, Calif.: University of California Press.

—— (1969b). *A Rhetoric of motives*. Berkeley, Calif.: University of California Press.

Burnett, Rosalie (1991). Accounts and narratives. In Barbara M. Montgomery and Steve Duck (Eds.), *Studying interpersonal interaction* (121-140).

Byrne, Geoff and Joan Byrne, Bradley J. Fair, Linda M. Fair, Lu Ann Horst, Annabelle Hoylman, Arthur S. Hoylman, B.D. Hoylman, Ed Kehr, Doris Martin, Wilmer G. Martin, Cheryl Mickley, Gary Mickley, Glenn E. Musselman, Lois Musselman, Leona Musselman, Melvin Musselman, Mildred Musselman, Diane Rider, Douglas Rider, Michael L. Rider, Roxanne Rider, Earl Schmidt, Elizabeth Schmidt, Dick Shaffer, Helen Shaffer, Lois Whisler (1995, August 29). [Letter to the editor]. *Gospel Herald*, 6.

Buker, Eloise A. (1990). Feminist social theory and hermeneutics: An empowering dialectic? *Social Epistemology, 4*(1), 23-39.

Cameron, W. S. K. (1996). On communicative actors talking past one another: The Gadamer-Habermas debate. *Philosophy Today 40* (spring), 160-168.

Campbell, Will (1977). *Brother to a dragonfly*. New York: Continuum Publishing Co.

Caputo, John D. (1987). *Radical hermeneutics: Repetition, deconstruction, and the hermeneutic project*. Bloomington and Indianapolis: Indiana University Press.

Charmaz, Kathy (1983). The grounded theory method: An explication and interpretation. In Robert M. Emerson (Ed.), *Contemporary field research* (109-126). Prospect Heights, Ill.: Waveland Press

Chen, Kuang-Hsin (1987). Beyond truth and method: On misreading Gadamer's praxical hermeneutics. *Quarterly Journal of Speech 73,* 183-199.

Clark, Michael J. (1997). *Defying the darkness: Gay theology in the shadows.* Cleveland: Pilgrim Press.

Clemens, Donella and Willis A. Miller, Philip C. Bergey, James M. Lapp, Addie Gehman (1997, October 14). [Letter to Franconia Conference delegates].

Clough, Patricia Ticineto (1994). *Feminist thought: Desire, power and academic discourse.* Oxford, England and Cambridge, Mass.: Blackwell.

Collins, Raymond F. (2000). *Sexual ethics and the New Testament: behavior and belief.* New York: Crossroad Publishing Co.

Comstock, Gary D. and Susan E. Henking (1996). *Que(e)rying religion: A critical anthology.* New York: Continuum.

Comstock, Gary David (1996). *Unrepentant, self-affirming, practicing: Lesbian/bisexual/gay people within organized religion.* New York: Continuum, 1996.

Cotlar, Andrew Howard (1986). The relation between sociological method and everyday life: Weber, Husserl, Schutz, and Gadamer. *Dissertation Abstracts International, A: The Humanities and Social Sciences,* 47(1), 329-A-330-A.

Council on Faith, Life, and Strategy issues statement on meaning of "dialogue" (1995, December 12). *Gospel Herald,* 10.

Crusius, Thomas (1995). Neither trust nor suspicion: Kenneth Burke's rhetoric and hermeneutics. *Studies in the Literary Imagination 28(2),* 79-90.

Cummings, Mary Lou (1995, May 9). Franconia designates Germantown as associate member. *Gospel Herald,* 10.

Czubaroff, Jeanine (n.d.). Rhetorical relationships: "Arguers as Lovers" revisited. Collegeville, Pa.: Ursinus College. Unpublished manuscript.

Czubaroff, J. and T. Whelan (1995). Theory and pedagogy of understanding. Philadelphia: Temple University Discourse Analysis Conference.

Deetz, Stanley (1978). Conceptualizing human understanding: Gadamer's hermeneutics and American communication studies. *Communication Quarterly, 26(2),* 12-23.

——— (1982a). Critical interpretive research in organizational communication. *Western Journal of Speech Communication 46,* 131-149.

—— (1982b, April) Humane discourse: A unitary principle for effectiveness and ethics in interpersonal interaction. Paper presented at Central States Speech Convention. Cited in Simons (n.d.:1).

—— (1983). Negation and the political function of rhetoric: A review essay. *Quarterly Journal of Speech 69*, 434-441.

—— (1992). Democracy in an age of corportate colonization: Developments in communication and the politics of everyday life. Albany, N.Y.: State University of New York Press.

Delegates gather to pray, express grief, and confer (1997, November). *Franconia Conference News*, 1.

Derrida, Jacques (1972). *Dissemination*. (Barbara Johnson, Trans.). Chicago: University of Chicago Press.

—— (1989a). Three questions to Hans-Georg Gadamer. In Diane P. Michelfelder and Richard E. Palmer (Eds.), *Dialogue and deconstruction* (Diane Michelfelder and Richard Palmer, Trans.) (52-55).

—— (1989b). Interpreting signatures (Nietzche/Heidegger): Two questions. In Diane P. Michelfelder and Richard E. Palmer (Eds.), *Dialogue and deconstruction* (Diane Michelfelder and Richard Palmer, Trans.) (58-71).

Derstine, Jim (1987, August 18). [Letter to the editor]. *Gospel Herald*, 594.

Dickens, David R. and Andrea Fontana (Eds.) (1994). *Postmodernism and social inquiry*. New York: The Guilford Press.

Dreyfus, Hubert L. and Paul Rabinow (1983). *Michel Foucault: Beyond structuralism and hermeneutics*, 2nd. ed. Chicago: University of Chicago Press.

Driedger, Leo and Donald B. Kraybill (1994). *Mennonite peacemaking: From quietism to activism*. Scottdale, Pa.: Herald Press.

Dudley, Bill (1992, November 3). [Letter to the editor]. *Gospel Herald*, 4.

Duck, Steve (1991). Diaries and logs. In Montgomery, Barbara M. and Steve Duck (Eds.), *Studying interpersonal interaction* (141-160).

Dyck, Cornelius J. (1993). *An introduction to Mennonite history: A popular history of the Anabaptists and Mennonites* (3rd ed.). Scottdale, Pa.: Herald Press.

—— (1995). *Spiritual life in Anabaptism: Classic devotional resources*. Scottdale, Pa.: Herald Press.

Eagleton, Terry (1983). *Literary theory: An introduction*. Minneapolis: University of Minnesota Press.

Elshtain, Jean Bethke (1995). The politics of difference. *Religious Studies News*, 10(2), 7-8.

Emerson, Robert M., Rachel I. Fretz, and Linda L. Shaw (1995). *Writing ethnographic fieldnotes*. Chicago: University of Chicago Press.

Engle, James R. (1997). Hard choices. *God leads a people home: Adult Bible study guide (fall)* (62-63). Scottdale, Pa.: Herald Press.

Finger, Thomas (1990). Grace. *Mennonite encyclopedia*, vol. 5. (352-353). Scottdale, Pa.: Herald Press.

Fish, Stanley (1989). Rhetoric. *Doing what comes naturally: Change, rhetoric, and the practice of theory in literary and legal studies* (471-502), Durham, N.C.: Duke University Press.

Foucault, Michel (1972). *The archaeology of knowledge, and the discourse on language.* (A.M. Sheridan Smith, Trans.). New York: Pantheon Books. Original work published 1971.

———— (1977). Nietzsche, genealogy, history. In Donald F. Bouchard (Ed.), *Language, counter-memory, practice.* (139-164). Original essay published 1971.

———— (1980a). Two lectures. In Colin Gordon (Ed.), *Power/Knowledge: Selected interviews and other writings 1972-1977* (78-108). (Colin Gordon et al, Trans.). New York: Pantheon Books.

———— (1980b). Truth and power. In Colin Gordon (Ed.), *Power/Knowledge: Selected interviews and other writings 1972-1977* (109-133).

———— (1984). What is enlightenment? In Paul Rabinow (Ed.), *The Foucault Reader* (32-50). New York: Pantheon Books.

———— (1987). The ethic of care for the self as a practice of freedom: An interview with Michel Foucault on January 20, 1984. In James Bernauer and David Rasmussen (Eds.), *The Final Foucault* (6-20). Cambridge, Mass.: The MIT Press.

———— (1990). *The History of Sexuality: Vol. 1. An Introduction.* (Robert Hurley, Trans.). New York: Vintage Books of Random House.

———— (1994a). *The birth of the clinic: An archaeology of medical perception.* (A.M. Sheridan Smith, Trans.). New York: Vintage Books of Random House. Original work published 1963.

———— (2000a). Omnes et singulatum: Toward a critique of political reason. In James D. Faubion (Ed.), *Essential works of Michel Foucault: Vol 3. Power* (Robert Hurley et al, Trans.) (298-325). New York: The New Press.

———— (2000b). So is it important to think? In James D. Faubion (Ed.), *Essential works of Michel Foucault: Vol 3. Power*(454-458).

[Franconia Mennonite Conference letter to delegates] (1997, October 14).

Friedman, Edwin H. (1985). *Generation to generation: Family process in church and synagogue.* New York: The Guilford Press.

Fulkerson, Mary McClintock (1994). *Changing the subject: Women's discourses and feminist theology.* Philadelphia: Fortress Press.

Gaboury, Glen A. (1992, December 15). [Letter to the editor]. *Gospel Herald*, 5.

Gadamer, Hans-Georg (1976). *Philosophical hermeneutics.* (David E. Linge, Trans. and Ed.). Berkeley: University of California Press.

———— (1980). *Logos* and *Ergon* in Plato's *Lysis. Dialogue and dialectic: Eight hermeneutical studies on Plato* (1-20) (P. Christopher Smith, Trans.). New Haven and London: Yale University Press.

———— (1981). *Reason in the age of science* (Frederick G. Lawrence, Trans.). Cambridge, Mass.: The MIT Press.

———— (1983). Appendix: A letter by Dr. Hans-Georg Gadamer. In Richard Bernstein, *Beyond objectivism and relativism: Science, hermeneutics, and praxis* (261-265).

———— (1984). The hermeneutics of suspicion. In G. Shapiro and A. Sica (Eds.), *Hermeneutics* (54-65). Amherst, Mass.: University of Massachussetts Press.

———— (1986). *The relevance of the beautiful and other essays* (Robert Bernasconi, Ed.; Nicholas Walker, Trans.). Cambridge: Cambridge University Press.

———— (1989a). Text and interpretation. In Diane P. Michelfelder and Richard E. Palmer (Eds.), *Dialogue and deconstruction* (Diane Michelfelder and Richard Palmer, Trans.) (21-51).

———— (1989b). Reply to Jacques Derrida. In Diane P. Michelfelder and Richard E. Palmer (Eds.), *Dialogue and deconstruction* (Diane Michelfelder and Richard Palmer, Trans.) (55-57).

———— (1992) *Hans-Georg Gadamer on education, poetry, and history.* Misgeld, Dieter and Graeme Nicholson (Eds.), (Lawrence Schmidt and Monica Reuss, Trans.). Albany, N.Y.: SUNY Press.

———— (1994). Heidegger's ways. (John W. Stanley, Trans.). Albany, N.Y.: SUNY Press.

———— (1994a). *Truth and method* (2nd, rev. ed.). (Joel Weinsheimer and Donald G. Marshall, Trans.). New York: Continuum. Original work published 1960.

———— (1994b). The historicity of understanding. In Mueller-Vollmer, Kurt. *The hermeneutics reader: Texts of the German tradition from the Enlightenment to the present* (256-292). New York: Continuum. Original work published 1967.

———— (1996). *The enigma of health: The art of healing in a scientific age* (Jason Gaiger and Nicholas Walker, Trans.). Stanford, Calif.: Stanford University Press.

———— (1997a). Reflections on my philosophical journey. In Lewis Edwin Hahn (Ed.), *The philosophy of Hans-Georg Gadamer* (3-63).

———— (1997b). Reply to Karl-Otto Appel. In Lewis Edwin Hahn (Ed.), *The philosophy of Hans-Georg Gadamer* (95-97).

———(1999). *Hermeneutics, religion, and ethics*. (Joel Weinsheimer, Trans.). New Haven: Yale University Press.

———(2000). *The beginning of philosophy*. (Rod Coltman, Trans.). New York: Continuum.

Gaede, Beth Ann (Ed.) (1998). *Congregations talking about homosexuality*. New York: The Alban Institute.

Gearhart, Sally Milton (1979). The womanization of rhetoric. *Women's Studies International Quarterly, 2*, 195-201.

Geertz, Clifford (1973). Thick descriptions: Toward an interpretive theory of culture. In Clifford Geertz (Ed.), *The interpretation of cultures* (1-32). New York: Basic Books.

——— (1980). Blurred genres: The refiguration of social thought. *The American Scholar*, 165-179.

Gendlin, E. T. (1997). The responsive order: A new empiricism. http://www.focusing.org/gendlin4.html (consulted September 25, 1997).

Germantown loses membership, pastor's credentials on January 1 (1997, November). *Franconia Conference News*, 1.

Germantown Mennonite Church's process in response to our two-year associate membership (1997). In *Praying for the Church Beyond Us* (41-42). [Semi-annual report, Franconia Mennonite Conference, Spring Conference Assembly, April 26].

Gies, Sally B. and Donald E. Messer (Eds.) (1994). *Caught in the crossfire: Helping Christians debate homosexuality*. Nashville: Abingdon Press.

Gitlin, Todd (1995). *The twilight of common dreams: Why America is wracked by culture wars*. New York: Metropolitan Books.

Glaser, Chris (1998). *Coming out as sacrament*. Louisille: Westminster/John Knox Press, 1998.

Godshall, Eileen (1987, September 29). [Letter to the editor]. *Gospel Herald*, 690.

Goss, Robert (1993). *Jesus acted up: A gay and lesbian manifesto*. New York: HarperSanFransisco.

Green, Jon (1987, August 18). [Letter to the editor]. *Gospel Herald*, 594.

Greenberg, David F. (1988). *The construction of homosexuality*. Chicago: University of Chicago Press.

Grenz, Stanley J. 1998. *Welcoming but not affirming: An evangelical response to homosexuality*. Louisville, Ky.: Westminster John Knox Press, 1998.

Griswold, Wendy (1987). *A methodological framework for the sociology of culture. Sociological Methodology, 17*, 1-35.

Grove, Clarence (1993, May 25). [Letter to the editor]. *Gospel Herald*, 4.

Habermas, Jurgen (1988). *On the logic of the social sciences*. (Shierry Weber Nicholson and Jerry A. Stark, Trans.). Cambridge, Mass.: The MIT Press. Original work published 1967.

——— (1994). Hermeneutics and the social sciences. In Kurt Mueller-Vollmer. *The hermeneutics reader: Texts of the German tradition from the Enlightenment to the present* (294-319). New York: Continuum. Original work published 1967.

Halperin, David M. (1995). *Saint Foucault: Toward a gay hagiography* New York: Oxford University Press.

Hanigan, James P. (1988). *Homosexuality: The test case for Christian sexual ethics*. New York: Paulist Press.

Hahn, Lewis Edwin (Ed.) (1997). *The philosophy of Hans-Georg Gadamer. The library of living philosophers, XXIV*. Chicago and La Salle, Ill.: Open Court Publishing Co.

Harder, Leland (1993). *Doors to lock and doors to open: The discerning people of God*. Scottdale, Pa.: Herald Press.

Hariman, Robert (1987, November). Friendship as a hermeneutical model. Des Moines, Iowa: Duke University. Paper presented at Speech Communication Association, Boston, Mass., 1-10.

Hart, Roderick P. (1990). *Modern rhetorical criticism*. New York: Harper-Collins Publishers.

Hauerwas, Stanley (1994a). Positioning: In the church and university but not of either. In *Dispatches from the front: Theological engagements with the secular*. Durham, S.C.: Duke University Press, 15.

——— (1994b, Spring). Storytelling: A Response to "Mennonites on Hauerwas." *Conrad Grebel Review* 12, 166-169.

Hays, Richard B. (1986, Spring). Relations natural and unnatural: A response to Boswell's exegesis of Romans 1. *Journal of Religious Ethics* 14, 184-215.

——— (1996). The moral vision of the New Testament: A contemporary introduction to New Testament ethics. New York: HarperCollins Publishers.

——— (1991, July). Awaiting the redemption of our bodies. *Sojourners 20*, 17-21.

——— (1997, February 26). Salvation by trust? Reading the Bible faithfully. *Christian Century*, 218-223.

Hefling, Charles (Ed.) (1996). *Our selves, our souls and bodies: Sexuality and the household of God*. Boston: Cowley Publications.

Hekman, Susan J. (1984). Action as a text: Gadamer's hermeneutics and the social scientific analysis of action. *Journal for the Theory of Social Behavior* 14(3), Oct, 333-354.

———— (1986). *Hermeneutics and the sociology of knowledge.* Notre Dame, Ind.: University of Notre Dame Press.

Helms, Dick (1987, September 22). [Letter to the editor]. *Gospel Herald*, 674.

Herald Press Catalog (2000-2001). Scottdale, Pa.: Herald Press.

Hershey, Harold B. (1992, November 3). [Letter to the editor]. *Gospel Herald*, 7.

Hockman, Cathleen (1995, April 18). Ilinois Conference wrestles with future of churches accepting homosexual members. *Gospel Herald*, 8-9.

Hollinger, Robert (1985a). Practical reason and hermeneutics. *Philosophy and Rhetoric, 18*, 113-122.

———— (Ed.) (1985b). *Hermeneutics and praxis.* Notre Dame, Ind.: University of Notre Dame Press.

Hostetler, Beulah S. (1987). *American Mennonites and Protestant movements: A community paradigm.* Scottdale, Pa.: Herald Press.

Huspek, Michael (1994). Critical ethnography and subjective experience. *Human Studies, 17*, 1, Jan, 45-63.

Jameson, Fredric (1984). Postmodernism, or the cultural logic of late capitalism. *New Left Review, 146*, 53-93.

Jones, Stanton L. and Mark A. Yarhouse (2000). *Homosexuality: The use of scientific research in the church's moral debate.* Downers Grove, Ill.: InterVarsity Press.

Jordan, Mark D. (1997). *The invention of sodomy.* Chicago: University of Chicago Press.

Jost, Walter and Michael J. Hyde (Eds.) (1997). *Rhetoric and hermeneutics in our time: A reader.* New Haven: Yale University Press

Juhnke, James C. (1990). *Mennonite experience in America: Vol. 3. Vision, doctrine, war: Mennonite identity and organization in America, 1890-1930.* Scottdale, Pa.: Herald Press.

Kasdorf, Julia (1997). Bakhtin, boundaries and bodies. *The Mennonite Quarterly Review 71*(2), 169-188.

Katz, Jack (1983). A theory of qualitative methodology: The social system of analytic fieldwork. In R. Emerson (Ed.), *Contemporary field research* (127-148). Prospect Heights, Ill.: Waveland Press

Kauffman, J. Howard and Leland Harder (1975). *Anabaptists four centuries later: A profile of five Mennonite and Brethren in Christ denominations.* Scottdale, Pa.: Herald Press.

Kauffman, J. Howard and Leo Driedger (1991). *The Mennonite mosaic: Identity and modernization.* Scottdale, Pa.: Herald Press.

King, Michael A. (1990). *Trackless wastes and stars to steer by: Christian identity in a homeless age.* Scottdale, Pa.: Herald Press.

——— (1997, Fall). Angels, atheists, and common ground: Toward a separatist and worldly postmodern Anabaptism. *Conrad Grebel Review* 15, 251-268.

——— (1998, January 6). What if "bias" isn't a bad word after all?" *Gospel Herald*, 1-3.

——— (2000). Valuing the story of power and telling a grander one: Anabaptism and power postmodernism in mutually enlarging conversation. In Susan Biesecker-Mast and Gerald Biesecker-Mast (Eds.) *Anabaptists and postmodernity.*

Kauffman, Richard A. (2000, May 2). A third way beyond fight or flight. *The Mennonite*, 6-8.

Kniss, Fred (1997). *Disquiet in the land: Cultural conflict in American Mennonite communities.* New Brunswick, N.J.: Rutgers University Press.

Kögler, Hans Herbert (1999). *The power of dialogue: Critical hermeneutics after Gadamer and Foucault.* (Paul Hendrickson, Trans.) Cambridge, Mass.: MIT Press. Original work published 1992.

Kontopoulous, Kyriakos M. (1995). The dark side of the fire: Postmodern critique and the elusiveness of the ideological. *Argumentation* 9(1), 5-19.

Kotva, Joseph J. Jr. (1989, Winter). Scripture, ethics, and the local church: Homosexuality as a case study. *The Conrad Grebel Review* 7, 41-61.

Kraus, C. Norman (Ed.). (2001). *To continue the dialogue: Biblical interpretation and homosexuality.* Telford, Pa.: Pandora Press U.S.

Kreider, Roberta (Ed.) (1998). *From wounded hearts: Faith stories of lesbian, gay, bisexual, and transgendered people and those who love them.* Gaithersburg, Md.: Chi Ro Press, 1998.

Krippendorf, Klaus (1980). *Content analysis: An introduction to its methodology.* Beverly Hills: Sage Publications.

Kunjam, Shant S. (1997, December 30). [Letter to the editor]. *Gospel Herald*, 4.

Lakoff, George (1996). *Moral politics: What conservatives know that liberals don't.* Chicago: University of Chicago Press.

Lakoff, George and Mark Johnson (1980). *Metaphors we live by.* Chicago: University of Chicago Press.

Lawrence, Jill (1996, December 16). Wanted: Good citizens, close communities. *Unites States Today*, 1-2A).

Landis, Steven E. (1997, December 30). [Letter to the editor]. *Gospel Herald*, 5.

Landis, Susan Mark (1993). *But why don't we go to war? Finding Jesus' path to peace.* Scottdale, Pa.: Herald Press.

Lentricchia, Frank (1983). *Criticism and social change.* Chicago: University of Chicago Press.

Lesher, Ruth Detweiler (1996, May 28). When to build fences and when to open the gates. *Gospel Herald,* 1-3, 8.

Liechty, Joseph C. (1980, January). Humility: The foundation of Mennonite religious outlook in the 1860s. *Mennonite Quarterly Review 54(1),* 5-31.

Linge, David E. (1976). Editor's introduction. In Linge, David E. (Ed.), *Philosophical hermeneutics.* Berkeley: University of California Press.

Lofland, J. and L.H. Lofland (1984). *Analyzing social settings: A guide to qualitative observation and analysis,* 2nd ed. Belmont, Calif.: Wadsworth.

Lowe, Lisa (1991). Discourse and heterogeneity: Situating Orientalism. In *Critical terrains: French and British Orientalisms* (1-29). Ithaca and London: Cornell University Press.

Lukes, Steven (1974). *Power: A radical view.* New York: Macmillan.

Lyon, Arabella (n.d.). *Intentions: Negotiated, contested, and ignored.* Philadelphia: Temple University. Unpublished manuscript.

Lyotard, Jean-Francois (1984). *The postmodern condition: A report on knowledge.* (Geoffrey Bennington and Brian Massumi, Trans.). Minneapolis: University of Minnesota Press.

Lyotard, Jean-Francois and Jean-Loup Thébaud (1985). *Just gaming.* Minneapolis: University of Minnesota Press.

MacMaster, Richard K. (1985). *Mennonite experience in America: Vol. 1. Land, piety, peoplehood: The establishment of Mennonite communities in America, 1683-1790.* Scottdale, Pa.: Herald Press.

Madison, Gary B. (1992, spring). Coping with Nietzsche's legacy: Rorty, Derrida, Gadamer. *Philosophy Today,* 3-19.

Mailloux, Stephen (1989). *Rhetorical power.* Ithaca: Cornell University Press.

―――― (1995). Persuasions good and bad: Bunyan, Iser, and Fish on rhetoric and hermeneutics in literature, *Studies in the Literary Imagination, 28(2),* 43-62.

Margolis, Joseph (1995a) Beyond postmodernism: Logic as rhetoric. *Argumentation 9,* 21-31.

―――― (1995b). *Historied thought, constructed world: A conceptual primer for the turn of the millennium.* Berkeley, Calif.: University of California Press.

Mast, Anita (1995, June 27). [Letter to the editor]. *Gospel Herald*, 5.

McGowan, Thomas G. (1989). The sociological significance of Gadamer's hermeneutics. *Dissertation Abstracts International, A: The Humanities and Social Sciences, 50*(3), Sept, 806A-807A.

McKerrow, Raymie E. (1989). Critical rhetoric: Theory and praxis. *Communication Monographs, 56*, 91-111.

McHoul, A. W. (1982). Hermeneutic and ethnomethodological formulations of conversational and textual talk. *Semiotica, 38*(1-2), 91-126.

McNeil, John J. (1995). *Freedom, glorious freedom: The spiritual journey to the fullness of life for gays, lesbians, and everybody else*. Boston: Beacon Press.

Metts, Susan, Susan Sprecher, and William R. Cupach (1991). Retrospective self-reports. In Barbara M. Montgomery and Steve Duck (Eds.), *Studying interpersonal interaction* (162-178).

Michelfelder, Diane P. and Richard E. Palmer (Eds.) (1989). *Dialogue and deconstruction: The Gadamer-Derrida encounter*. Albany, N.Y.: SUNY Press.

Miller, Willis (1997). Report of Overseer Advisory Committee, March 10, 1997. In *Praying for the Church Beyond Us* (40). [Semi-annual report, Franconia Mennonite Conference, Spring Conference Assembly, April 26].

Miller, Willis, Hubert Schartzentruber, Libby Caes, Joe Haines, John Ruth, Carl Yusavitz (Overseer Advisory Committee); James L. Derstine, Richard Lichty, Anita Bender, George Hatzfeld, John Linscheid, Ra-Mona Stahl, Tina Swartz Burkholder (Germantown Congregational Representatives) (1997). Draft proposal for a Germantown Mennonite Church relationship with Franconia Mennonite Conference. In *Praying for the Church Beyond Us*. (43-45). [Semi-annual report, Franconia Mennonite Conference, Spring Conference Assembly, April 26].

Misgeld, Dieter (1985). On Gadamer's hermeneutics. In Hollinger, Robert (Ed.). *Hermeneutics and praxis*. Notre Dame: University of Notre Dame Press.

—— (1991). In Hugh J. Silverman (Ed.), *Gadamer and hermeneutics* (163-177). New York and London: Routledge.

Mollenkott, Virginia Ramey (1992). *Sensuous spirituality: Out from fundamentalism*. New York: Crossroad Publishing.

Montgomery, Barbara M. and Steve Duck (Eds.). (1991a). *Studying interpersonal interaction*. New York: The Guilford Press.

Montgomery, Barbara M. and Steve Duck (1991b). Methodology and open dialogue. In Barbara M. Montgomery and Steve Duck (Eds.), *Studying Interpersonal interaction* (318-336).

Nelson, John S., Allan Megill, and Donald N. McCloskey (Eds.) (1987). *The rhetoric of the human sciences: Language and argument in scholarship and public affairs.* Madison, Wis.: The University of Wisconsin Press.

Nicholson, Graeme (1991). In Silverman, Hugh J. (Ed.), *Gadamer and hermeneutics* (151-162). New York and London: Routledge.

―――― (1997). Truth in metaphysics and in hermeneutics. In Lewis Edwin Hahn (Ed.), *The philosophy of Hans-Georg Gadamer* (309-320).

Okin, Susan Moller (1989). *Justice, gender and the family.* New York: Basic Books.

Ontario Consultants on Religious Tolerance (2000). http://www.religioustolerance.org/hom_chur2.htm and related links (consulted December 6, 2000).

O'Reilly, David (1997, October 17). Mennonite denomination expels church for taking gay members. *Philadelphia Inquirer*, R1, R4.

Orr, Jack C. How shall we say: "Reality is socially constructed through communication?" *Central States Speech Journal, 29*, 265-274.

―――― (1990). Critical rationalism: Rhetoric and the voice of reason. In Richard A. Cherwitz (Ed.), *Rhetoric and Philosophy* (105-148). Hillsdale, N.J.: Lawrence Erlbaum Associates.

Palmer, Tom G. (1987). Gadamer's hermeneutics and social theory. *Critical Review, 1*(3), 91-108.

Palmer, Richard E. (1997). What hermeneutics can offer rhetoric. In Walter Jost and Michael J. Hyde (Eds.), *Rhetoric and hermeneutics in our time* (108-131).

Peachey, Lorne (1995a, January 17). Conference leaders explore various options for work with differing views on homosexuality. *Gospel Herald*, 9.

―――― (1995b, August 29). For everything there is a season. *Gospel Herald*, 16.

―――― (1996a, October 1). Who's to go: Liberals or conservatives? *Gospel Herald*, 16.

―――― (1996b, November 26). Consultation on military and church membership finds issue also involves economics and education. *Gospel Herald*, 12.

Perelman, Chaim and L. Olbrechts-Tyteca (1969). *The new rhetoric: A treatise on argumentation.* (J. Wilkinson and P. Weaver, Trans.). Notre Dame, Ind.: Notre Dame Press.

Praying for the Church Beyond Us (1997). [Semi-annual report, Franconia Mennonite Conference, Spring Conference Assembly, April 26].

Price, Tom (2000, November 30). Evangelist calls church to share faith amid diversity. *Mennonite Weekly Review, 7.*

Pronk, Pim (1993). *Against nature?: Types of moral argumentation regarding homosexuality.* Grand Rapids, Mich.: Wm. B. Eerdmans.

Radcliffe, Krista (1995). Listening to Cassandra: A materialist-feminist exposé of the necessary relations between rhetoric and hermeneutics, *Studies in the Literary Imagination 28*(2), 63-78.

Rationale and proposed action (1997) [Franconia Conference position paper]. 1-2

Recommendation for delegate action (1997). [Statement from Franconia Mennonite Conference Leaders issued to delegates]. April 24.

Redekop, Calvin (1998). *Leaving Anabaptism: From Evangelical Mennonite Brethren to Fellowship of Evangelical Bible Churches.* Telford, Pa.: Pandora Press U.S.

Reimer, Carla (1993, April 27). Listening Committee members reflect on task. *Gospel Herald,* 10.

Rempel, Ron (1995, February 14). Participants tell stories and air views at MCEC workshop on homosexuality. *Gospel Herald,* 5.

Ricoeur, Paul (1991). *From text to action: Essays in hermeneutics, II.* (Kathleen Blamey and John B. Thompson, Trans.). Evanston, Ill.: Northwestern University Press. Original work published in French, 1986.

——— (1997). Rhetoric—poetics—hermeneutics. In Walter Jost and Michael J. Hyde (Eds.), *Rhetoric and hermeneutics in our time* (60-82).

Rorty, Richard (1979). *Philosophy and the mirror of nature.* Princeton, N.J.: Princeton University Press.

——— (1989). *Contingency, irony, solidarity.* Cambridge, England: Cambridge University Press.

——— (1991). *Objectivism, relativism, and truth: Philosophical papers,* vol. 1. Cambridge, England: Cambridge University Press.

Rosenau, Pauline Marie (1992). *Post-modernism and the social sciences: Insights, inroads, and intrusions.* Princeton: Princeton University Press.

Rothberg, Donald (1986). Gadamer, Rorty, hermeneutics, and truth: A response to Warnke. *Inquiry 29,* 355-361.

Ruth, John (1984). *Studies in Anabaptist and Mennonite history: Vol. 26. Maintaining the right fellowship: A narrative account of the oldest Mennonite community in North America.* Scottdale, Pa.: Herald Press.

Satinover, Jeffrey (1996). *Homosexuality and the politics of truth.* Grand Rapids, Mich.: Baker Books.

Sawatsky, Rodney J. (1992). The one and the many: The recovery of Mennonite pluralism. In Walter Klaassen (Ed.), *Anabaptism revisited: Essays on Anabaptist-Mennonite studies in honor of C.J. Dyck.* Scottdale, Pa.: Herald Press.

Say, Elizabeth A. and Mark R. Kowalewski (1998). *Gays, lesbians, and family values*. Cleveland: Pilgrim Press.

Scheibler, Ingrid (2000). *Gadamer: Between Heidegger and Habermas*. Lanham, Md.: Rowman & Littlefield Publishers, Inc.

Schlabach, Theron F. (1988). *Mennonite experience in America: Vol. 2. Peace, faith, nation: Mennonites and Amish in nineteenth-century America*. Scottdale, Pa.: Herald Press.

Schmidt, Thomas E. (1995). *Straight and narrow?: Compassion and clarity in the homosexuality debate*. Downers Grove, Ill.: InterVarsity Press.

Schott, Robin (1991). Whose home is it anyway? A feminist response to Gadamer's hermeneutics. In Silverman, Hugh J. (Ed.), *Gadamer and hermeneutics* (202-212).

Schmidt, Lawrence K. (1996). Recalling the hermeneutic circle. *Philosophy Today 41*, 263-272.

Schrag, Calvin O. (1996). In Jost, Walter and Michael J. Hyde (Eds.), *Rhetoric and hermeneutics in our time* (132-148).

Scott, Robert L. (1967). On viewing rhetoric as epistemic. *Central States Speech Journal 18*, 9-17.

——— (1973). On *not* defining "rhetoric." *Philosophy and Rhetoric 6*, 81-96.

——— (1976). On viewing rhetoric as epistemic: Ten years later. *Central States Speech Journal*, 258-266.

Shenk, David (1997, June 17). No one mingles in "global village." *USA Today*, 13A.

Shenk, Steve (1987, July 28). Mennonites condemn militarism, apartheid, homosexual practice. *Gospel Herald*, 532-534.

Shusterman, Richard (1989). The Gadamer-Derrida encounter: A pragmatist perspective. In Diane P. Michelfelder and Richard E. Palmer (Eds.), *Dialogue and deconstruction* (215-221).

Siker, Jeffrey S. (Ed.) (1994a). *Homosexuality in the church: Both sides of the debate*. Louisville, Ky.: Westminster John Knox Press.

——— (1994b, July). How to decide? Homosexual Christians, the Bible, and Gentile inclusion. *Theology Today 51*, 219-234.

Silverman, Hugh J. (Ed.) (1991). *Gadamer and hermeneutics*. New York and London: Routledge.

——— (1991). Introduction. In Hugh J. Silverman (Ed.), *Gadamer and hermeneutics* (1-10).

Simons, Herbert W. (n.d). What are good friends for? Towards a friendship model of scholarly conversation. Philadelphia: Temple University. Unpublished manuscript.

——— (1985). Chronicle and critique of a conference. *Quarterly Journal of Speech 71*, 52-64.

—— (Ed.) (1989). *Rhetoric in the Human Sciences.* London: Sage Publications.

—— (Ed.) (1990) *The rhetorical turn: Invention and persuasion in the art of inquiry.* Chicago: University of Chicago Press.

Soards, Marion L. (1995). *Scripture and homosexuality: Biblical authority and the church today.* Louisville, Ky.: Westminster John Knox Press.

Smith, Barbara Herrnstein (1997). *Belief and resistance: Dynamics of contemporary intellectual controversy.* Cambridge, Mass.: Harvard University Press.

Smith, P. Christopher (1991). *Hermeneutics and human finitude: Toward a theory of ethical understanding.* New York: Fordham University Press.

Smith, Ralph R. and Russel R. Windes (1997). The progay and antigay issue culture: Interpretation, influence and dissent. *Quarterly Journal of Speech 83*, 28-48.

—— (2000). *Progay/antigay: The rhetorical war over sexuality.* Thousand Oaks, Calif.: Sage Publications, Inc.

Smucker, Marcus G. (1990). Prayer. *Mennonite encyclopedia*, vol. 5. (717-718). Scottdale, Pa.: Herald Press.

Snyder, C. Arnold (1995). *Anabaptist history and theology: An introduction.* Kitchener, Ont.: Pandora Press.

Sokolowski, Robert (1997). Gadamer's theory of hermeneutics. In Hahn, Lewis Edwin (Ed.), *The philosophy of Hans-Georg Gadamer* (223-234).

Sommer, Susan (1997, April 15). Illinois Conference places two churches "under discipline." *Gospel Herald*, 9.

Solano, José (1998, January 6). [Letter to the editor]. *Gospel Herald*, 5.

Spradley, J. P. (1980). Making an ethnographic record. In *Participant Observation* (63-72). New York: Holt, Rinehart and Winston.

Stewart, John (1978). Foundations of dialogic communication. *Quarterly Journal of Speech 64*, 183-201.

—— (Ed.) (1986). *Bridges not walls: A book about interpersonal communication.* New York: Random House.

—— (1995). *Language as articulate contact: Toward a post-semiotic philosophy of communication.* Albany, N.Y.: State University of New York Press.

—— and Milt Thomas (1986). Dialogic listenings: Sculpting mutual meanings. In John Stewart (Ed.), *Bridges not walls: A book about interpersonal communication* (180-197).

Stuart, Elizabeth with Andy Braunston, Malcolm Edwards, John McMahon, and Tim Morrison (1997). *Religion is a queer thing: A guide to the Christian faith for lesbian, gay, bisexual and transgendered people.* Cleveland: Piligrim Press.

Steuber, Karsten R. (1994). Understanding truth and objectivity: A dialogue between Donald Davidson and Hans-Georg Gadamer. In Brice R. Wachterhauser (Ed.), *Hermeneutics and Truth* (172-189).

Stoltzfus Jost, Ruth and Timothy (1995, February 21). [Letter to the editor]. *Gospel Herald*, 8.

Studies in the Literary Imagination 28(2), 63-78.

Stutzman, Ervin Ray (1993). Appendix B: The Mennonite Church: Social organization. In From nonresistance to peace and justice: Mennonite peace rhetoric, 1951-1991 (366-371). (Doctoral dissertation, Temple University, 1993).

Sullivan, Andrew and Joseph Landau (Eds.) (1997) *Same-sex marriage: Pro and con.* New York: Vintage Press.

Swartley, Willard M. (1983). *Slavery, Sabbath, war, and women: Case issues in biblical interpretation.* Scottdale, Pa.: Herald Press.

———— (1990). Biblical interpretation. *Mennonite encyclopedia*, vol. 5. (80-83). Scottdale, Pa.: Herald Press

Tillich, Paul (1954). *Love, power, and justice: Ontological analyses and ethical implications.* London: Oxford University Press.

Toews, Paul (1996). *Mennonite experience in America: Vol. 4. Mennonites in American society, 1930-1970: Modernity and the persistence of religious community.* Scottdale, Pa.: Herald Press.

Toulmin, Stephen (1964). *The uses of argument.* London: Cambridge University Press.

Tracy, David (1984). Creativity in the interpretation of religion: The question of radical pluralism. *New Literary History 15(2)*, 289-309.

Wachterhauser, Bruce R. (Ed.) (1994a). *Hermeneutics and truth.* Evanston, Ill.: Northwestern University Press.

———— (1994b). Gadamer's realism: The "belongingness" of world and reality. In Brice R. Wachterhauser (Ed.), *Hermeneutics and truth* (148-171).

Warner, Rebecca (1991). Incorporating time. In Montgomery, Barbara M. and Steve Duck (Eds.), *Studying interspersonal interaction* (82-102).

Warnke, Georgia (1986). Hermeneutics and the social sciences: A Gadamerian critique of Rorty. *Inquiry, 28*, 339-357.

———— (1987). *Hermeneutics, tradition and reason.* Stanford, Calif.: Stanford University Press.

———— (1990). Walzer, Rawls, and Gadamer: Hermeneutics and political theory. In Kathleen Wright (Ed.), *Festivals of interpretation: essays on Hans-Georg Gadamer's work* (136-160).

———— (1993a). Feminism and hermeneutics. *Hypatia 8(1)*, 81-98

———— (1993b). *Justice and interpretation.* Cambridge, Mass.: The MIT Press.

———— (1994). Hermeneutics, tradition, and the standpoint of women. In Brice R. Wachterhauser (Ed.), *Hermeneutics and Truth* (206-226).

Weaver, J. Denny (1996, May 21). Making sure which game we are playing. *Gospel Herald*, 1-3.

———— (1997). *Studies in Anabaptist and Mennonite history: Vol. 35. Keeping salvation ethical: Mennonite and Amish atonement theology in the late nineteenth century.* Scottdale, Pa.: Herald Press.

———— (2000). *Anabaptist theology in face of postmodernity: A proposal for the third millennium.* Telford, Pa.: Pandora Press U.S.

Weaver, Valerie (1996, May 7). If we can't evangelize, we can't exist. *Gospel Herald*, 1-3.

———— (1997a, October 21). Franconia delegates vote to remove Germantown church from conference. *Gospel Herald*, 9.

———— (1997b, November 4). We're losing more than 120 members. *Gospel Herald*, 16.

Weber, Robert Philip (n.d). *Basic content analysis* (2nd ed). Unpublished monograph, Harvard University.

Weed, Elizabeth and Naomi Schor (Eds.) (1997). *Feminism meets queer theory: Books from differences.* Bloomington, Ind.: University of Indiana Press.

Weinsheimer, Joel C. (1985). *Gadamer's hermeneutics: A reading of* Truth and Method. New Haven: Yale University Press.

Williams, Karen Jane (1992, February). Problems inherent in applying Gadamer's philosophical hermeneutics to the study of conversation. Paper presented at the Annual Meeting of the Western States Communication Association (63rd, Boise, Idaho), 3-6.

———— (1995). Toward a hermeneutic ethnomethodology of conversation: An integration of Gadamer and Garfinkel. (Doctoral dissertation, University of Washington, 1995).

Witten, Marcia (1992). Guarding the castle of God: Religious speech in the context of secularity: An examination of the sermon discourse of two Protestant denominations. (Doctoral dissertation, Princeton University, 1992).

White, James Boyd (1984). *When words lose their meaning: Constitutions and reconstitutions of language, character, and community.* Chicago: University of Chicago Press.

———— (1987). Rhetoric and law: The arts of cultural and communal life. In Nelson et al. (Eds.), *The rhetoric of the human sciences* (298-318).

Wright, Kathleen, (Ed.) (1990). *Festivals of interpretation: Essays on Hans-Georg Gadamer's work.* Albany, N.Y.: State University of New York Press.

Yoder, J. Otis (1993, June 15). [Letter to the editor]. *Gospel Herald*, 5.

THE INDEX

THE AUTHOR

Michael A. King, Telford, Pennsylvania, is pastor, Spring Mount (Pa.) Mennonite Church (1997-); publisher, Pandora Press U.S.; and founding editor, *DreamSeeker Magazine*. He has been pastor in a variety of congregations in diverse settings.

He is author of *Trackless Wastes and Stars to Steer By: Christian Identity in a Homeless Age* (Herald Press, 1990), of many articles published in a wide variety of magazines and journals, including *The Christian Century* and *Christian Ministry*, and of "Kingsview" columns in *Christian Living* (1989-1997) and *DreamSeeker Magazine* (2001-). He is co-author, with Ronald J. Sider, of *Preaching about Life in a Threatening World* (Westminster, 1997).

King holds a Ph.D. (1998) in rhetoric and communication from Temple University, Philadelphia; an M.Div. (1982) from Eastern Baptist Theological Seminary, Philadelphia; and a B.A. (1976) in Bible and philosophy from Eastern Mennonite University (EMU), Harrisonburg, Virginia. He is a member of the Franconia Conference (Mennonite Church USA) Faith and Life Advisory Council, chair of Haverim, an EMU alumni group supporting the EMU Bible and Religion Department, and a member of the Eastern Mennonite Seminary Preaching Institute steering committee.

The oldest of nine children, King was born in 1954 in Sellersville, Pennsylvania, but soon taken to Cuba by his missionary parents, Aaron and Betty King. He lived in Cuba until age five, then in Mexico until college years. King is married to Joan Kenerson King, of Olean, New York, a family therapist and registered nurse who serves as consultant in various areas of public health policy. Michael and Joan have individually and jointly served as speakers and resource persons in many settings. They are parents of Kristy (b. 1981), Katie (1984), Rachael (1988) and share homemaking.